CW00829524

THE ARCHAEOLOGY OF
MEDIEVAL RURAL SETTLEMENT
IN IRELAND

The Archaeology of
Medieval Rural Settlement
in Ireland

Kieran Denis O'Conor

Discovery Programme Monograph No. 3

First published in 1998
by the Royal Irish Academy
19 Dawson St, Dublin 2.

Copyright © The Royal Irish Academy 1998.

All rights reserved. No part of this book may be reprinted or reproduced or utilised in any electronic, mechanical or other means, now known or hereafter invented, including photocopying and recording, or otherwise without either the prior written consent of the publishers or a licence permitting restricted copying in Ireland issued by the Irish Copyright Licensing Agency Ltd, The Writers' Centre, 19 Parnell Square, Dublin 1.

ISBN 1-874045-61-5

British Library Cataloguing-in-Publication Data.
A catalogue record for this book is available from the British Library.

Editor: Emer Condit
Cover design: Geraldine Garland

Typeset in Ireland by Wordwell Ltd.
Origination by Wordwell Ltd, The Type Bureau and Grants.
Printed by Colour Books.

Cover images—based on wall-paintings in St Bridget's Church, Clare Island, Co. Mayo, which are presently under conservation by Christoph Oldenbourg and Madeleine Katkov. (Photography courtesy of Christoph Oldenbourg and Madeleine Katkov.)

An Chomhairle Oidhreachta / The Heritage Council

The Discovery Programme gratefully acknowledges the financial contribution of The Heritage Council towards the cost of publishing this book.

Discovery Programme/Royal Irish Academy, Dublin 1998

Contents

Acknowledgements

I am grateful to those who critiqued drafts of this report, namely David Sweetman (my external referee), Terry Barry, Edel Bhreathnach, John Bradley, Howard Clarke, George Eogan, Clare Foley, Amanda Kelly, Jeremy Knight, Alan Lane, Noel Lynch, Karena Morton, Ronan O'Flaherty and Aidan O'Sullivan. Any mistakes, eccentricities and oddities in the text, however, are mine.

I am indebted, again, to Amanda Kelly for her help and support in the production of this report. Special thanks are also due to Paul Synnott and Barry Masterson, who were involved in the image-processing. Perhaps I should also thank them both for their continual patience with my lack of word-processor knowledge! I am also grateful to Ronan O'Flaherty and Kathleen O'Sullivan for their administrative support, without which this report could not have been written.

Con Brogan, John Scarry and Tony Roche of *Duchas*, The Heritage Service (Department of Arts, Heritage, Gaeltacht and the Islands) provided most of the photographs that accompany the text. Others were generously supplied by the Cambridge University Committee for Aerial Photography, Con Manning, Leo Swan, and the National Library of Ireland. I would also like to thank the *Journal of the Royal Society of Antiquaries of Ireland*, the Cork Archaeological and Historical Society, the *North Munster Antiquarian Journal*, Terry Barry, John Bradley, Rose Cleary, Christina Fredengren, Robert Higham, Peter Scholefield and Stafford Borough Council for permission to reproduce Figs 7–8, 12–16 and 21.

I thank Tom McNeill and Mark Gardiner, both of Queen's University, Belfast, who spent part of a morning and a full afternoon of their time suggesting ideas, themes and potential regions for any future project on medieval rural settlement in Ireland. I am also grateful to Victor Buckley, Archaeological Survey of Ireland, for his continual support in the production of this report. I am indebted to Caroline Sandes, who kindly gave me permission to refer to her forthcoming paper on proposals for future research on medieval pottery in Ireland.

Many other people assisted with the completion of this report and readily gave their advice and help. These include Grenville Astill, Michael Aston, Niall Brady, Gabriel Cooney, Claire Cotter, Kathryn Daly, Gareth Derbyshire, Martin Doody, Penny Dransart, Christopher Dyer, Nancy Edwards, Maria Fitzgerald, Elizabeth FitzPatrick, Joe Flannery, Christina Fredengren, Hugh Gallagher, Eoin Grogan, Mark Hennessy, Michael Herity, Robert Higham, John Kenyon, Michael Moore, Roderick and Teresa Morton, Niamh O'Callaghan, Finola O'Carroll, O'Conor Don and Madam O'Conor, Rory O'Conor, Raghnall Ó Floinn, Barry O'Reilly, Denys Pringle, Steve Ripon, Geoffrey Stell, and the librarians of the Royal Irish Academy and University College Dublin. I am grateful to Christoph Oldenbourg and Madeleine Katkov, who provided the photographs of the late medieval wall-paintings in St Bridget's Church, Clare Island, Co. Mayo, which are used in the cover design. I would also like to acknowledge the work of Emer Condit and Nick Maxwell of Wordwell Ltd in the preparation of this publication.

Finally, I thank my wife Karena and my sons Eoin and Hugh for their support.

List of plates

List of figures

PREFACE

Many of the sights, sounds and events of everyday life in the Irish countryside today were also known to rural folk in medieval Ireland. Despite these shared experiences, however, the nature of medieval rural settlement remains one of the least understood aspects of Irish archaeology, for a number of reasons. Medieval archaeology as a whole is a relatively new study in comparison to other branches of Irish archaeology, and most of the archaeological work on the subject over the last two decades or so has been carried out in what were the major urban centres of medieval Ireland. The Directorate and Council of the Discovery Programme therefore commissioned an archaeologist, Kieran O'Conor, to carry out a study on medieval rural settlement in Ireland, and specifically to isolate questions and priorities for future research.

The monograph begins by examining the history of medieval rural settlement studies in Ireland and then moves on to consider the subject-matter thematically. The topics considered include the role of castles as country houses and manorial centres, English peasant settlement, and society in Gaelic-dominated parts of medieval Ireland. Strategies for tackling the various questions identified are considered in detail, and the volume includes an extensive bibliography.

This study is the first step in a major new research project to be carried out by the Discovery Programme on medieval rural settlement in Ireland. It is hoped that it will be welcomed by all students of the medieval period in Ireland and elsewhere.

George Eogan

INTRODUCTION

Ireland is still essentially a rural country, despite the massive growth in its towns and cities over the last few decades; about 42% of the population of the Republic of Ireland live in rural areas. Furthermore, vast numbers of city dwellers were brought up on farms in country districts but had to leave to find work in towns, especially Dublin. The thousands of cars leaving Dublin every Friday evening and returning late on Sunday night are testimony to the love of native place which is so deeply ingrained in the Irish psyche. Many other urban dwellers are the offspring of countryfolk who moved to cities to find employment, and will remember long summer vacations spent on farms belonging to their grandparents or other near relatives. This all means that the division between urban and rural life is still not as marked in Ireland as it is in other western European countries, especially ones that industrialised early, where whole communities have come to exist which have no close family links with the countryside. Agriculture is still the main industry in Ireland and rural issues are never far from the main news.

Medieval Ireland was also rural in nature, with anything up to 95% of the population living outside true towns. This report examines the nature of rural settlement and life throughout this period. Furthermore, it isolates questions on the subject that need to be addressed by future research, and suggests ways in which these questions could be answered. It is hoped that this report will start a process which will eventually lead to a better understanding of the medieval period in Ireland and elsewhere. Many of the ideas put forward here may be revised by future work on medieval rural settlement in Ireland. Lastly, it is hoped that the subject of this report will be of interest to modern Irish people, given that so many of them have a rural background.

Medieval rural settlement is defined here as meaning all settlements and settlement forms, regardless of function or status, that lay outside true towns during the period from the late eleventh and twelfth centuries through to the second half of the seventeenth century.

The last years of the eleventh century and all of the twelfth century are seen by the present writer as marking the final end of the Early Christian period and the beginning of the medieval period in Ireland. Events such as the reform of the Church, the related introduction of various Continental religious orders and new architectural styles and concepts, the increase in trade with Britain and Europe, the growth in urbanism and the arrival in 1169 of the Anglo-Normans (who brought a new language and culture in their train, and whose coming linked Ireland politically to England for the next 750 years) all occurred in the late eleventh and twelfth centuries. Many of these events still affect Irish society today. The present writer tends to the view that the late eleventh and twelfth centuries were a time of great change and the beginning of a new era—the medieval period.

It is somewhat more difficult to justify the late seventeenth century as the end of the medieval period. Political historians normally, but not exclusively, view the year 1534, which marked the end of the Kildare hegemony over the island and saw the start of the Tudor reconquest of Ireland, as marking the end of the Middle Ages in this country. However, it must be remembered that archaeologists study the material remains of the past and they realise that culture and society rarely change overnight. So when did the medieval period in Ireland end in archaeological terms? This is a difficult question to answer as it has never been addressed properly by Irish archaeology. However, certain medieval settlement forms, such as various types of castles, crannogs and cashels, appear to be finally abandoned in the second half of the seventeenth century. There is therefore a certain amount of evidence to suggest, in archaeological terms, that the latter period rather than the early sixteenth century represents the end of the Middle Ages in this country. It might be added that something similar was suggested 32 years ago in the Preface to *An Archaeological Survey of County Down* (Jope *et al.* 1966).

Kieran O'Conor, Discovery Programme, January 1998.

1. THE HISTORY OF MEDIEVAL RURAL SETTLEMENT STUDIES IN IRELAND

1.1—Introduction

The term *'Medieval rural settlement in Ireland'* is defined in this report as meaning all settlements, regardless of status or function, that lay outside true towns during the period from *c*. AD 1100 until the late seventeenth century. The aim of this chapter is to review both the archaeological and the historical work that has been carried out on this subject since 1900.

1.2—Medieval rural settlement studies, 1900–97

1.2a—1900–40

Given the inclusive definition of medieval rural settlement in Ireland, the main debate within the subject during the first two decades of this century was concerned with the identification of mottes as Anglo-Norman castles (Fig. 1; Pl. 1; Orpen 1906a; 1906b; 1907b; 1907c; 1908a; 1908b; 1908c; 1909c; 1909d; 1910a; 1910b; 1910c; 1911–20, i, 341; ii, 343–4; Westropp 1904; 1905). This was part of a wider debate on the function and origins of mottes going on throughout the British Isles at this time (Armitage 1912; Counihan 1990; 1991). Masonry castles were also the focus of some academic attention (Crawford 1909; Fleming 1909; Kelly 1913; Leask 1914; Orpen 1907a; 1909a; 1909b; Westropp 1907a; 1907b; 1908; 1909; 1911). Much research was also carried out on ecclesiastical art and architecture during these two decades (Champneys 1910; Crawford 1919; Langrishe 1906; Lawlor 1917; Leask 1916; Macalister 1913; Westropp 1900–2; 1904–5; 1915).

Pl. 1—*The motte at Knockgraffon, Co. Tipperary. Timber defences would originally have surmounted the motte mound.* (Photo: *Dúchas*, The Heritage Service.)

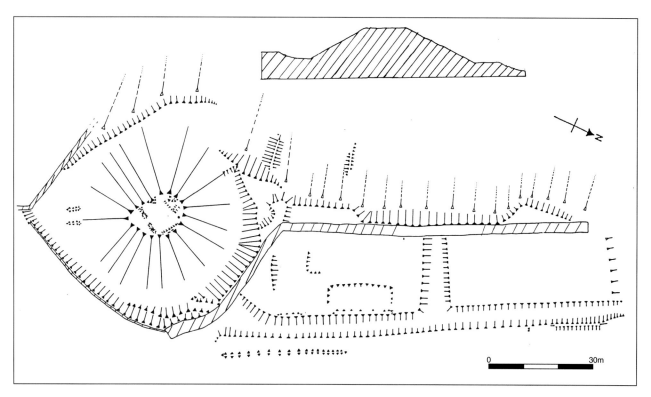

Fig. 1—*Plan of the motte castle at St Mullin's, Co. Carlow* (after O'Conor 1993).

Masonry castles and tower-houses continued to receive some attention from scholars during the 1920s and 1930s (Davies and Swan 1939; Lawlor 1923; 1928; Fitzpatrick 1927; 1935; Gleeson 1936a; 1936b; Gleeson and Leask 1936; Leask 1937). The major relevant publication of the period was surely Harold Leask's analysis of Anglo-Norman castles in Ireland, which appeared in the *Archaeological Journal* (Leask 1936). Motte castles were no longer the focus of academic interest during the 1920s and 1930s. This was partly due to Goddard Orpen's death in 1932 at the age of 80, as he was the great scholar of earthwork castles in Ireland. Unfortunately, he seems to have published very little in the last ten years of his life (Counihan 1991, 57–8). However, Vere Gordon Childe did excavate a motte castle at Doonmore, Co. Antrim, during the 1930s (Childe 1938). This was the first motte castle to be excavated scientifically in Ireland. Some research work was done on other mottes in the same region at this time (Lawlor 1938; 1939). The deserted Anglo-Norman settlement at Lisronagh, Co. Tipperary, also received some attention (Curtis 1936; P. Lyons 1937), and a minor excavation was carried out in 1934 on what the present writer feels was a small nucleated medieval settlement at Ballynamona, Co. Limerick (Ó Ríordáin 1936).

While little work was done on medieval rural settlement prior to the Second World War, some important research was published on the subject during this period. In particular, Orpen's very decisive identification of mottes as Norman castles was of long-term value to Irish medieval archaeology, as well as having important implications for the study of earthwork castles in Britain. The period also saw the beginning of Leask's work on medieval architecture, which was to culminate in major publications on this subject over the next two decades.

1.2b—1940–70

Leask's *Irish castles and castellated houses*, published in 1941, dealt with the phenomenon of castle-building in Ireland right down to the seventeenth century. It remained the main work on Irish castles until recently, despite the fact that Leask intended it to be merely an interim statement on the subject (McNeill 1997, 2). It concentrated on the architecture of masonry castles in Ireland, barely touching on the question of earthwork castles (Pls 2–3; Leask 1941). Various articles published in the 1940s and

Pl. 2—*The thirteenth-century masonry castle at Castleroche, Co. Louth.* (Photo: *Dúchas,* The Heritage Service.)

Pl. 3—*The fifteenth-century tower-house at Dunsoghly, Co. Dublin.* (Photo: *Dúchas,* The Heritage Service.)

Pl. 4—*The circular keep at Dundrum, Co. Down, built around 1205. Dundrum Castle was excavated by Dudley Waterman during the 1950s.* (Photo: Con Manning.)

1950s indicate that interest in stone castles continued throughout this period (M. Clarke 1944; Davies 1947; Leask 1943; 1944; 1951; 1953; Waterman 1951; 1956; 1958b). The fieldwork for *An Archaeological Survey of County Down* (Jope *et al.* 1966) was carried out in the 1950s and early 1960s, and a programme of excavations was undertaken in conjunction with the survey to elucidate the function and date of the different monument types visible in the Down landscape (e.g. Waterman 1954a, 103). A series of excavations of motte castles took place in Down, mainly during the 1950s (Dickinson and Waterman 1959; Waterman 1954a; 1954b; 1955; 1959a; 1959b; 1963), along with certain masonry castles of general Anglo-Norman date (Pl. 4; Waterman 1951; 1955; 1964; Waterman and Collins 1952). This work made County Down one of the foremost places for castle research in Europe during the 1950s and 1960s (McNeill 1997, 2), and laid the foundation for more recent work by Ulster-based scholars on castles in Ireland and elsewhere (e.g. Graham 1988b; McNeill 1992a; 1997a).

Two important excavations of Gaelic medieval high-status habitation sites were published during the 1940s and 1950s: the O'Brien settlement at Clonroad More, Ennis, Co. Clare, and the O'Neill crannog site of Island MacHugh, Co. Tyrone (Davies 1950; Hunt 1946). The artefactual assemblages from these sites are important because they provide information about the material culture of Gaelic Ireland during the medieval period. Another contribution to the study of medieval rural settlement was the publication of the excavation report of two medieval peasant longhouses at Caherguillamore, Co. Limerick (Ó Ríordáin and Hunt 1942). This excavation provided important information about the morphology of ordinary houses in Anglo-Norman-controlled parts of the country, as well as providing an insight into peasant life in medieval Ireland. It was first suggested at this time that medieval Gaelic peasants lived in small nucleated settlements similar to later clachans. These can be defined as unplanned clusters of houses and outbuildings inhabited by people who were commonly related to one another (Proudfoot 1959).

Medieval ecclesiastical art and architecture continued to be of interest to scholars during the 1940s and early 1950s (Davies 1948; Hunt 1950; Leask 1948; Mooney 1955; 1956; 1957), culminating in Leask's publication of his three-volume work *Irish churches and monastic buildings* between 1955 and 1960, still regarded as a major source for the study of medieval ecclesiastical architecture in this country (Pls 5–6).

An Archaeological Survey of County Down, published in 1966, contained many descriptions and plans of extant medieval sites in County Down (Jope *et al.* 1966). Both masonry and earthwork castles continued to receive some attention from scholars during the 1960s (Addyman 1965; de Paor 1962; Hunt 1960; Waterman 1968). The first and only scientific excavation of a motte castle in the Republic took place at Lurgankeel, Co. Louth, during the early 1960s in advance of development (*Oibre* 1965,

Pl. 5—*The great Benedictine monastery at Fore, Co. Westmeath, founded by Hugh de Lacy around 1185.* (Photo: *Dúchas,* The Heritage Service.)

Pl. 6—*Rosserk Abbey, Co. Mayo, founded by the Franciscan Third Order Regular sometime just before 1441.* (Photo: *Dúchas,* The Heritage Service.)

22). Unfortunately this site has never been published properly. Bunratty Castle, Co. Clare, was also excavated by the OPW prior to conservation, but it too was never published by its excavator.

Ecclesiastical architecture and sculpture continued to attract interest (de Paor 1967; 1969; Henry 1966; Rae 1966; Roe 1968). The excavations of the Cistercian monasteries of Mellifont, Co. Louth, and Holycross, Co. Tipperary, along with the Augustinian abbey of Ballintober, Co. Mayo, were initiated by the OPW during the 1960s. Mellifont was the only one of these investigations to be published (de Paor 1969).

Certain publications appeared in this decade that are of relevance to our understanding of settlement and society in medieval Gaelic Ireland (Hayes-McCoy 1964; Rynne 1963). Otway-Ruthven's *A history of medieval Ireland,* published in 1968, included a chapter on rural settlement in Anglo-Norman-controlled parts of medieval Ireland, based mainly on information from the surviving documentary sources, with little discussion of the available archaeological evidence (Otway-Ruthven 1968, 102–25). The 1960s also saw the first identification of a medieval pottery kiln in Ireland—at Downpatrick, Co. Down (Pollock and Waterman 1963). Furthermore, the first excavation in Ireland of a true moated site occurred in this decade, when in 1967 Robin Glasscock excavated a moated site at Kilmagoura, Co. Cork (Glasscock 1968). Again, the excavation report of this site has yet to be published.

Large numbers of monuments of medieval date survive in the Irish landscape today. Considering the size of this resource, it could be argued at first glance that really very little work was carried out on medieval rural settlement between *c.* 1940 and *c.* 1970. Nevertheless, despite this lack of sustained research, publications that are still regarded as important by Irish archaeology did appear during this 30-year period.

1.2c—1970–87

The 1970s saw a marked increase in publications relating to aspects of medieval rural settlement in Ireland. Earthwork castles were yet again the centre of a certain amount of academic attention. As in Britain, articles appeared on the subject of motte castles during this decade (Culleton and Colfer 1974–5; Glasscock 1975; Glasscock and McNeill 1972; McNeill 1975b; Talbot 1972). It was first suggested during the 1970s that ringwork castles as well as mottes existed in medieval Ireland (Fanning 1973–4; Twohig 1978). Reports also appeared on the excavations of three large Anglo-Norman masonry castles (Fanning 1975; Sweetman 1978; 1979). A comprehensive report of the excavation of a tower-house at Dunboy Castle, Co. Cork, was published in 1978 (Gowen 1978). Other useful work on tower-houses and stone castles appeared during this period (Claffey 1974–5; Maguire 1974; McNeill 1977; Ó Danachair 1977–9). Ecclesiastical art and architecture, as well as medieval figure sculpture, continued to arouse much interest (Harbison 1971; 1973; 1975b; 1977; Hunt 1974; Stalley 1971; 1973; 1975; 1977; Rae 1970; 1971). Excavation reports on two Augustinian priories also appeared in the 1970s (Fanning 1976; Waterman 1979), and the Clontuskert report included a plan of the field system adjacent to the priory at the site (Fanning 1976, 122).

The study of medieval rural settlement in Ireland broadened out into aspects of the subject that had not received much attention prior to 1970, and almost invariably this research was carried out by Ulster-based academics. There was a major debate amongst scholars during the 1970s as to whether or not ringforts were constructed and occupied during the medieval period in Gaelic-dominated areas of the country (Pl. 7; Barrett and Graham 1975; Lynn 1975a; 1975b; McNeill 1975a; Proudfoot 1977). Moated sites, particularly in south-eastern Ireland, were also the subject of intensive research in the 1970s (Barry 1977; 1978; 1979; Glasscock 1970). The question of nucleated settlements of village form and 'rural boroughs' (which can be defined as villages with urban legal status) in Anglo-Norman parts of medieval Ireland was examined by academics at this time (Buchanan 1970; Glasscock 1970; 1971; Graham 1975; 1977a; 1977b; 1978; 1979; A. Simms 1979). Another medieval pottery kiln was recognised in Ulster in the 1970s (Simpson *et al.* 1979).

Pl. 7—*Ringfort at Lisnabin, Co. Westmeath.* (Photo: Leo Swan.)

Various books relating to the history of medieval Ireland appeared in the early 1970s as part of the *Gill History of Ireland* series. They concentrated mainly on political history, although they contain much information of value to the study of medieval rural settlement in its broadest sense (Dolley 1972; Lydon 1973; MacCurtain 1972; Ó Corráin 1972; Watt 1972). Nicholls's *Gaelic and Gaelicised Ireland in the Middle Ages* (1972) remains of immense importance in understanding the nature of Gaelic settlement and society throughout the medieval period up to the seventeenth century.

The 1980s saw the continuation of this interest in various aspects of rural settlement in medieval Ireland. Two important publications appeared in this decade prior to 1987 which contributed greatly to our archaeological understanding of the period. The most prominent of these was T. E. McNeill's *Anglo-Norman Ulster* (1980), a major archaeological and historical analysis of the Anglo-Norman Earldom of Ulster. This interdisciplinary regional study of a marcher lordship contains much that is of value to the scholar of medieval rural settlement in both Anglo-Norman and Gaelic Ireland. The second was Brian Graham's small monograph *Anglo-Norman settlement in Ireland* (1985), which gave a concise and comprehensive overview of the research that had been carried out up to then by historians, historical geographers and archaeologists on medieval Ireland, including rural settlement (Graham 1985b).

Earthwork castles still received a lot of attention from scholars in the years before 1987 (Barry 1983; Barry *et al.* 1984; Graham 1980; McNeill 1980, 65–9, 84–9). The excavation report of the motte and raised rath at Rathmullan, Co. Down, appeared in the early 1980s (Lynn 1981–2). The *partial* ringwork at Ferrycarrig, Co. Wexford, was exca-

Pl. 8—*Moated site at Grove, Co. Kilkenny. The original buildings within a moated site were built of wood or clay and wood. Moated sites had timber defences but were not defensive enough to be called castles.* (Photo: *Dúchas, The Heritage Service.*)

vated during the mid-1980s (Bennett 1984–5; Cotter 1987; 1988). Publications on masonry castles and tower-houses continued to appear (Craig 1982, 60–7, 95–150; Lynn 1985–6; McNeill 1980, 71–6; 1981; 1983; O'Keeffe 1985–6; 1987), including the report of the excavation of Adare Castle, Co. Limerick (Sweetman 1980). Ecclesiastical art and architecture continued to attract some interest (Craig 1982, 35–59, 68–94; King 1984; Stalley 1984).

Moated sites continued to be analysed and investigated archaeologically in the years immediately prior to 1987 (Pl. 8; Barry 1981; Doody 1987; Sweetman 1981; Yates 1983). Interest in the question of nucleated villages within Anglo-Norman areas of medieval Ireland continued (K. J. Edwards *et al.* 1983; Graham 1985a; McNeill 1980, 84–9; A. Simms 1983). A paper on medieval agricultural practices in Anglo-Norman Kildare was published in 1985 (Hall *et al.* 1985). The report of the excavation of two medieval peasant houses at Lough Gur, Co. Limerick, appeared in 1983 (Cleary 1983). Another apparently thirteenth-century house was excavated at Tildarg, Co. Antrim, in 1982 (Brannon 1984; Barry 1987, 82). The excavation of a medieval house at Jerpoint Church townland, Co. Kilkenny, was published in 1989 (Foley 1989).

Historians also produced important research during the 1980s on medieval rural settlement in Ireland. Empey's (1982; 1983) work on the settlement history of the Anglo-Norman cantred of Knocktopher, Co. Kilkenny, is of immense importance in understanding the nature of certain archaeological monuments, such as motte castles and moated sites, as well as creating a picture of what a medieval manorial centre looked like in south-east Ireland. Research was also published on the nature of Anglo-Norman and Gaelic settlement in Tipperary (Empey 1985; Hennessey 1985; Nicholls 1985). The last chapter of Alfred Smyth's *Celtic Leinster* is of value when trying to understand Gaelic survival and settlement during the medieval period (Smyth 1982, 102–17). Robin Frame's *Colonial Ireland, 1169–1369*, while dealing mainly with political history, also has a chapter on settlement (Frame 1981, 69–91). Most of the actual excavation work during this decade was carried out in advance of development and was not orientated towards research.

1.2d—1987

The year 1987 was extremely important for the study of medieval rural settlement in Ireland. Primarily, it saw the publication of T. B. Barry's *The archaeology of medieval Ireland,* which offered the first synthesis of all work ever carried out on the medieval period in Ireland up to that year. Its appearance marked a watershed in the study of medieval archaeology in this country. Large parts of this book discussed various aspects of medieval rural settlement from an archaeological rather than a historical perspective (Barry 1987, 37–115, 139–203). Conrad Cairns's monograph *Irish tower-houses, a Co. Tipperary case study,* also published in this year, was a major contribution to our understanding of this monument type, of which at least 3000–3500 once existed in the Irish landscape—possibly many more (Cairns 1987, 5; Barry 1993b, 211). Other publications appeared in 1987 that were of importance to the study of the medieval period in general and medieval rural settlement in particular. This year saw the publication of the first edition of *A New History of Ireland, Volume II. Medieval Ireland, 1169–1534,* edited by Art Cosgrove (the second edition of this volume appeared in 1994). A number of essays by historians and historical geographers within this book are concerned with the nature of rural settlement in both Anglo-Norman and Gaelic regions of medieval Ireland (Glasscock 1987; Nicholls 1987; Watt 1987a; 1987b). Two further articles within the volume are of relevance to the economy of medieval rural Ireland (Down 1987; Childs and O'Neill 1987). One paper discusses the nature of medieval architecture and sculpture in Ireland (Rae 1987). George Cunningham's *The Anglo-Norman advance into the south-west midlands of Ireland, 1185–1221,* also published in 1987, is a comprehensive regional study of the development of Anglo-Norman power and settlement in the Tipperary, south Offaly and south-west Laois area. It contains numerous plans and descriptions of rural medieval sites. Roger Stalley's *The Cistercian monasteries of Ireland* also appeared in 1987; the Cistercian monastic movement was clearly very important in the shaping of the medieval landscape, as this order brought new land into agricultural use. The publication of these books and articles was a major contribution to the study of medieval rural settlement and society in Ireland, making 1987 an important landmark in Irish medieval archaeology.

1.2e—Discussion: medieval rural settlement studies in Ireland, 1900–87

This review of the research on various aspects of medieval rural settlement carried out by scholars in Ireland between 1900 and 1987 raises a number of different points. Firstly, it is true to say that little real interest in the subject was shown by archaeologists between 1900 and *c.* 1970. A review of the actual *archaeological* papers (defined here as meaning substantial articles dealing with some aspect of the physical remains of the past) published in the *Journal of the Royal Society of Antiquaries of Ireland* and the *Proceedings of the Royal Irish Academy* between 1900 and 1970 indicates that Irish archaeologists were primarily interested in researching the prehistoric and Early Christian periods. This should not obscure the fact that important work on the general subject of medieval rural settlement was published during these 70 years. As noted above, the historian Goddard Orpen's research on motte castles and the architect Harold Leask's work on masonry castles and churches, abbeys and friaries are still of immense value to the student of the medieval period in Ireland. There was always some work being done on medieval archaeology throughout these seven decades, even if it tended to be obscured at times by greater amounts of research on other periods. Furthermore, after *c.* 1950 there was a spectacular growth in the amount of work carried out on medieval archaeology in east Ulster. This did not happen elsewhere in Ireland.

The tendency amongst Irish archaeologists before *c.* 1970 to concentrate largely on the prehistoric and Early Christian periods has been noted before (Barry 1987, 1; O'Conor 1992, 3–4). There are some immediately obvious reasons for this which are relevant to the discipline of archaeology as a whole. These include the natural bias of archaeologists towards studying periods for which there is little or no documentary evidence, where their discipline and methods of enquiry will have the most impact. The large-scale survival in the field throughout Ireland of prehistoric and Early Christian monuments and landscapes would intrigue any scholar, compelling him or her to study them further. Furthermore, the surviving artefacts from these periods are amongst the most fascinating from non-Classical Europe. Indeed, Early Christian Insular art, as seen on metalwork, stone sculpture and illuminated manuscripts, is regarded as one of the most accomplished artistic styles ever (N. Edwards 1990, 132). It must be presumed that the existence of large numbers of impressive prehistoric and Early Christian artefacts and monuments within Ireland influenced scholars to some extent in choosing these periods for research, inhibiting the growth of an interest in medieval archaeology in this country until quite recently.

The development of medieval archaeology was also slow in Britain before *c.* 1950. For example, Glyn Daniels's *A hundred years of archaeology*, which examines the development of the discipline in Britain and elsewhere, includes no discussion on the medieval period (Daniels 1950). Prehistory was really the prime concern of mainstream archaeology in Britain and elsewhere prior to the 1950s. University departments of archaeology reflected this bias, and medieval archaeology only began to be regularly taught in British universities from the early 1970s onwards (H. Clarke 1984, 9). Therefore, at first glance, there was nothing especially unique about the lack of work on medieval archaeology in Ireland, at least before 1950. However, it was realised in Britain after 1950 that archaeology had a distinctive role to play in helping to understand the nature of the medieval period in that country (*ibid.*, 15–16), partly because the excavations of bomb-sites in London and elsewhere had revealed a certain amount of information about the origins of urbanism in Britain from the Roman period onwards. Furthermore, the excavations of certain medieval rural sites, such as the deserted village of Wharram Percy, Yorkshire, produced dramatic evidence for life in the countryside during the whole period (*ibid.*, 131, 168–9). The numerous excavations of earthwork and masonry castles in Down during the 1950s and 1960s seem to be a reflection in Ulster of this upsurge in interest in medieval archaeology seen throughout Britain and, indeed, elsewhere in Europe after *c.* 1950. As noted, this work was to lay the foundation for further work by Ulster-based scholars on medieval rural settlement in general after *c.* 1970 (sections 1.2b, 1.2c).

However, this upsurge in archaeological work was not really seen in the Republic of Ireland after 1950 up to the 1970s, with the exception of some papers on the traditional topics of castles and ecclesiastical sites and the excavation of a few medieval sites in advance of conservation or development (section 1.2b). In the context of medieval rural settlement, Ulster-based or Ulster-educated academics dominated the study throughout the 1970s and beyond (section 1.2c).

While there are a number of reasons why little work was done on medieval archaeology in Ireland up to the 1950s, this discussion has not yet properly explained why medieval archaeology was slower to develop in the Republic than in Ulster. It is obvious that the tensions, trends and enthusiasms apparent within any particular society will in some way be reflected in that culture's intellectual and artistic work (T. Brown 1981, 9). Robin Frame, in the introduction to *Colonial Ireland,* stated that 'the Anglo-Norman invasion of Ireland in the twelfth century has normally been regarded as the first act in the prolonged, frequently miserable drama of relations between England and Ireland' (Frame 1981). These two points are important as it has been argued that the lack of work on medieval archaeology over much of this century is due in large measure to Ireland's recent history. The pre-Viking part of the Early Christian period and prehistory were seen by Irish nationalists as eras free from Norse interference or Anglo-Norman and English domination—halcyon days of great cultural and spiritual achievement for the Irish people, which could be attained again now that the Republic had won its independence (Barry 1987, 1). Indeed, many symbols of Irish national identity were taken from the prehistoric and Early Christian periods. Even today the Republic's coinage and stamps draw heavily from motifs and artefacts associated with these pre-Norman eras. The importance of the prehistoric and Early Christian periods to Irish national life explains why at least some archaeologists in Ireland over much of this century, and in the Republic in particular, were uninterested in the medieval period, often seeing it as merely a branch of English archaeology (Ó Floinn, forthcoming, 111–112). Furthermore, it is clear that at least some archaeologists in the 1970s and very early 1980s viewed the rich Hiberno-Norse and Anglo-Norman excavations at Wood Quay, Dublin, with hostility and as unimportant for Irish archaeology (Wallace 1984, 133; Woodman 1995, 285–6). Certainly, this negative attitude helps to explain why so little sustained archaeological work was done on the medieval period in Ireland, in particular in the Republic. The emphasis on the prehistoric and Early Christian periods was partly an archaeological reflection of the nationalism that pervaded much of Irish society for a large part of this century.

R. A. S. Macalister was appointed to the chair of Celtic Archaeology at University College Dublin in 1909, and was to teach archaeology there until 1943 (Herity and Eogan 1977, 13). The best expression of the relationship between Irish nationalism, glorification of both the prehistoric and Early Christian periods and lack of sympathy towards the medieval period is seen in his book *The archaeology of Ireland* (Macalister 1928). He clearly saw the medieval period as one of decline for Ireland, stating: 'as we review the products of medieval Ireland, we see everywhere a sad decline from the achievements of Celtic Ireland. All the skill, all the devotion to labour, these are snuffed out like the flame of a candle' (Macalister 1928, 356). Macalister seems to have viewed the arrival of the Anglo-Normans in Ireland in a negative light. He believed that the achievements of the Anglo-Normans, as well as the medieval period in general, were things related solely to England:

> 'In speaking of the antiquities of the period, it will be unnecessary to make more than passing allusions to those remains which are English in all but geographical situation. Such subjects as cross-legged effigies, pavement tiles, Plantagenet coins, arms and armour, and the like, are a branch of English archaeology and even then their extension to Ireland is much more a matter of English than of Irish interest' (*ibid.*).

He also believed that the cultural achievements of the prehistoric and Early Christian periods in Ireland should act as an example and give confidence to the newly independent state. In the concluding paragraph of his book, he writes:

> 'In these tempestuous days of ours, the young Free State of Ireland trims her argosy, and sets forth in courage and aspiration to voyage over the uncharted seas of the future. Four thousand years ago her people guided the first faltering steps of the Folk of the North on the way of civilisation. Twelve hundred years ago they shepherded a war-broken Europe upon the way of learning and the way of life. May she prove worthy of her ancient past; may she find that once more she has a mission to a bewildered, rudderless world: and may God be her speed in its fulfilment' (Macalister 1928, 357).

Such sentiments, expressed by arguably the most prominent Irish archaeologist of his day, help us to understand why little sustained research was carried out on medieval archaeology in the Republic until quite recently. Conversely, it might be added that Goddard Orpen, the historian who carried out so much work on medieval archaeology in the first two decades of this century, was very definitely loyalist in his sympathies (Flanagan 1989, 1–2; McNeill 1997, 2). Indeed, it has recently been suggested that

Orpen's Unionism and staunch belief in British institutions may have hindered the development of castle studies in Ireland and exacerbated the tendency to see them as symbols of Anglo-Norman and later English military domination (McNeill 1997, 2).

This argument helps to explain why the main impetus to medieval archaeology in general, and medieval rural settlement in particular, in Ireland came mainly from Northern Irish or Ulster-based archaeologists and historical geographers from the 1950s through to the 1970s (Barry 1987, 1). Obviously, given the political and cultural situation in Northern Ireland, the universities and institutions there had closer academic and intellectual links with Britain. As noted, in England interest in medieval archaeology, including the study of deserted villages and moated sites, grew in the 1950s, blossoming into a whole series of excavations of urban and rural sites in the 1960s and 1970s. Therefore, at one level, it would appear that the large-scale excavation of medieval sites in east Ulster during the 1950s, and the increased research on medieval rural settlement after 1970 by mainly Ulster-based academics, was a reflection of academic trends and interests apparent in Britain at that time. However, it is also fair to say that the emotional ties that existed between society in the Republic and the prehistoric and Early Christian periods during the 1950s through to the 1970s were far stronger than they were in the North. Unionist scholars would have been far more receptive to studying the medieval period owing to their cultural background, which saw both the link with England and that country's historical involvement with Ireland as positive (McNeill 1997, 2).

However, Barry stated that by the mid-1980s interest in medieval archaeology had grown in the Republic. He believed that this was partly a reflection of the State's growing involvement since the 1960s and 1970s with such international institutions as the United Nations and the EEC, arguing that this increased contact with the outside world allowed scholars to take a more varied approach to interpretations of the past (1987, 1–2). More specifically, Barry saw the excavations at the Viking and medieval site at Wood Quay, Dublin, during the 1970s and 1980s as a catalyst in changing attitudes to medieval archaeology in Ireland. Overall, he stated that by 1987 there was an acknowledgement of the contributions made by the Norse and the Anglo-Normans to the development of Irish society (*ibid.*, 2). In 1987 Barry was clearly optimistic for the future of medieval archaeology in Ireland as a whole.

1.2f—1987–97

What is the current state of research into medieval archaeology in Ireland ten years after the publication of Barry's *The archaeology of medieval Ireland*? Was the writer too optimistic in believing that medieval archaeology had come of age in Ireland in the years immediately before 1987? Certainly, the prominence once attached to the prehistoric and Early Christian periods would now be considered anachronistic by most of the Republic's archaeological community. For example, in the period 1987–94, twelve MA theses submitted to the Departments of Archaeology at University College Cork (UCC), University College Dublin (UCD) and University College Galway (UCG) dealt with some aspect of the medieval period. A further four dealt with Hiberno-Norse material from the Dublin excavations. Furthermore, of twelve PhDs completed by scholars from the Republic on some aspect of Irish archaeology between 1987 and 1997, seven have dealt with medieval topics (Jordan 1990; FitzPatrick 1998; Long 1997; McAuliffe 1991b; Murtagh 1993; O'Conor 1993; O'Keeffe 1991). Lectureships in medieval archaeology have existed at Trinity College, Dublin, and Queen's University, Belfast, since 1978 and 1948 respectively. Medieval archaeologists were appointed to lectureships at St Patrick's College, Maynooth, in 1996 and UCC and UCG in 1997. This all bodes well for the future study of medieval archaeology in Ireland.

The collection of basic data relating to the study of medieval archaeology has also progressed since 1987. Almost 54% of the 1779 mostly rescue excavations carried out in the period 1987–96 investigated sites of medieval or suspected medieval date in both urban and rural areas, although it must be remembered that many of these digs were

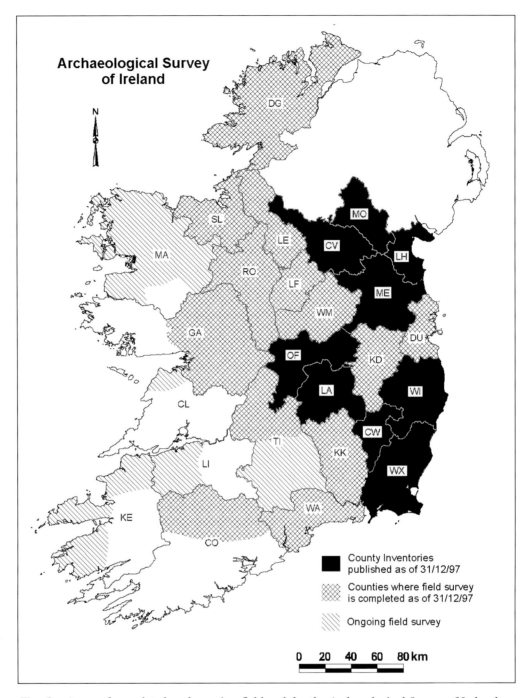

Fig. 2—*Areas of completed and ongoing fieldwork by the Archaeological Survey of Ireland.*

very small in scale and have produced little in the way of artefacts or structures (Bennett 1988; 1989a; 1990; 1991; 1992; 1993; 1994; 1995; 1996; 1997). The Archaeological Survey of Ireland has also done a large amount of fieldwork throughout the Republic over the last ten years. Fieldwork has been completed in twenty counties and is ongoing in Clare, Limerick, Tipperary and Mayo (Fig. 2). Thousands of comprehensive descriptions, sketch-plans and photographs of archaeological sites from all over the country now exist in the files of the Archaeological Survey, including reports on all the medieval sites visited over this period. In all, it is estimated that the archaeologists working for the Archaeological Survey have so far visited, identified and described 100,000 sites of all periods (V. Buckley, pers. comm.). Short descriptions of many of these monuments have been published in various county inventories since 1987 (Brindley and Kilfeather 1993; Buckley and Sweetman 1991; Gosling 1993; Grogan and Kilfeather 1997; Moore 1996; O'Brien and Sweetman 1997; O'Donovan

13

1995; Power *et al.* 1992; 1994; 1997; Sweetman *et al.* 1995). Furthermore, the Urban Archaeological Survey produced a number of reports on settlements in Ireland that had urban status during the medieval period, including rural boroughs, in the years after 1987 (Bradley and Dunne 1988a; 1988b; 1988c; 1989a; 1989b; 1989c; 1989d; 1990; Bradley and King 1988; 1989a; 1989b; 1990; Bradley *et al.* 1989a; 1989b).

This review of work carried out in a general way on medieval archaeology since 1987 indicates three points. Firstly, it is clear that the medieval period is a popular choice for research amongst PhD students. Secondly, there are now five full-time academic posts in medieval archaeology throughout Ireland. Thirdly, a considerable amount of fieldwork and excavation has been carried out on medieval sites all over the country since 1987, and consequently much more basic information concerning the archaeology of medieval Ireland exists now than in 1987. It could therefore be argued that the study of medieval archaeology in Ireland is in a strong position at present—more so than ten years ago.

However, a more detailed analysis of the current state of medieval archaeology in this country indicates that the *academic* and *intellectual* study of the whole period has not greatly progressed since 1987. For example, while a variety of books published over the last few years offer comprehensive and valuable new interpretations of the archaeology of the prehistoric and Early Christian periods (Harbison 1988; O'Kelly 1989; Edwards 1990; Mytum 1992; Cooney and Grogan 1994; Raftery 1994), no archaeological work offering a comprehensive overview of the medieval period in Ireland has been published since 1987, despite the large amount of excavation and survey work carried out at medieval sites all over the country since then. Barry's book remains the sole textbook on medieval archaeology in Ireland. Articles concerned with some aspect of the medieval period are underrepresented in the four major Irish archaeological journals. An analysis of all the archaeological papers published in the *Proceedings of the Royal Irish Academy*, the *Journal of the Royal Society of Antiquaries of Ireland*, the *Ulster Journal of Archaeology* and the *Journal of Irish Archaeology* shows only sixteen articles dealing with the medieval period since 1987. In comparison, these journals have published 137 articles dealing with the prehistoric and Early Christian periods over the last decade. Furthermore, a review of the papers published in *Medieval Archaeology* indicates that Graham's (1988b) article on Irish earthwork castles is the only comprehensive article published on Irish medieval archaeology (as opposed to papers on the Early Christian period) in this journal over the last ten years.

Therefore, despite the large amount of survey work, postgraduate research into the medieval period and excavation of medieval sites, these figures suggest that very little of this work is actually being published either in book form or as articles for major academic journals. This imbalance may change now that provision has been made for new lectureships in medieval archaeology within the Irish university system. In theory, academics have both the facilities and the time needed to produce major publications offering overviews of subjects and periods, unlike archaeologists working privately or for the State services. Perhaps the *next* ten years will be important for the development of medieval archaeology as a whole in this country.

What work has actually been undertaken since 1987 on the specific subject of medieval rural settlement in Ireland, as opposed to medieval archaeology as a whole? An analysis of all the excavations carried out over the last decade at medieval sites all over Ireland shows that the overwhelming majority were urban in character (Bennett 1988; 1989a; 1990; 1991; 1992; 1993; 1994; 1995; 1996; 1997), primarily a response to urban renewal and development—with a large amount of the funding for these developments coming from the EU. Furthermore, there has never been a long-term research excavation of a medieval rural (or indeed urban) site in Ireland comparable to those at the passage graves of Carrowmore, Co. Sligo, Newgrange and Knowth, Co. Meath, or at Moynagh Lough crannog, Co. Meath. The Discovery Programme itself, since its inception in 1991, has focused its research on the later prehistoric period.

Given the lack of concentrated archaeological research on medieval rural settlement, what publications have come out since 1987 that are of at least some relevance to the subject? Firstly, a large number of papers have been written on the subject of castles. Anglo-Norman masonry castles have received a certain amount of attention from scholars over the last ten years (Hodkinson 1995; Holland 1993–4; 1997; Mallory and McNeill 1991, 252–9; Manning 1990; McNeill 1990a; 1990b; 1993; 1997; B. Murtagh 1993; O'Conor 1996; 1997; O'Keeffe 1990b; Stalley 1992; Sweetman 1992a; 1992b; 1995). A number of articles on earthwork castles or timber castles have also appeared in the last decade (Graham 1988b; 1991; McNeill 1989–90; 1991; 1997, 56–74; Mallory and McNeill 1991, 259–62; O'Conor 1987–91; 1992; O'Keeffe 1990a; 1995a). Research on tower-houses has also been published since 1987 (Barry 1993b; 1995; Cairns 1991; Jordan 1990–1; McAuliffe 1991a; 1991b; MacCurtain 1988; McNeill 1992b; Mallory and McNeill 1991, 289–92; B. Murtagh 1994; O'Keeffe 1995b; Sweetman 1992a; 1995, 36–42). Many good descriptions and plans of masonry castles, earthwork castles and tower-houses were published in the *Archaeological Survey of County Louth* (Buckley and Sweetman 1991). A number of papers on rural settlement patterns, monument types and the economy of both Anglo-Norman and Gaelic Ireland have also been published by various historians, historical geographers and archaeologists over the last ten years (Barry 1988; 1993a; 1996; Empey 1988; 1990; Graham 1988a; 1993; Flanagan 1992–3; Holland 1994; 1997; Lucas 1989; Mallory and McNeill 1991, 289–92; O'Conor 1998; O'Keeffe 1996; A. Simms 1988a; 1988b). This review shows two things. Firstly, medieval archaeologists interested in non-urban archaeology are largely concerned with researching the phenomenon of castles in Ireland. Secondly, such work as does exist on rural medieval society and settlement patterns has been done as much by historians and historical geographers as by archaeologists.

1.3—Conclusions

Irish archaeologists have tended to concentrate their research on the prehistoric and Early Christian periods over much of this century. There were a number of reasons for this situation, common to the discipline of archaeology as a whole throughout Europe. The lack of substantial work on medieval archaeology was at least partly due in this country to the influences of Irish nationalism. It is fair to say that in some quarters there was a lack of sympathy towards the medieval period—as in the case of Professor Macalister. However, despite this, important research did get published on various aspects of medieval archaeology in the period 1900–70 (sections 1.2a–e). Specifically, a series of excavations of medieval sites, especially earthwork castles, took place in County Down during the 1950s and early 1960s. This led east Ulster, in these years, to become one of the prime places in Europe for castle research. Interest in medieval rural settlement grew after 1970. Again, Ulster-based archaeologists and historical geographers dominated this study at first. It was argued that this growth in research from the 1950s onwards was partly a reflection in Ulster of academic interest current in Britain at that time. It was also argued that Ulster academics may have been more responsive than their Southern colleagues to this shift in academic interests owing to their political and cultural background. Certainly, archaeologists in the Republic had become more responsive to medieval archaeology by the mid-1980s, possibly owing to changes in society as a whole (sections 1.2c–e). However, despite a large amount of survey and excavation—the latter overwhelmingly in urban areas—this upsurge has not resulted in a large number of publications on the period over the last ten years. The present writer feels that this has been largely due to the fact that most medieval archaeologists have tended to work either privately or for the State services, perhaps making it more difficult for them to publish their research in comparison to academics. The recent creation of a number of new university posts in medieval archaeology will hopefully mean a larger number of publications on the period in the future (section 1.2f).

A review of the publications dealing with some feature of medieval rural settlement in Ireland indicates that there has been a strong tendency to publish articles on castles and ecclesiastical art and architecture over much of this century (Pls 1–6; sections 1.2a–c). In more recent times, since *c.* 1970, work has been carried out on other, more varied aspects of medieval rural settlement in Ireland (section 1.2c). However, a large amount of the research undertaken on the subject since 1970 has come either from an analysis of the surviving manorial documents by historians or from extensive field-work, as often carried out by historical geographers as by archaeologists. There has been little in the way of excavations of medieval rural monument types in Ireland, certainly in terms of published reports of such investigations, with the exception of east Ulster (sections 1.2c–f; Barry 1996, 136). This will be discussed in more detail in Chapter 5 and Appendix I (sections 5.1, I.4b–f, I.5a). The main point here is that excavation, as opposed to other methods of enquiry about the past, has been distinctly under-utilised in the study of medieval rural settlement throughout most of Ireland (Barry 1996, 136).

One last point relevant to the study of archaeology as a whole in this country needs to be raised here. Unlike the related disciplines of history and historical geography, little attempt has been made by Irish archaeologists to try to understand the ideological influences which have affected the practice of archaeology up to the present day (Cooney 1995). Certainly, very little has been done to analyse comprehensively the processes which have affected Irish archaeology over time, although there are some notable exceptions to this (e.g. Cooney 1995; 1997; Woodman 1995). Perhaps a detailed modern study of the way archaeology and antiquarianism have evolved in Ireland since the beginning of the eighteenth century or even earlier should become a priority for the discipline of archaeology. Certainly, in the context of this report, it is felt that more work is needed on the development of medieval archaeology in Ireland. Certain specific questions need to be asked of this research. Firstly, to what extent did nationalism retard the growth of medieval archaeology in Ireland? Secondly, what other processes and influences affected the development of the study in this country? Thirdly, have certain modern scholars (including the present writer) placed too much emphasis on the negative effect of nationalism on medieval archaeology in Ireland? Certain ideas related to these questions were briefly discussed in this chapter. Nevertheless, it is suggested that more detailed research and thought are required on this whole subject.

2. CASTLES: COUNTRY HOUSES AND MANORIAL CENTRES

2.1—Introduction

England has some thousands of medieval parish churches dotted throughout its landscape today. They are clearly the most prominent reminder at a local level of the medieval period in that country, especially as much of the rural population of modern England still worship in them. They provide rural communities there with an unbroken link with the past, and their continued existence adds much to the serenity of the English countryside. Conversely, owing to the internally troubled and more religiously complex nature of Irish history, the vast majority of medieval parish churches in Ireland are now either completely demolished or in ruins or their sites are presently occupied by Church of Ireland churches built mainly between 1800 and 1830 by the Board of First Fruits. Indeed, many of these latter buildings are now themselves in decay owing to a decline in the Church of Ireland population in many country areas since the second half of the nineteenth century. The available archaeological evidence suggests that the vast majority of medieval parish churches in this country were small and simple in plan, with almost no decoration (Barry 1987, 140). This all means that the sites of medieval parish churches throughout Ireland are often lonely and insignificant places today, quite unlike the situation in England. It might also be added that the cathedrals of medieval Ireland were mostly no bigger than large parish churches in England (Barry 1987, 143).

Instead, the principal visible reminder of the medieval period in the Irish landscape today must surely be castles. It must be remembered that the term *castle,* like the appellations *megalithic tomb* or *barrow,* covers a number of diverse types of field monuments, which often look very different to one another. The popular image of the castle today is of a large masonry fortress (e.g. Higham 1989, 50). This ignores the fact that many medieval castles were constructed of earth and timber.

Masonry and earthwork castles in Ireland—late twelfth to early fourteenth century

The first phase of stone castle-building in Ireland was carried out between *c.* 1180 and *c.* 1310–20, mainly by Anglo-Norman lords (Sweetman 1995, 5, 8). This is really the period when the great masonry castles of Ireland were built, some of them up to several acres in extent. Such fortresses carried a wide variety of defences and domestic accommodation, such as large keeps, mural towers, fine twin-towered gatehouses and curtain-walls looped for archery (Pls 9–10; Leask 1941, 12–74; Sweetman 1995; McNeill 1997, 17–55, 81–168). Until the work of the Archaeological Survey of Ireland is complete, it will not be certain exactly how many masonry castles were constructed in the period from the late twelfth century through to the early fourteenth century. Just under 100 have been recognised in the landscape by various scholars to date (Fig. 3). It has been suggested to the present writer that this figure may eventually rise to about 150, as more will be recognised by the various field archaeologists working for the Archaeological Survey (D. Sweetman, pers. comm.).

It is continually forgotten, however, even by archaeologists, that the majority of castles built throughout Ireland and western Europe in the twelfth and thirteenth centuries were made of earth and timber (O'Conor, forthcoming). These fortresses are mostly known to the discipline of archaeology as *earthwork castles,* although it is noteworthy that some English archaeologists now prefer to call them *timber castles* (e.g.

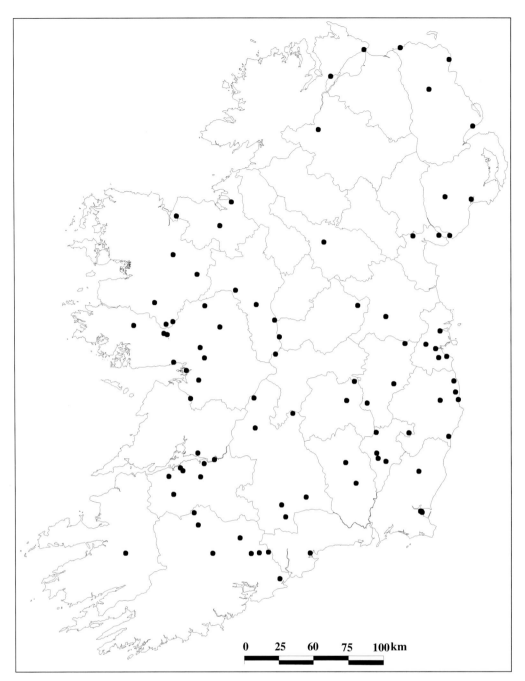

Fig. 3—*Interim distribution map of masonry castles of late twelfth- to early fourteenth-century date in Ireland* (Discovery Programme).

Higham and Barker 1992, 352). Earthwork or timber castles are basically divided into two types. The first is the motte, which can be described as a mound of earth whose flat summit would once have held wooden buildings and defences. Sometimes a defended enclosure known as a bailey was attached to its base. Again, the defences surmounting the bailey's banks and the buildings within it were also usually built of timber or clay and timber. It has been argued that at least 476 mottes were constructed in Ireland during the late twelfth, thirteenth and possibly very early fourteenth centuries (Pls 11–12; Fig. 4; O'Conor 1992, 3). The second type is called the ringwork. Most ringworks can be described as circular or oval areas defined by an earthen bank and ditch (Pl. 13; Fig. 5). The original defences and buildings around and within these ringworks were also made of timber or clay and wood. About 63 probable and possible ringworks can be identified today in the Irish landscape (*ibid.*). This means that at least

Pl. 9—*Dunamase Castle, Co. Laois. The first phase of this castle dates to the late twelfth century. However, excavation has shown that an important pre-Norman fortress existed here prior to the erection of the masonry castle. The second phase of the castle seems to have been built under the auspices of William Marshal the Elder around 1210. Anglo-Norman castles such as this had complex defences and often enclosed large areas.* (Photo: *Dúchas*, The Heritage Service.)

Pl. 10—*Ballymoon Castle, Co. Carlow, probably built in the early fourteenth century. The earthworks of what appears to be a deserted village occur around this castle.* (Photo: *Dúchas*, The Heritage Service.)

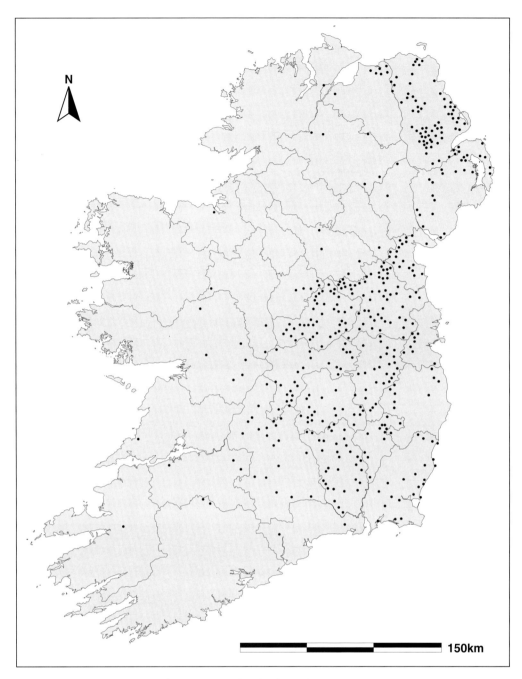

Fig. 4—*Distribution map of mottes in Ireland* (after O'Conor 1993).

525 earthwork or timber castles were built in medieval Ireland. This may even be a minimal figure, as new earthwork castles are still being recognised by the Archaeological Survey of Ireland.

In all, this suggests that at least 630 masonry and earthwork castles of various sorts were built in Ireland between the late twelfth century and the first years of the fourteenth century, mainly by Anglo-Norman lords. This figure is likely to increase as the results of ongoing fieldwork are published. It may rise to about 700 castles.

Tower-houses
The tower-house is another, later type of castle. Its principal element was generally a tall, rectangular or square masonry tower, mostly between three and five storeys in height (Pl. 14; Fig. 6). There was usually a vault over the ground floor, which was normally used for storage. Tower-houses were also entered by a doorway at this level.

Pl. 11—*The motte at Rathmore, Co. Kildare. This motte castle was built on the site of an important pre-Norman centre. The early nineteenth-century church beside the motte marks the location of the medieval parish church. A borough once existed here but there are no visible surface remains of earthworks in the fields around the motte. (Photo: Kieran O'Conor.)*

Pl. 12 —*The motte at Ballinphull, Co. Sligo. (Photo: Kieran O'Conor.)*

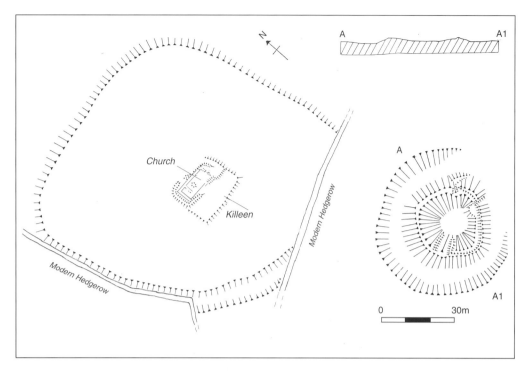

Above: Fig. 5—*Plan of the ringwork castle at Ballyorley, Co. Wexford* (after O'Conor 1993).

Pl. 13—*The ringwork castle at Rathangan, Co. Kildare. The historical sources and the earthwork's morphology and siting suggest that this ringwork was carved out of a pre-existing ringfort.* (Photo: Cambridge University Committee for Aerial Photography.)

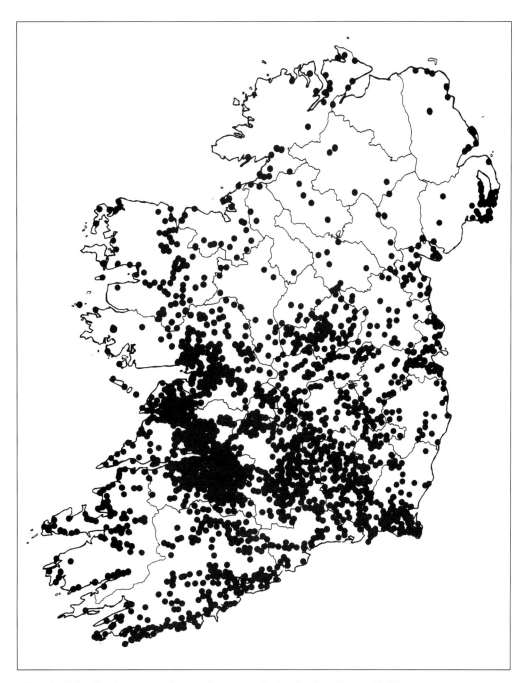

Fig. 6—*Distribution map of tower-houses in Ireland* (after Barry 1987).

The upper floors were often lit by fine windows and contained fireplaces, suggesting that these rooms were used for entertaining guests and as bedchambers. Garderobes are also associated with these uppermost rooms. Some tower-houses had thatched clay-walled halls beside them, which were also used for feasting and for the carrying out of administrative duties. The battlements on these tower-houses had stepped merlons and machicolations of various types. A certain number of tower-houses had a stone-walled enclosure, known as a bawn, around them or attached to them (Pl. 15; Barry 1987, 186; Cairns 1987, 13–20; McNeill 1997, 211–23). Documentary evidence suggests that some tower-houses also had bawns defended by wooden palisades, sod walls and even thick hedges (Barry 1987, 186; Cairns 1987, 17). A few bawns had circular towers at their corners, which allowed defensive fire to be brought to bear along the external faces of their curtain-walls. Gun-loops also occur in the walls of some bawns (Cairns 1987, 16–17). However, most bawns are not seriously defensive. The majority did not have angle-towers. Their gateways were mostly simple entranceways rather than

Pl. 14—*Tower-house at Rockstown, Co. Limerick.* (Photo: *Dúchas*, The Heritage Service.)

Pl. 15—*The tower-house and bawn at Aughanure, Co. Galway, built by the O'Flahertys in the sixteenth century.* (Photo: *Dúchas*, The Heritage Service.)

scientifically defended gatehouses. Many bawns are really too large for realistic defence. Most were simply enclosures designed to prevent theft rather than to hold off a concerted attack. The defences at these castles were usually concentrated on the tower itself (McNeill 1997, 217). Indeed, many tower-houses do not seem to have had actual bawns beside them (*ibid.*, 222).

It has been argued on historical grounds that tower-houses first started to be built in Ireland during the early fourteenth century (Barry 1987, 186; Cairns 1987, 8–9). However, no tower-house has yet been architecturally or archaeologically dated to this period. It has recently been postulated that, while a few tower-houses in Ireland date from the late fourteenth century, the fashion for building them here really began in the early fifteenth century (McNeill 1997, 226). It appears on present evidence that the very first tower-houses in Ireland were built by men of Anglo-Norman descent (Barry 1987, 188; Cairns 1987, 9). The first Gaelic-built ones are seen in the first years of the fifteenth century (*ibid.*). Tower-houses stopped being built in Ireland around 1650 (Cairns 1987, 3, 6). They seem to have been finally abandoned for non-defensive dwellings in the last years of the seventeenth century (McNeill 1997, 228–9).

It has been suggested that between 3000 and 3500 tower-houses were built in this country (Barry 1987, 186; Cairns 1987, 3, 21). An analysis of the OS six-inch maps for the whole country reveals many places marked as 'Castle (site of)'. No visible surface remains of these castles exist today. There are also hundreds of largely seventeenth-century historical references to castles at sites where no traces now exist above ground level. Using this evidence, Barry (1996, 140) suggested that anything up to 7000 tower-houses were built in Ireland between the fourteenth and seventeenth centuries. Whatever the exact number, Ireland was clearly the most castellated part of the British Isles around 1600 (Cairns 1987, 21).

Fortified houses

The fortified house developed from the tower-house (Pl. 16). This form of castle began to be built in the late sixteenth century and ceased to be erected around 1650. The most spectacular examples of fortified houses, such as Rathfarnham Castle, Co. Dublin, consist of large rectangular blocks with massive square towers at each corner. Far more emphasis is placed on domestic accommodation in fortified houses than in tower-houses. However, features such as gun-loops, flanking defence and machicolations indicate that fortified houses were also designed to repel attack. Very often this type of castle has an attached bawn (Power *et al.* 1994, 233–7; Sweetman 1995, 42–4; Sweetman *et al.* 1995, 124–6). It is not certain how many fortified houses once existed in the Irish countryside. Laois has twelve examples (Sweetman *et al.* 1995, 124–6), mid-Cork has about ten, while Cavan has only two (O'Donovan 1995, 235; Power *et al.* 1997, 233–7). The final figure will only be known when fieldwork throughout the country has been completed by the Archaeological Survey. Perhaps up to 200 fortified houses exist in the Irish countryside today, and maybe even more.

Summary

Between 4000 and 8000 structures that can be classified as castles may have been built in Ireland between the late twelfth century and the mid-seventeenth century. These include mottes, ringworks, Anglo-Norman masonry castles, later tower-houses and fortified houses. What links these monument types under the common term 'castle'? In effect, what were castles?

The function of castles

A castle, whether of earth and timber or of stone, was both a well-defended fortress capable of withstanding quite serious attack and a private residence, usually of someone of importance in medieval society, at least at a local level. It was both a stronghold and a house belonging to an individual, be he the lord of just one manor or a major magnate who controlled vast estates. The main military function of a castle was to protect its owner, his family and his retainers against sustained attack. It is believed that castles were the means by which territory was taken and held during the whole medieval period. It was very hard to break a lord's hold on a district once he held its castles. Castles, then, were military fortifications designed to repel attack and to withstand sieges, if only for a few hours (D.C. King 1988, 1–13; O'Conor, forthcoming). It is held that castles, even timber ones, were far more fortified than other medieval defensive sites, such as moated sites. For example, new research suggests that many, if not most, earthwork or timber castles had quite serious defences, such as mural towers

Pl. 16—*The seventeenth-century fortified house at Glinsk, Co. Galway, built by the Burkes.* (Photo: Kieran O'Conor.)

and palisades looped for archery. The formidable nature of the defences on most of these earth and timber fortresses seems to be the reason why they are referred to as castles in the surviving sources in exactly the same way as complex masonry ones (Figs 7–8; Barker and Higham 1982; 1988; Higham and Barker 1992, 159–61, 326, 334–7; O'Conor 1996, 111–12; forthcoming).

Therefore castles of all types were fortresses. Yet they were also dwellings and had peaceful functions as well (King 1988, 4–5). For example, a castle was the centre or *caput* of its owner's estate or manor. It was usually a working farm throughout most of the British Isles, and the lord's demesne land (the area within the manor kept and farmed directly by the lord), if it existed, was mostly cultivated from here. A building or room within the castle, or an edifice just outside its gate, served as a court-house for the manorial tenants where petty agricultural disputes were resolved. This made the castle a centre of rural administration and justice (King 1988, 5; O'Conor, forthcoming; Pounds 1990, 201). It must also be remembered that many Anglo-Norman manorial centres in medieval Ireland never had castles located at them. Presumably the lord's residence at these places was an undefended manor house, built of timber or clay and wood. Such a structure would be difficult to locate in the modern landscape, simply because it would have left no trace above ground (Barry 1987, 93–4). The main point here, however, is that castles had peaceful as well as military functions. The many hundreds of castles dotted throughout the Irish landscape today were once residences and farm centres in much the same way as contemporary undefended manor houses or later country houses of eighteenth- and nineteenth-century date. This is often forgotten in the popular imagination, which sees castles as purely military strongholds rather than as lively centres of working farms and rural administration.

2.2—Castles as manorial centres

Irish scholarship, in contrast, has always acknowledged in a general way that castles were both private residences and well-defended fortresses. For example, Leask (1941), Sweetman (1995) and McNeill (1997) comprehensively analysed the architectural

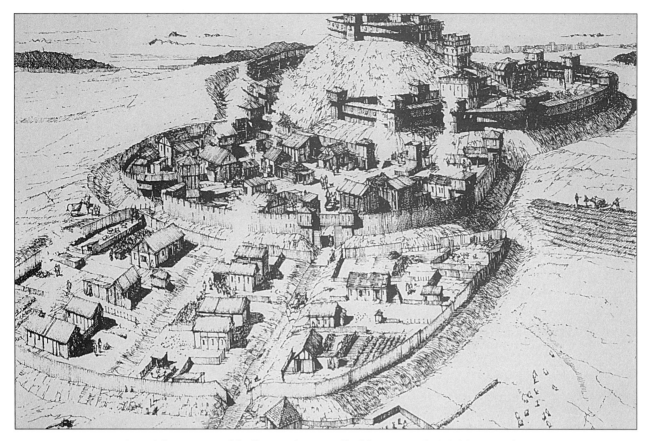

Fig. 7—*Reconstruction of the motte and bailey castle at Stafford by Peter Scholefield* (© Stafford Borough Council).

Fig. 8—*Reconstruction of part of the bailey at Hen Domen, Powys* (Barker and Higham 1988).

evidence for living accommodation in Irish masonry castles of all dates, as well as discussing their defensive features. The excavated evidence for domestic buildings in earthwork castles in Ireland has also been reviewed in recent years (O'Conor 1992, 4–5; 1993, 369–75; forthcoming). Indeed, there is general agreement amongst Irish archaeologists and historians that most castles marked the centres of estates and that farming was carried out from many of them (e.g. Barry 1987, 186; Cairns 1987, 25; O'Conor, forthcoming).

However, very little archaeological work has been carried out in Ireland on the nature and layout of the farm buildings around, beside and within castles of all sorts. There are a number of reasons for this.

Firstly, most of these buildings were built of wood or a mixture of clay and wood. Naturally, these have decayed over time and leave no trace above ground level today. Furthermore, it must also be presumed that many buildings around and within Irish castles were destroyed in the endemic warfare that characterised Ireland up to the late seventeenth century. This warfare became more violent and bloody in the century and a half after *c.* 1530 during the English reconquest of Ireland (McNeill 1997, 228). Medieval farm buildings simply do not seem to exist in the Irish landscape today, unlike in England. Secondly, there has been comparatively little excavation at castle sites in Ireland, and most investigations have been small in size with limited goals. Therefore it is no surprise that little is known in archaeological terms about ancillary agricultural and administrative buildings beside or within Irish castles. The excavations of most Anglo-Norman masonry castles have been carried out in advance of conservation work either by the Office of Public Works in the Republic or by the Department of the Environment in Northern Ireland. While these excavations produced many interesting results, most were small in scale and limited to specific areas of the castle under conservation and consolidation.

For example, Ballyloughan Castle, Co. Carlow, was excavated in 1955 while conservation work was being carried out on the site by the OPW (Pl. 17; de Paor 1962, 1). This castle consists of a more or less square courtyard, about 45m by 45m in area, once delimited by a curtain-wall. Square angle-towers stand at the north-eastern and south-western corners of this enclosure. Presumably angle-towers also once existed at the other two corners. A twin-towered gatehouse stands midway along the south curtain-wall (de Paor 1962; McNeill 1997, 114–16). The castle, which was built about 1300, also had a ditch around it (de Paor 1962, 7). Excavation took place only at the points within the castle that needed conservation—the north-east angle-tower and part of the gatehouse (de Paor 1962, 3). Only a tiny fraction of the large courtyard area was excavated. Therefore the part of the castle where it is likely that undefended wooden and clay-walled farm and administrative buildings once existed was not investigated.

There has never been an excavation of a large Anglo-Norman masonry castle which specifically set out to find ancillary farm buildings within or around it. Furthermore, owing to the fact that few tower-houses have been excavated in Ireland despite their large numbers, hardly anything is known about the physical nature of the farm buildings around these later castles either (Barry 1987, 190; McNeill 1997, 222). It was noted above that most of the castles in use in Ireland between the late twelfth and early fourteenth centuries were earthwork castles (section 2.1). Yet only a handful of motte and ringwork castles have been excavated to date on this island, and most of these investigations, which took place mainly in the 1950s and early 1960s, were small in scale. For example, the excavation of the important motte castle at Dromore, Co. Down, consisted of nothing more than a couple of trenches across the summit of the mound (Waterman 1954b). The excavation of baileys and off-mound habitation beside free-standing mottes (i.e. mottes without baileys) is negligible (Barry 1987, 38–9).

The archaeological evidence, therefore, for most castles functioning as the centres of demesne farms on manors or as the agricultural cores of later freehold estates is minimal. Fieldwork and excavation have both contributed little to our knowledge of the farmyards that once existed within or beside most castles in Ireland. At present it

Pl. 17—*Ballyloughan Castle, Co. Carlow, built about 1300.* (Photo: *Dúchas*, The Heritage Service.)

is the existing historical evidence, which comes mainly from references found in surviving manorial extents and accounts, that best illustrates the fact that most castles once functioned as administrative and farm centres. In many ways this is surprising as there is a dearth of such economic records in Ireland in comparison to the huge wealth of documentation relating to the manorial economy in England (Down 1987, 439). For example, no extents or accounts survive for the first 80–100 years or so of manorial development in Ireland after 1169 (*ibid.*, 455).

Some references suggest that a plethora of what appear to be timber or clay-walled farm and administrative buildings once existed around many castles. Probably the most famous reference comes from an extent of the manor of Inch, near Thurles, Co. Tipperary, made in 1303. A variety of manorial buildings stood around the motte castle there in that year, including a hall, a wooden chapel, a kitchen, a fish-house, stables, a granary, a sheepcote, a dovecote and a malt-kiln. A mill and fish-ponds also apparently existed at the site, or at least nearby. A castle garden, presumably for growing herbs, fruit and vegetables, is also referred to in this extent (*Red Bk. Ormond*, 52–3; Empey 1985, 80). An almost equally famous reference to buildings within and around a motte castle comes from an extent of the manor of Knocktopher made in 1312, which states that a palisade, a *bretesche* (a timber tower), a hall, a chamber and a chapel with an attached storeroom existed at or lay within the castle at this date. There was also a kitchen within an outer gate. Another chamber or building and a *bretesche* lay outside this gate. A cruck-built wooden grange and a byre lay in the lower courtyard of the castle (seemingly a reference to the bailey). A masonry-built hall was also standing in this 'lower courtyard'—apparently the only stone building in the whole castle complex. Other timber buildings existed in this part of the castle too. A dovecote, three fruit and herb gardens and two mills also occurred beside this castle (*Red Bk. Ormond*, 127–31; Empey 1982, 332). Unfortunately the motte and bailey at Knocktopher were levelled around 1980 in the course of farm development (Nicholls 1982, 370).

There are many other references to agricultural buildings beside or within sites that can be identified as castles. The only surviving Irish pipe roll is full of references to farming activities being carried out from various Anglo-Norman masonry and earthwork castles in royal hands (Davies and Quinn 1941). The 'haggard' or farmyard

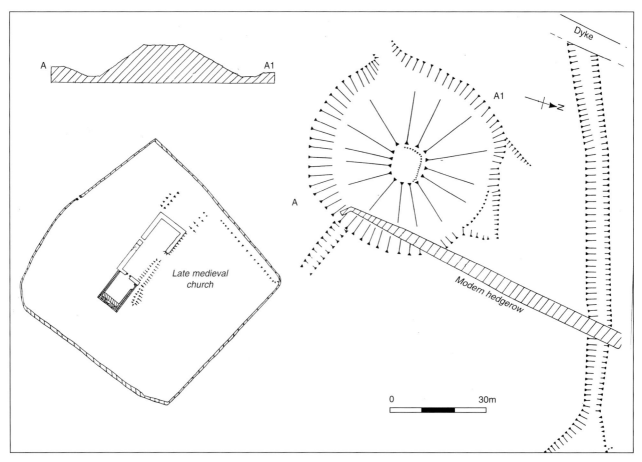

Fig. 9—*Plan of the motte castle at Cloncurry, Co. Kildare* (after O'Conor 1993).

of the castle of 'Ryban' in County Kildare is mentioned in 1297 (*Cal. Justic. Rolls Ire.*, I, 180). A motte was levelled at Castlereban South around 1900 (Fitzgerald 1896–9, 168; Orpen 1907b, 253). Part of the bailey still survives at the site today (O'Conor 1993, 472). This appears to be the thirteenth-century castle of 'Ryban' (O'Conor 1987–91, 15). A 1304 extent of the manor of Cloncurry, Co. Kildare, also indicates that a series of domestic and farm buildings existed here. A thatched hall and another small building lay beside the motte (*mota*) in a 'courtyard'. Beside this courtyard and motte was a farmyard containing two eight-post barns, a corn-drying kiln, a cow-byre, a dovecote and a threshing house (*Red Bk. Ormond*, 27–31; O'Loan 1961, 14–15). No buildings or earthworks, except for the remains of the medieval parish church and a probable hollow way, exist beside the free-standing motte at Cloncurry today (Fig. 9). In 1305 Agnes Fitzgerald claimed that John fitz Thomas Fitzgerald had attacked her at Rathmore—the *caput* of a rich County Kildare manor. He had taken livestock and corn, as well as destroying farm equipment and agricultural and domestic buildings (*Cal. Justic. Rolls Ire.*, ii, 75–8, 240–1). Presumably these farm buildings lay around the large motte extant at Rathmore today (Pl. 11). Furthermore, a mill is mentioned at Rathmore in a 1331 extent of the possessions of Richard Fitzgerald, earl of Kildare (*Red Bk. Kildare*, no. 131).

A 1307 extent of the manor of Lough Merans, Co. Kilkenny, states that a *bretesche*, a granary, stables and a sheepfold, all made of wood, existed at the manorial centre there in that year (*CDI*, v, no. 668; *CIPM*, iv, no. 435). The *caput* of this manor seems to have been a motte carved out of a promontory which jutted into a lake, with an attached bailey (Orpen 1911–20, iii, 93). Another 1307 extent mentions a thatched sheepfold and two watermills, amongst other timber and stone buildings, at the *caput* of the manor of Old Ross, Co Wexford (*CDI*, v, no. 617; *CIPM*, iv, no.434; *Cal. Justic.*

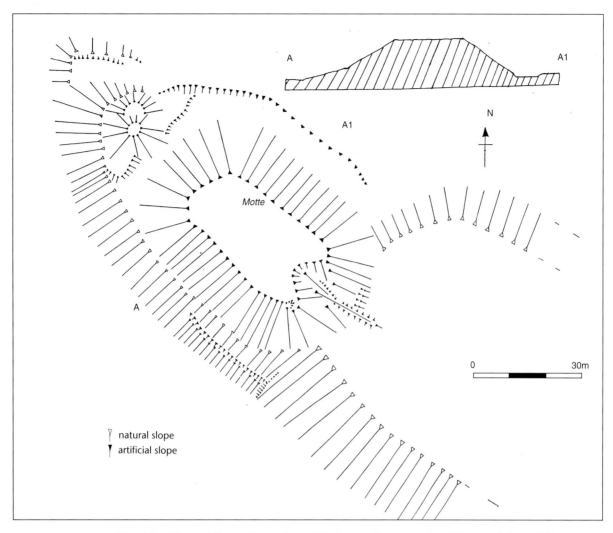

natural slope
artificial slope

0   30m

Fig. 10—*Plan of the motte castle at Westcourt Demesne, Co. Kilkenny* (after O'Conor 1993).

Rolls Ire., ii, 347). The centre of this manor seems to be marked by the motte extant at Springpark, Old Ross, today, which has a levelled bailey beside it (Pl. 18; Moore 1996, 93). A hall, a wooden dairy or byre and a palisade are also incidentally referred to at the site in 1280–1 (Hore 1900–11, i, 15). A 1307 extent of the manor of Callan, Co. Kilkenny, mentions the castle at the manorial centre. A series of wooden domestic buildings lay 'within' this castle (*CDI*, v, no. 659; *CIPM*, iv, no. 435), which is apparently the motte extant at Westcourt Demesne, lying near the left bank of the King's River on the outskirts of modern Callan (Fig. 10). Presumably these buildings originally lay on the very large motte summit there, which has an area of *c.* 800m², as the site appears never to have had an attached bailey. Apparently beside the castle, but not within it, lay a farmyard or haggard in which there was a large wooden barn, a building for housing oxen and stone-built stables. Two watermills are also mentioned (*CIPM*, iv, no. 435).

The *caput* of the medieval manor of 'Dunfert' seems to be represented today by the circular earthwork enclosure at Danesfort, Co. Kilkenny (Orpen 1909d, 321). It is probably best to describe this site as a ringwork castle (O'Conor 1993, 709–10). A number of timber buildings seem to have existed within this enclosure in 1307, including a hall, a dairy, a granary and several other wooden structures. A watermill, a dovecote and a rabbit warren also occurred at the site but presumably outside the bounds of the enclosure (*CDI*, v, no. 667; *CIPM*, iv, no. 435). Indeed, a ruined masonry dovecote still exists just to the north-east of the site, although this structure appears to be of seventeenth- or eighteenth-century date. An inquisition into the lands of Roger

Pl. 18—*The motte at Springpark, Old Ross, Co. Wexford. Farm buildings once stood around the mound here during the medieval period.* (Photo: Kieran O'Conor.)

Bigod in 1307 stated that at 'Forth' (Castlemore, Co. Carlow) there was a grange (barn?) of ten forks and a watermill, amongst other timber and masonry buildings (*CDI*, v, no. 617; *CIPM*, iv, no. 434; *Cal. Justic. Rolls Ire.*, ii, 346). Presumably most of these buildings (apart from the watermill) lay within the motte and bailey castle extant at Castlemore today (Fig. 11). It was noted above (section 2.1) that castles were centres of rural administration and justice throughout the medieval period. A manorial court seems to have been held within this latter castle during the thirteenth century at least (*CDI*, iii, no. 593). A manorial court dealing with agricultural disputes between the tenants of

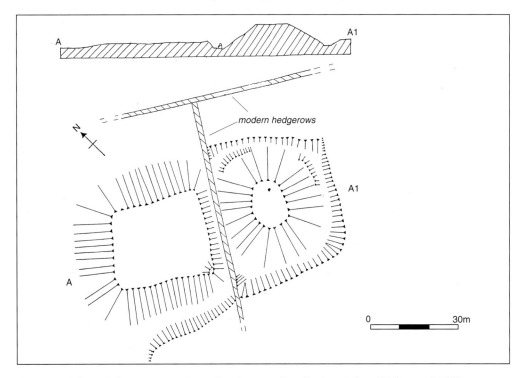

Fig. 11—*Plan of the motte castle at Castlemore, Co. Carlow* (after O'Conor 1993).

the manor of Kill, Co. Kildare, was still being held within the motte and bailey there as late as 1540, long after the site had been deserted as a residence and farm centre (*Ext. Ir. Mon. Possessions*, 39). Presumably a timber building in which this manorial court took place still stood somewhere within the site at this late date.

A 1324 inquisition into the lands of Aymer de Valence indicates that he had held the manor of Odagh, Co. Kilkenny, in demesne. A large motte exists at Odagh today which appears never to have had a bailey. This motte (*mota*) is directly referred to in the 1324 inquisition as it had two thatched buildings on its summit, which had an area of *c.* 1300m². There seems to have been a barn at the site, as well as a watermill (*CIPM*, vi, no. 518). A 1326 extent of the manor of Ballymore belonging to the archbishop of Dublin (Ballymore Eustace, Co. Kildare) states that within the castle there was a hall, various buildings or rooms used for accommodation, a kitchen, a chapel, a granary, stables and a grange (barn?) (*Archbishop Alen's Reg.*, 189–92).

Most later tower-houses also functioned as the centres of working farms. For example, a list of the goods in use at the tower-house of Castletown, Co. Limerick, in 1642 includes a large quantity of farm equipment such as carts and ploughs. Brewing and distilling gear is also mentioned, as well as oxen (Cairns 1987, 24). The fact that tower-houses are generally sited in non-defensive locations on good agricultural land must also be taken as an indication that the vast majority of these fortresses were also farms (Barry 1987, 188–9; Cairns 1987, 24; O'Dowd 1991, 79).

These are just a few of the many surviving references to agricultural and administrative buildings associated with castles in medieval Ireland. Apart from clearly indicating that many castles functioned as farm centres, they also raise a number of other points.

Mills

Anglo-Norman lords clearly derived a large amount of their annual manorial income from their mills, which were often located beside castles, as seen from the references outlined above (Hennessy 1996, 121, 124; Mallory and McNeill 1991, 263; McNeill 1980, 40, 88, 188). Mills are frequently mentioned in the surviving sources and were clearly important places in the rural landscape throughout the areas controlled by the Anglo-Normans. What form did these structures originally take? Historical references to windmills exist from the late twelfth century onwards in England, where windmill mounds of medieval date are a well-recognised archaeological monument. These mounds would have been surmounted by timber-built windmills during their period of use (Beresford and St Joseph 1979, 64–5). Yet windmill mounds are almost non-existent in Ireland. One possible windmill mound of medieval date was identified at Agher, Co. Meath, within a deserted settlement beside a motte castle (Moore 1987, 164).

Another windmill mound exists within the bounds of the deserted medieval settlement at Rinndown, Co. Roscommon. This mound, however, has a masonry windmill of cylindrical shape built on top of it. It has been suggested that the earliest windmills of this type in Ireland date from the seventeenth century (Moore 1996, 192). Two other types of stone-built windmill survive in the Irish countryside today—the tapering windmill and the conical windmill. These seem to have evolved at a somewhat later date than the cylindrical windmill. The conical windmill seems to have first appeared, in Wexford at least, during the late eighteenth century (*ibid.*). At present there is no exact figure for the numbers of post-medieval stone-built windmills extant in the Irish countryside. Seven examples exist in modern County Roscommon and 23 were identified in County Wexford (*ibid.*, 192–5).

The main point in the present context is that stone-built or wooden windmills were not really a feature of medieval Ireland. It is clear from both fieldwork and the surviving documentary evidence that timber-built watermills, whether of the vertical or horizontal variety, were the preferred type. Silted-up mill-races can still be seen beside a number of Leinster mottes (O'Conor 1993, 364–5). Presumably at least some of these mill-races and the watermills that lay along them were in use while the earthwork castles were occupied. However, despite their importance to the manorial economy of medieval Ireland, no rural watermill of Anglo-Norman date has ever been excavated in this country.

Fish-ponds

Medieval fish-ponds are a fairly common field monument in the English countryside today, often occurring at sites that functioned as manorial or monastic centres during the medieval period (e.g. Aston 1988), but it appears on present evidence that recognisable medieval fish-ponds are rare in Ireland. It has been suggested that fish-ponds may have occurred beside the fifteenth-century Dominican priory at Tulsk, Co. Roscommon (O'Conor *et al.* 1996, 68–9). A long, rectangular fish-pond exists beside the fifteenth-century tower-house at Leamaneh, Co. Clare, to which a seventeenth-century house is attached (Mon. No. CL016-032). A long, rectangular fish-pond occurs near the site of a castle at Kilkee Upper, Co. Clare (Westropp 1918). Possible medieval fish-ponds can be seen at Caherass and Old Abbey, Co. Limerick (*ibid.*). The reference to fish-ponds at Inch in 1303 suggests that at least some Anglo-Norman manorial centres had them (*Red Bk. Ormond*, 52–3). Certainly, a fish-pond was under construction at Limerick in 1211–12 (Davies and Quinn 1941, 70–1). Fish-ponds are also mentioned in 1243 on de Burgo lands in Tipperary (Hennessey 1996, 122). However, the scant physical evidence for fish-ponds of medieval date in the Irish landscape today seems to suggest that very few existed here during the medieval period, unlike the situation in England. Why was this, given the importance of fish in the medieval diet? How did Anglo-Norman lords and their manorial tenants in medieval Ireland obtain their fish? Water-filled fosses around castles or moated sites in medieval England, primarily defensive in function, were sometimes also used as fish-ponds (e.g. Platt 1978, 188), and this may have happened in some cases in medieval Ireland. For example, the motte at Aghaboe, Co. Laois, is sited on low-lying ground close to a stream, and is surrounded by a wide fosse, now silted up. Other ditches radiating out from this fosse seem to have had no real defensive purpose, but it appears that they all once held water (Orpen 1909d, 335). Perhaps these ditches once acted as both a fish-pond and a defensive barrier around the motte. Part of the original ditch running across the narrowest part of the promontory jutting out into Lough Ree at the deserted medieval town at Rinndown, Co. Roscommon, seems to have been dug out and turned into a fish- or duck-pond. Rinndown Castle lies just to the north of this feature, along the ditch.

Another explanation for the lack of straightforward fish-ponds in this country could be that there was greater exploitation of river, lake and sea fish on the manors of Anglo-Norman-controlled parts of medieval Ireland in comparison to England. For example, quite an amount of evidence for sophisticated medieval fish-traps and fish-weirs has been discovered recently in sheltered coastal and estuarine areas of Ireland (O'Sullivan 1994; 1995a; 1995b; 1997).

Rabbit-farming

The reference to a warren at 'Dunfert' (Danesfort, Co. Kilkenny) in 1307 is an indication that rabbit-farming took place on at least some Anglo-Norman manors in medieval Ireland. Other references to rabbit warrens on Anglo-Norman manors occur in the surviving sources (e.g. F. Kelly 1997, 137). Cigar-shaped earthworks known as pillow-mounds exist all over the English countryside today. These were constructed for rabbits to burrow into and live in so that they could be culled at regular intervals for their meat and fur. It was once held that these earthworks were of medieval date (Aston 1985, 115). No pillow-mound has yet been recognised in Ireland, despite the evidence for medieval rabbit-farming here. More recent work in England now suggests that most pillow-mounds date from the sixteenth century and later (*ibid.*). Presumably rabbit-farming on medieval English manors was carried out in suitable fields, probably protected by a palisade to keep out predators such as foxes. Rabbit-farming may also have been carried out in this way at manorial centres in medieval Ireland. It seems that pillow-mounds were not yet part of the cultural assemblage of England or Wales when Anglo-Norman and English colonists came to Ireland in the late twelfth and thirteenth centuries.

The dating of motte and ringwork castles

The references outlined above to buildings around, within and on mostly motte castles, including descriptions of what appear to be timber towers, raise an important point which is essential for our understanding of the role this form of earthwork castle played in medieval Ireland. Leask (1941, 11, 24) seems to have been the first to believe that mottes were built in the late twelfth century only as temporary fortifications, as he regarded them as unsuitable for permanent residences. He believed that they were replaced by masonry castles around *c.* 1200, without giving any specific examples to support his view. The work of the Archaeological Survey of Ireland in recent years clearly shows that the vast majority of mottes in this country do not have masonry castles of thirteenth- or early fourteenth-century date beside them or on them. It might be added that a fair number have or had later tower-houses beside them—a castle type shown above to be really post-1400 in date in Ireland (Brindley and Kilfeather 1993, 78–9; Buckley 1986, 86–8; Buckley and Sweetman 1991, 281–98; Moore 1987, 156–61; 1996, 90–4; O'Brien and Sweetman 1997, 132–4; O'Conor 1993, 417–703; Sweetman *et al.* 1995, 101–3; Stout 1984, 111–13).

The references discussed above to what appear to be wooden buildings and defences in use at certain motte castles in Ireland during the period 1300–20 suggest that many of these castles were still in use as both residences and fortresses between 100 and 150 years after they were first built (O'Conor 1987–91, 13–25; 1992, 6; 1993, 330–7, 375–84; forthcoming). Research elsewhere in the British Isles also indicates that most motte castles were built as permanent fortifications and residences, in use as purely wooden fortresses for anything up to 200 years (e.g. Barker and Higham 1982; 1988; Higham 1989; Higham and Barker 1992). Indeed, recent work in Ireland suggests that many Anglo-Norman masonry castles had ringwork rather than motte precursors. Evidence for what appear to be earlier ringwork castles was found during the excavations of Limerick Castle, Trim Castle, Ferns Castle, Kilkenny Castle and probably Carlow Castle and Adare Castle, Co. Limerick (Barry 1983, 307; 1987, 49; Murtagh 1993; O'Conor 1997; Sweetman 1978; 1979; 1980; K. Wiggins, pers. comm.). It must also be remembered, however, that not all ringworks were pulled down at a later date to make way for large masonry castles. For example, the ringwork castle at Rathangan, Co. Kildare, seemingly carved out of a pre-Norman ringfort, appears to have still been used by the Fitzgeralds as a timber castle in the early fourteenth century (Pl. 13; *Red Bk. Kildare*, no. 122; O'Conor 1987–91, 15). The excavator of the ringwork at Pollardstown, Co. Kildare, which marks the *caput* of a historically attested Anglo-Norman manor, suggested that the range of artefacts found in the quite deep habitation layers indicated that this earthwork castle was occupied from the late twelfth century through to the fourteenth century. It must be added that many of these finds could also be fifteenth-century in date (Fanning 1973–4; O'Conor 1993, 719–20). The main point in the present context is that masonry castles were not built over these ringworks in the very late twelfth century or early in the thirteenth century. They continued as earthwork castles until they were abandoned completely.

Furthermore, Leask's (1941, 11, 25) belief that mottes stopped being erected in Ireland after the very early years of the thirteenth century is now open to question. Although many mottes were still in use as timber castles over many parts of lowland England in the first years of the fourteenth century, few appear to have been built in that country after *c.* 1150 (King 1988, 26; Kenyon 1990, 8). The available evidence, however, suggests that motte castles were built at far later dates than this in other, more troubled parts of Britain. A number of mottes in Wales were postulated as dating from the period *after* the Edwardian conquest of 1282–3 and were erected as a reaction against a rise in casual violence and lawlessness (King 1988, 143–5). Scotland also appears to have had a longer history of motte construction than most of England. The excavator of the motte of Castlehill of Strachan, Kincardineshire, dated the initial phase of occupation at this site to *c*. 1250 (Yeoman 1984, 340–4). The erection of Roberton motte, Lanarkshire, apparently took place in the very late thirteenth or early fourteenth century, during the troubled times of the Scottish War of Independence (Haggarty and Tabraham 1982, 61–2). There is a certain amount of evidence, therefore, that mottes continued to be built after *c*. 1250 in areas of Britain that suffered from troubled internal conditions.

It must be stated that the few excavated examples of motte castles in Ireland, which occur mainly in east Ulster, indicate a date in either the very late twelfth or early thirteenth century for their initial erection, although many continued to be occupied into the fourteenth century (Barry 1987, 38–9; Lynn 1981–2, 112–14, 166–9). Despite this assertion, McNeill (1980, 69) has argued on distributional grounds that mottes continued to be built in parts of east Ulster until *c*. 1250. The second half of the thirteenth century saw the beginnings of a revival of Gaelic power in Ireland, which manifested itself both militarily and culturally throughout the country. This movement, known as the Gaelic Resurgence, really gathered pace in the fourteenth century, especially after the ravages of the Bruce Invasion and the Black Death on the Anglo-Norman colony (Lydon 1987b; K. Simms 1989, 74–103). This century, especially its second half, was an age of territorial retreat for the Anglo-Norman/English colony in Ireland. Warfare became endemic in regions that had been comparatively peaceful up to the mid-thirteenth century. The fourteenth century also witnessed the growing Gaelicisation of many Anglo-Norman families (Frame 1981, 111–35; K. Simms 1989, 74–103). By 1500 Ireland consisted of a large number of virtually independent lordships, controlled either by Gaelic lords or by men of Anglo-Norman descent, now for the most part largely Hibernicised in their culture and outlook, jostling for power amongst themselves (Richter 1988, 191–2). It was not until the seventeenth century that Ireland was fully reconquered by the English government (Canny 1989; MacCurtain 1972, 89–192).

What began the Gaelic Resurgence? It has been argued that a number of different factors caused this movement throughout Ireland, each giving momentum to the others. Gaelic Ireland began to perfect its military tactics against the Anglo-Normans in the later thirteenth century (section 4.3). This was helped by the emergence of a group of competent leaders throughout Gaelic Ireland at the same time. The process was aided by a weakening of the colonial government, which was ruthlessly exploited by Edward I for resources to carry on his campaigns elsewhere. The late thirteenth and early fourteenth centuries also saw a very definite Irish sense of grievance against the racist attitudes of certain Anglo-Norman or English settlers, and a fear that many of the latter still had a desire to take more Irish lands (Lydon 1987b, 241–3). However, the immediate spur to the Gaelic Resurgence in many parts of the country may have been sheer economic necessity. Such things as cattle murrain, bad harvests and overpopulation may have caused the Irish to begin raiding richer Anglo-Norman areas from the second half of the thirteenth century onwards (Lydon 1987b, 243). For example, Leinster was a very prosperous and peaceful region for most of the thirteenth century. Many towns and rich Anglo-Norman manors had been set up there during the late twelfth and early thirteenth centuries. There seems to have been little real trouble between the Irish septs of the region and the colony up to *c*. 1270. But despite this appearance of peace and plenty, the Gaelic Resurgence was to occur in Leinster too. The main catalyst for this trouble appears to have been actual famine and cattle murrain in 1271. Warfare and raiding were to be relatively common in Leinster for the rest of the thirteenth century, with the Irish of the region defeating a number of colonial armies sent against them. This warfare and raiding was to intensify throughout the fourteenth century, with large areas of Leinster returning to Irish control or at least cultural

Pl. 19—*The motte at Aghaboe, Co. Laois. The historical sources and possibly the site's morphology suggest that this motte was built either in the late thirteenth or even early fourteenth century.* (Photo: Kieran O'Conor.)

domination (Lydon 1987b, 256–61, 264–7). It has been argued that a number of motte castles in Leinster were erected in either the late thirteenth or the early fourteenth century as a reaction against the Gaelic Resurgence in the region (Pl. 19; O'Conor 1987–91, 13–25; 1993, 316–30). Therefore, it is suggested that while many, if not most, mottes in Ireland were erected in either the late twelfth or very early thirteenth century, some continued to be built even beyond 1300.

When were motte and ringwork castles finally abandoned in Ireland? The motte and bailey at Liddel Strength, Cumberland, was still in use as a timber castle in the mid-fourteenth century (King 1988, 30). The motte at Sycharth, Denbigh, was still occupied as late as 1400, with its timber buildings and defences being burnt by the English in 1403 (Hague and Warhurst 1966; Higham and Barker 1992, 144–6; Kenyon 1990, 22). These examples suggest that timber castles continued to be occupied throughout parts of Britain into the late fourteenth or even early fifteenth century. As noted, the historical evidence suggests that earthwork castles were still very much in use in Ireland during the first quarter of the fourteenth century. The evidence from the few motte castles excavated in Ireland, which lie mostly in east Ulster, suggests that at least some of these were abandoned at some stage in the fourteenth century, presumably owing to the pressures of the Gaelic Resurgence in the area, which saw various Anglo-Norman settlements being deserted (e.g. Waterman 1954a, 122; 1959a, 169). This might suggest that it was the reconquest of certain areas by the Gaelic Irish throughout the fourteenth century that led to the abandonment of many earthwork castles. Alternatively, earthwork castles and their adjacent settlements could have been deserted owing to the economic and social upheavals of the fourteenth century.

Very little can be said with authority at present about when mottes and ringworks were finally abandoned as both fortresses and residences. Were mottes finally abandoned in more secure areas of the Anglo-Norman colony during the course of the fourteenth century as well? Certainly, rich agricultural areas such as modern Kildare, Meath and south Tipperary seem to have been regularly raided by Gaelic septs from along their borders throughout the fourteenth century. However, despite these attacks, these regions remained under the control of lords of Anglo-Norman descent up to the seventeenth century. It might be added that there were internal upheavals and feuding in these areas amongst the Anglo-Normans themselves. Such lawless and violent conditions were to continue in many areas throughout the fifteenth and sixteenth centuries.

As noted, quite a few mottes have or had tower-houses located beside them. It was shown above that the overwhelming majority of tower-houses in this country were built after 1400 (section 2.1). The juxtaposition of some mottes with tower-houses must surely be taken as an indication that the former were in use until they were replaced by the latter as defended residences at some stage in the fifteenth century, given the troubled internal conditions of late medieval Ireland. Many other mottes, however, in districts that were dominated by Anglo-Norman families up to the seventeenth century, never had tower-houses beside them. Again, it is possible that these places continued to be used as castles throughout the fifteenth century and possibly later, until conditions in these areas were sufficiently stable to allow them to be finally abandoned or for their defences to be allowed to decay (O'Conor 1987–91, 25–8).

It is therefore possible that in the unsettled conditions of late fourteenth- and fifteenth-century Ireland some mottes continued as castles and defended manorial residences. King (1988, 29–30), partly thinking of the mid-fourteenth-century use of earthwork castles on the Scottish border, stated that there was no such thing as an 'obsolete' castle. Although fortifications could be out of date in any given period, this did not mean that these fortresses could not provide defence for their occupants against attack. The main point in the context of late fourteenth- and fifteenth-century Ireland is that an earthwork or timber castle would have been a perfectly adequate defence for a minor lord and his family in the localised, small-scale warfare of late medieval Ireland. It must be admitted, however, that this view is based more on logic than on hard archaeological evidence.

2.3—Conclusions

2.3a—Castles: country houses and manorial centres—current state of knowledge

Castles of all sorts occur in large numbers throughout Ireland today. These include mottes, ringworks, large Anglo-Norman masonry castles and tower-houses. At least 4000 castles were built in Ireland between the twelfth and seventeenth centuries, probably many more, although it must be remembered that over three-quarters of these were tower-houses, overwhelmingly built in this country after 1400. The Irish landscape today contains far more castles than other parts of the British Isles, even Scotland (section 2.1).

There has always been a tendency in the popular mind to view castles as purely military centres. This view is further complicated in Ireland by the fact that castles have often been seen as symbols of English domination (section 2.1) (McNeill 1997, 2). Yet castles can be defined as strongly defended private residences, usually of someone of importance in medieval society, even if only at a local level. Certainly, castles were designed to protect their owners against attack, but they were also homes in which people lived out their lives. Castles were the administrative centres of their owners' manors and estates, as well as the centres of working farms. For example, most Anglo-Norman castles, certainly those located outside the earldom of Ulster, were the centres of demesne farms—the lands within manors farmed directly by their lords. The surviving historical sources indicate that a variety of administrative and farm buildings lay within and around many castles in Ireland. These buildings have decayed or been destroyed over time, leaving castles standing isolated in the landscape today. This makes it easy to forget that these places were once vibrant centres of medieval life (sections 2.1, 2.2).

Almost three-quarters of the castles built in Ireland by Anglo-Norman lords had earth and timber defences. The vast majority of these earthwork castles were mottes (at least in their final form). The evidence suggests that mottes and most ringworks were built as permanent castles, usually marking the *capita* of manors. These were the centres from which the Anglo-Normans controlled many parts of Ireland from the late twelfth century through to the fourteenth century, and possibly even later in some districts. The rural economy of Anglo-Norman-controlled areas of medieval Ireland was to a large extent run from these earthwork castles. Their importance has been continuously underestimated by Irish scholars this century, who have tended to place more emphasis on masonry castles. Only one motte castle has ever been excavated in the Republic—the motte at Lurgankeel, Co. Louth—and the results of this excavation have never been published, bar one small note about 30 years ago (*Oibre* 1965, 22).

As in other troubled areas of the British Isles in the medieval period, such as Scotland and Wales, there is a certain amount of evidence to suggest that some motte castles were built throughout the thirteenth century, even into the very early fourteenth century. Many earthwork castles were deserted during the course of the fourteenth century, perhaps as a result of the Gaelic reconquest of the areas in which they lay or possibly because of economic vicissitudes and the long-term effects of the Black Death. However, it is the present writer's opinion that some earthwork castles continued to be used as defended residences into the fifteenth century in districts that remained under the control of families of Anglo-Norman descent. They were then either replaced by tower-houses or their defences were allowed to decay owing to an improvement in the local military situation (section 2.2).

2.3b—Castles: country houses and manorial centres—priorities for future research
Clearly, one of the main priorities for future research into medieval rural settlement in Ireland is to use excavation to shed more light on the fact that most castles were not just fortresses but the centres of working farms and rural administration as well. Another priority must surely be to target a motte for long-term excavation, in order to better understand the important role played by this type of castle in Anglo-Norman Ireland.

It is possible that both of these research aims could be welded into one. The thorough excavation of a carefully chosen motte castle would answer a variety of questions raised in this chapter. As these places were mostly residences, this excavation would shed light on the physical layout of an Anglo-Norman manorial centre. Much information could be gained on the nature and variety of the agricultural buildings associated with a demesne farm. This would mean in turn that such an excavation would have the potential to yield information on the manorial economy and agrarian history of Anglo-Norman Ireland, especially during the very late twelfth and early thirteenth centuries, the general period for which there is a lack of surviving economic and social records (section 2.2).

The nature of the timber defences associated with motte castles could also be examined in such a project. This would help in understanding why these sites are called castles in the sources and why they were such a popular choice of castle from the late twelfth century through to the early fourteenth century. Another important question for this excavation would be the issue of when mottes were finally abandoned in this country. The motte chosen would have to be located at a known manorial centre in a part of eastern Ireland well settled by English tenants, where the historical sources suggest clear evidence for demesne farming throughout the thirteenth and early fourteenth centuries. Since it is quite likely that the Anglo-Normans built their motte castles at pre-existing Irish lordly centres (section 4.2c; Flanagan 1993), such an excavation could also yield much information about Irish society immediately prior to their arrival.

3. ENGLISH PEASANT SETTLEMENT ON ANGLO-NORMAN MANORS

3.1—Introduction

The surviving documentary sources relating to the socio-economic development of Anglo-Norman manors in Ireland date mainly from the late thirteenth century onwards (Glasscock 1987, 212; Otway-Ruthven 1965, 778; 1968, 109, 115). Far less historical evidence survives for the early period of Anglo-Norman settlement (Otway-Ruthven 1965, 77). Therefore the information contained in these later sources (mainly manorial extents and various inquisitions post-mortem into the possessions of certain tenants-in-chief of the king) has to be used to reconstruct the social and economic development of Anglo-Norman settlement in Ireland during the late twelfth century and the first half of the thirteenth century.

The evidence from these extents and inquisitions shows that by the late thirteenth century many of the areas conquered by the Anglo-Normans since 1169 contained large numbers of peasants of mainly English origin, with some Welsh and Flemings, side by side with tenants of Gaelic Irish stock (Bartlett 1993, 144–8; Down 1987, 443–4; Duffy 1997, 83–4; Glasscock 1987, 213–21; Otway-Ruthven 1965, 77–83; 1968, 113–15). Specifically, these documentary sources suggest that by about 1270 a substantial part of the peasant population was of English descent in the present counties of Louth, Meath, Dublin, Kildare and Kilkenny, along with the southern halves of Wexford and Tipperary and parts of Cork, Limerick and Kerry (Glasscock 1987, 221; Otway-Ruthven 1965, 77; 1968, 113–15). For example, in 1304 over 50% of the tenants on the manor of Cloncurry, Co. Kildare, appear to be of English descent (*Red Bk. Ormond*, 27–34). Again, the population of the manor of Moyaliff, Co. Tipperary, was overwhelmingly of English origin in 1305 (*Red Bk. Ormond*, 64–7). The situation was the same on a wide range of manors throughout eastern and south-eastern Ireland (Otway-Ruthven 1965, 79–83). It has been argued that by about 1300 anything up to 50% of the population in lowland parts of the latter regions were the descendants of mostly English peasant colonists (Otway-Ruthven 1968, 115). Placename evidence also indicates that these areas saw widespread English colonisation (Jones-Hughes 1970, 247; Watt 1987a, 311). However, outside these regions of eastern Ireland there was little in the way of peasant immigration from England or elsewhere (Bartlett 1993, 144–8).

When did this substantial movement of mainly English peasants to Ireland actually take place? It is generally held that this immigration happened in the first two generations after the year 1169, perhaps peaking in the two decades after 1200 (Otway-Ruthven 1968, 113–14). However, very little is actually known about the colonisation process (Duffy 1997, 84), owing to a lack of archaeological excavation at Anglo-Norman manorial centres and of surviving documentary sources for this early period (e.g. Bartlett 1993, 144–5). For example, it is unclear how many peasants were involved in this migration and how long it took (Glasscock 1987, 221–2; Graham 1985b, 16; 1993, 73). Where these peasants actually came from in England and Wales is again a matter of some obscurity (Graham 1993, 73). It is now generally thought that they were recruited from the regions and estates that their lords in Ireland originally hailed from in western England and Wales (Eagar 1988; Graham 1993, 73).

It might be added that this peasant movement into Ireland is paralleled in other parts of Europe, such as the lands of the West Slavs east of the Elbe, which were settled by German-speaking peoples in the thirteenth century. Therefore this colonisation of

Ireland by mainly English peasants can be seen as part of a wider phenomenon of expansion of settlement and population out from the developed areas of Europe into more peripheral regions (Barry 1987, 73; Duffy 1997, 84–5; Otway-Ruthven 1965, 77; 1968, 109; A. Simms 1988a; 1988b, 291).

The next question must surely be why these peasants moved from the relatively peaceful lands of western England and south Wales to a potentially hostile and unfamiliar country. The available historical sources strongly suggest that there was a labour shortage in Ireland in the decades after 1169. There seems not to have been enough people available to work the new Anglo-Norman manors (Otway-Ruthven 1968, 115). By about 1200, or slightly later, many Anglo-Norman lords needed men to work their new Irish lands (Graham 1985b, 16; K. Simms 1989, 60). Conversely, the twelfth and early thirteenth centuries were periods of population growth in England and Wales, with subsequent pressure on settled land (Glasscock 1987, 212, 221; Graham 1985b, 16; Platt 1978, 91–3; K. Simms 1989, 60–1), and it must be presumed that both the availability of land and the potential for employment in Ireland were major enticements for people to leave England or Wales. Anglo-Norman lords also offered these peasants the chance of increasing their social status by moving to Ireland (Barry 1987, 73; 1996, 135; Duffy 1997, 83–4; Glasscock 1987, 212; Graham 1985b, 16; McNeill 1980, 89–91; Otway-Ruthven 1951, 1; 1968, 116–18). An English villein could become a free tenant simply by coming to Ireland, with all the hereditary rights and personal freedom that this entailed (Otway-Ruthven 1968, 116–17).

Furthermore, settlements at the centres of certain Anglo-Norman manors contained at least some tenants of burgess status. These settlements, which were never more than agricultural villages, are termed 'rural boroughs' by scholars today to distinguish them from true towns of the medieval period (Fig. 12). The traditional view is that Anglo-Norman lords gave these settlements urban rights as part of an overall attempt to attract English settlers to Ireland by offering them burgess status (Barry 1987, 73; 1996, 135; Duffy 1997, 83–4; Glasscock 1987, 223; Graham 1985a, 5; McNeill 1980, 89–91; Otway-Ruthven 1968, 116–18). A more recent theory, however, argues that urban rights may only have been granted to individual tenants at many of these places and not to the settlements themselves (H. Clarke, pers. comm.). Burgesses held their own burgage plots at a very low fixed rent and also leased other lands from their lords, probably as tenants-at-will. They had their own court or hundred, where they could decide many of their own affairs, as the judgements there were passed by fellow burgesses (Otway-Ruthven 1951, 1; 1968, 112–13; Graham 1993, 81). Therefore, the creation of numerous 'rural boroughs' or the granting of burgess status to individual tenants at certain Anglo-Norman manorial centres meant that the freedoms and increased prestige associated with burgage tenure lured many English tenants to Ireland and helped to populate the nascent manors. However, the foundation of many boroughs throughout Ireland by the Anglo-Normans during the late twelfth and early thirteenth centuries was not solely a ploy to attract settlers. It has been shown that the creation of boroughs was a well-established method by which lords increased their manorial incomes through the imposition of market tolls and by changing their peasants' agricultural surplus into direct cash to pay rent for their lands (Graham 1985a, 5–6; 1993, 82; K. Simms 1989, 60–1).

Another inducement for settlers to come to Ireland was that labour services were far lighter on Irish manors than on English ones. The lord's demesne land on most manors in Ireland was worked by labourers who were normally paid in cash or in kind and who usually belonged to the cottier class of manorial tenant. Labour services did not play a large part in the cultivation of the lord's home farm in medieval Ireland (Otway-Ruthven 1951, 9–10; 1968, 110, 118). However, despite all these attractions to emigrate, it is also possible that certain tenants were pressurised in some way by their lords in England or Wales to move to Ireland in order to populate new manors.

These various enticements to bring English settlers over to Ireland around the year 1200 seem to have been successful in the eastern part of the country. By *c.* 1250, if not

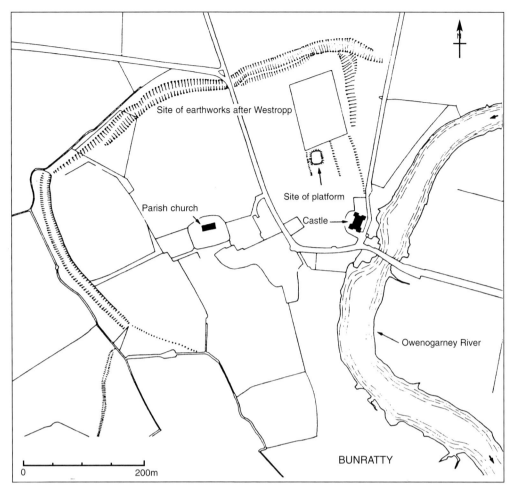

Fig. 12—*Plan of the site of the rural borough of Bunratty, Co. Clare* (after Bradley 1988).

considerably earlier, the peasant population of some parts of rural Ireland was divided into two ethnic groups, each having a different language and culture (Glasscock 1987, 222; A. Simms 1988a, 27).

It is the purpose of this chapter to examine the settlement forms and material culture associated with this influx of English peasants in the late twelfth and thirteenth centuries.

3.2—Villages and rural boroughs at Anglo-Norman manorial centres

3.2a—General theories

One constant theme running through the study of medieval rural settlement in Ireland over the last 30 years or so concerns the nature of the settlement pattern within Anglo-Norman manors. Documentary sources such as manorial extents, which, as noted, date mainly from the late thirteenth century onwards in Ireland, are not particularly helpful when attempting to understand the settlement forms or monument types that once existed on Anglo-Norman manors. They list the tenants on any given manor, their status, the lands they held, and the rents and labour services paid and given for them (Edwards *et al.* 1983, 352; Graham 1985a, 11; 1985b, 17). Arguably, their main interest for the discipline of archaeology is the information they sometimes give about the usually timber buildings associated with the lord's demesne or home farm at the manorial centre, which often occurred beside a motte or within its adjacent bailey (sections 2.2, 2.3). However, they do not usually indicate where the various grades of tenants actually lived within the manor or what settlement forms existed within its bounds (Graham 1985a, 11; 1985b, 10, 17–20). Neither do they describe the physical nature of the farmsteads and cottages lived in by these tenants. Manorial extents are primarily fiscal records and are not usually informative about the material culture of the peasants living and farming within the physical boundaries of the manor.

Despite these flaws in the available documentary records, it was held without question for many years that English peasants on Anglo-Norman manors lived in villages or rural boroughs clustered around a church and the lord's manor-house— which in Ireland was often located in some form of castle. It was presumed also that large open fields, divided into strips and with common grazing land beyond, surrounded these English-style villages in Ireland. This settlement model saw the inhabitants of these villages travelling out each day to cultivate their scattered strips, based on a yearly rotation of wheat, oats and fallow, or, alternatively, to work on their lord's demesne land either for cash or as part of their labour services (Duffy 1997, 111–12; Glasscock 1970; 1971; Graham 1975; Otway-Ruthven 1951; 1965; 1968, 107–18). The sites of about 3000 deserted villages occur in the English countryside today (Rowley and Wood 1982, 5). Many are or were until recently marked by rectilinear earthworks representing the remains of tofts and crofts, hollow ways and the footings of deserted houses. These features are usually juxtaposed with a church and the earthworks of a manor house (*ibid.*, 28–30).

Conversely, the earthworks of deserted villages or rural boroughs are rare in Ireland, the greatest number occurring in the southern part of County Tipperary. The fact that village earthworks do not occur in any great numbers did not deter certain scholars from believing that nucleated settlements were once widespread in all the parts of medieval Ireland that were at one time under Anglo-Norman control. Glasscock (1970, 171) argued that all sites in the regions of Ireland once held by the Anglo-Normans where medieval churches were located, be they parish churches or chapels of ease, marked the locations of deserted villages or rural boroughs, even if no earthworks of deserted peasant settlements exist there today. It might be added that earthwork castles frequently occur in juxtaposition with these church sites, being seen as representing the location of the lord of the manor's residence and the centre of his demesne farm. Graham (1975, 224–8), using this method combined with the evidence from various historical sources, suggested that about 98 villages and up to eight rural boroughs of Anglo-Norman date once existed in the present county of Meath.

Therefore up to the 1970s scholars in Ireland believed that in the decades after 1169 the Anglo-Normans brought the typical nucleated village of the English midlands to Ireland with them. These academics held that the physical appearance of these villages or rural boroughs consisted of a church, frequently juxtaposed with a timber castle, which was usually a motte and the centre of the lord's demesne farm, surrounded by many peasant houses filled with mainly English-speaking settlers. Furthermore, it was taken for granted that large open fields occurred beyond these villages. However, it was realised even in the 1950s that there were some differences between Anglo-Norman manors in Ireland and the typical manors of the English midlands. It was understood that the Gaelic Irish tenants on these manors, called 'betaghs' in the surviving manorial sources, lived in house clusters, possibly like later clachans, in townlands away from these nucleated English-style villages (Buchanan 1970, 150; Graham 1975, 244; Otway-Ruthven 1951, 3, 12; 1965, 76; 1968, 110–12). These Gaelic Irish betaghs apparently farmed their land in common, seemingly working it on an indigenous infield–outfield method like the later rundale system. Betaghs also owed labour services and rents to the lord of the manor (Glasscock 1987, 211; Graham 1985b, 23–4; 1993, 76; Otway-Ruthven 1951, 3; 1968, 110–13, 117; A. Simms 1983, 145; K. Simms 1989, 63).

This picture of English-style villages surrounded by large open fields in Anglo-Norman-controlled areas of medieval Ireland has been questioned and modified over the last two decades. The first attack on this model came from an in-depth regional study which examined the settlement patterns and organisation of the earldom of Ulster. It was shown that nucleated settlements of village form did not usually occur at manorial centres in Anglo-Norman areas of Ulster, except perhaps at the odd *caput* that had the status of a borough. It was argued that the evidence suggests that only the lord's residence, mostly located on a motte top, his mill (or one of them), and a church occurred at these places. Tenants lived out in townlands within the bounds of the manor and were mostly, if not all, of Gaelic Irish stock. These peasants came to their estate centres only to pay rent, attend the lord's court and get their corn ground at his mill (McNeill 1980, 84–8). Furthermore, the available historical and archaeological evidence suggests that Anglo-Norman lords in Ulster did not engage in demesne farming. It appears that all the land within any given manor was divided into rent-paying parcels worked by Irish tenants. The rent itself was paid in kind, most likely in measures of corn. There was therefore no need for the various ancillary farm buildings usually associated with demesne farming beside the residences of Anglo-Norman lords in east Ulster, unlike the situation throughout eastern and south-eastern Ireland. This is seen as one of the main reasons why so few baileys exist beside Ulster mottes today (McNeill 1980, 88).

McNeill showed, therefore, that the *capita* of Anglo-Norman manors in Ulster were really only administrative in function and were not centres of population or agricultural production, because the Anglo-Norman conquest there had not been accompanied by a corresponding movement of English peasant colonists into the region (McNeill 1980, 88). The Anglo-Norman conquest of east Ulster was a military takeover of an existing Irish system of agricultural production, which the conquerors seem to have intensified but kept intact. Large open fields were not introduced to the region. The conquest of east Ulster merely saw the removal of Gaelic Irish lords and their replacement by Anglo-Norman ones, at least in lowland parts of the region. Gaelic Irish peasants still remained scattered throughout the townlands that made up the manor and continued to work the land they had always occupied for their new lords (Graham 1993, 74; McNeill 1980, 88).

It must be remembered today that McNeill did not originally intend his 1980 model of rural settlement in Anglo-Norman Ulster to undermine the theory that English peasants in medieval Ireland lived in relatively large villages at manorial centres. He seems to have believed that villages of English style existed at the *capita* of Anglo-Norman manors in the parts of the colony that had seen substantial peasant immigration from England and Wales, noted above as being large parts of Leinster and Munster. He also stated that demesne farming had taken place at these manorial centres in eastern and south-eastern Ireland (McNeill 1980, 83). One important aspect of his work on the earldom of Ulster was that it provided a model of rural settlement for other areas of Ireland that had been conquered by the Anglo-Normans but saw little corresponding English peasant settlement. This model of a dispersed rural settlement pattern within the geographical bounds of manors, with the land being occupied and tilled by mainly Irish tenants, is especially applicable to border regions and agriculturally marginal areas of Anglo-Norman Ireland (Barry 1988; A. Simms 1988a, 34). For example, the settlement pattern on Anglo-Norman manors in the present county of Westmeath was mainly dispersed during the medieval period (Meenan 1985). Something similar even existed in marginal areas of medieval Leinster, in regions such as present Laois (Empey 1990, 89). It must be stated, however, that demesne farming does appear to have been carried out from manorial centres in both Laois and Westmeath, so in this respect the physical appearance of the *capita* in these two areas was different from those in east Ulster (section 2.2).

Yet what about the parts of the colony that did experience large-scale colonisation and settlement by peasants from western Britain? It is certainly clear that the Anglo-Normans took over pre-existing Gaelic Irish land divisions and territorial boundaries in their attempts to quickly develop their lands and new manors after 1169 (Frame 1981, 70–1; A. Simms 1988a, 33–4), presumably because it would have taken too long and been too complicated to create their own divisions. The long-term effect of McNeill's work in Ulster was that it caused various scholars, mainly historical geographers, to look again at the settlement pattern on manors throughout eastern Ireland and specifically to examine the extent to which the pre-existing townland system, in place long before 1169, affected the way Anglo-Norman lords developed their lands in the late twelfth and thirteenth centuries.

Edwards *et al.* (1983) and A. Simms (1983), looking at the evidence from the Dublin manors of Newcastle Lyons and Esker, strongly argued that the pre-existing townland system militated against the formation of large, nucleated, English-style villages in areas heavily colonised by peasants from parts of Britain where this settlement form was the norm. This model argues that demesne farming was carried out from manorial centres in much the same way as it was in the English midlands. This meant that a considerable number of farm buildings were associated with the lord's residence, be it a motte, masonry castle or undefended manor house (sections 2.2, 2.3). Various cottars and tenants-at-will, who owed labour services to their manorial lord and were invariably of English origin, lived in cottages on their crofts or gardens beside the lord's residence, his mill and the manorial church (which was mostly the parish church). Burgesses, where they existed, would also have lived at these manorial centres. This model also holds, however, that English free tenants and their dependants always lived on compact holdings in townlands of their own well away from the manorial centres. Therefore this theory holds that while villages did exist at many manorial centres in eastern Ireland, there were also numerous English tenants living in dispersed settlements within the geographical bounds of manors from the earliest period of Anglo-Norman settlement onwards. The fact that the free tenants did not live at the manorial centres meant that villages in Anglo-Norman Ireland were never as large as those seen over large parts of England and on the Continent (Edwards *et al.* 1983; A. Simms 1983; 1988a, 33–5; 1988b).

There has been some criticism of this model, as it is based on sources that date from the fourteenth century at the earliest (Graham 1985a, 6). It has been suggested that the phenomenon of English free tenants living out in townlands of their own away from manorial centres can be explained as part of a secondary colonisation of marginal lands that took place over the course of the thirteenth century. Alternatively, it has been argued that this phenomenon is linked to a decline in village life after *c.* 1300, when the free tenants made a decision to leave manorial centres and move out into the fields and lands around these settlements—perhaps as part of the general trend towards pastoral farming seen in Ireland throughout the fourteenth century (Graham 1985a, 6–10, 13; 1985b, 16–17; 1993, 74).

What is the archaeological evidence for the manorial villages and 'rural boroughs' of Anglo-Norman Ireland? Can previous archaeological work be of help in understanding the development and decline of these villages?

3.2b—The evidence for the field remains of deserted medieval villages and rural boroughs in Ireland

Archaeological fieldwork can be defined as the analysis and recording of the remains of past human activity without excavation. The earthworks of deserted settlements do exist in the Irish countryside today, although they are not numerous (Pls 10 and 20). Some of these village remains are clearly late medieval or post-medieval in date. However, as this chapter is really concerned with English peasant settlement in Ireland during the period *c.* 1169–1350, only earthworks located at historically attested or known Anglo-Norman manorial centres will be discussed. A review of the work of Glasscock (1970, 168–74), Graham (1975; 1985b, 126–9) and Barry (1987, 72–83) indicates how few of these centres have earthworks at them today. The available historical evidence suggests that many of these latter sites were deserted in the seventeenth century, and it is believed that the earthworks at such places represent the remains of the last phase of occupation (Barry 1987, 76; 1988, 354; 1993a, 118; 1996, 137; Glasscock

1987, 223–4; A. Simms 1983, 147). Overall, certain scholars have tried to argue that many of the nucleated settlements set up by the Anglo-Normans in the late twelfth and early thirteenth centuries were finally deserted in the seventeenth century, although they realised that there was considerable shrinkage in the size of these places during the troubles and changes of the fourteenth century (Barry 1996, 137; Graham 1975, 223–4, 245–6).

The only problem with this hypothesis is that if villages were finally deserted in the seventeenth century, why are there so few deserted settlement remains at the overwhelming majority of these sites, unlike the situation in England? Surely, if many of these sites were continuously occupied for anything up to 500 years, some trace would remain above ground today? Yet earthworks at the sites of Anglo-Norman manorial centres are rare in the parts of eastern Ireland where villages, some of which were rural boroughs, are believed to have existed, at least in the thirteenth or early fourteenth century. Only the remains of a church site and usually an earthwork castle (invariably a motte) occur at sites at which the historical sources suggest there was once a manorial village or rural borough. No earthworks representing the remains of tofts, crofts, houses or roadways exist at the vast majority of these sites. For example, Castlemore, Co. Carlow, was the site of a rural borough, being the *caput* of an important Marshal and later Bigod manor during the thirteenth and fourteenth centuries (Orpen 1906b; 1907b, 247; 1911–20, ii, 231). Apparently 80 burgesses and 29 cottars lived here in 1283, when the manor was held by the Bigods, earls of Norfolk, as lords of Carlow (Orpen 1906b, 379). A 1307 inquisition into the lands of Roger Bigod at the time of his death suggest that there were 79 burgage holdings and 29 cottars here at this date (*CDI*, v, no. 617; *CIPM*, iv, no. 434; *Cal. Justic. Rolls Ire.*, iii, 19–20). Yet the only visible surface remains at the site today consist of a motte castle and an overgrown burial-ground, which marks the site of the historically attested medieval church (Fig. 11). No remains of a deserted settlement can be seen at the site. A totally flat field exists between the motte and the church. A similar situation exists at what were the *capita* of the overwhelming majority of Anglo-Norman manors in eastern Ireland (Pl. 11; Fig. 9; O'Conor 1993, 418–770).

How can this be explained if villages of some form once existed at the majority of these sites? Is this lack of earthworks an indication that something like McNeill's Ulster model of dispersed settlement throughout the manor, with no peasants living at the manorial centre, is applicable even to heavily colonised parts of Leinster, Meath and Munster? The answer to this last question must be no, since there are valid archaeological reasons why no deserted village earthworks can be seen at the sites of these manorial centres today. Villages that were deserted at an early stage in England, during the thirteenth and fourteenth centuries, rarely leave any trace above ground level today, except perhaps for the church and the remains of the manor house, if it were located in a moated site or early castle (Rowley and Wood 1982, 27). A similar pattern prevails elsewhere in Britain. For example, the visible surface remains at the rural borough of Rattray, Buchan, occupied from the thirteenth century through to the fifteenth century, consisted solely of a motte and church site. A series of peasant houses were uncovered during the course of the excavation there, along with a smithy and a pottery (Murray and Murray 1993). Presumably sites such as Rattray were not occupied long enough for earthwork features such as hollow ways to develop and hence leave little trace in the modern landscape.

Thus it is possible that the reason why so few historically attested manorial centres in eastern Ireland have the earthworks of peasant settlements beside them is because these villages or rural boroughs were deserted prior to *c.* 1400 or even considerably earlier. There is certainly much evidence to support this hypothesis of early village desertion in eastern Ireland, especially during the fourteenth century. It has traditionally been held that the combined effects of the Gaelic Resurgence, the Bruce Wars and famine in the period 1315–18, the Black Death (which had a worse effect on Anglo-Norman areas than on Gaelic ones), and the trend towards pastoralism seen after *c.* 1300 all contributed towards the decline and desertion of many Anglo-Norman settlements in the fourteenth century (Barry 1987, 168–79; Curtis 1938, 223–318; Frame 1981, 111–35; Lydon 1973, 47–122; 1987b; 1987c; Orpen 1911–20, iv, 160–249; Otway-Ruthven 1968, 225–308; Richter 1988, 158–71; A. Smyth 1982, 111–17; K. Simms 1989, 74–96). These factors must have been behind the considerable exodus of peasants and labourers of English descent out of Ireland to England during the fourteenth and very early fifteenth centuries (Cosgrove 1987a, 529–30, 1987b, 553; Lydon 1987b, 268; Richter 1988, 167; K. Simms 1989, 89). However, certain areas, notably in south Tipperary and Kilkenny, were not that badly affected by the troubles of the fourteenth century and remained stable and prosperous throughout the late medieval period (Barry 1988, 351). Indeed, the fact that some of the best examples of deserted settlements occur in south Tipperary may be due to its stability during the medieval period, with these settlements being occupied continuously from the thirteenth up to the seventeenth century. The historical sources, however, suggest that large parts of the colony experienced decay and decline throughout the fourteenth century.

The rarity of earthworks means that little is known about the original layout of these villages and rural boroughs during the medieval period. Furthermore, most of the few sites where village earthworks survive have not been properly planned and analysed by archaeologists, and some are under threat today from agricultural development (Barry 1987, 76). In Ireland archaeological fieldwork has been of little value in understanding the nature of nucleated rural settlements in Anglo-Norman-controlled areas.

3.2c—The excavated evidence for medieval villages in Ireland
What does excavation tell us about these nucleated settlements at various Anglo-Norman manorial centres? The answer is very little, since so few of these sites have been excavated up to the present and any investigations have been small in scale.

Caherguillamore, Co. Limerick
Two medieval houses were excavated in 1940 at Caherguillamore, Co. Limerick, in an area of limestone rock outcrop (Fig. 13). The earliest reference to the site is in 1287, when the *vill,* land and castle of *Cahir a Gillimo* are mentioned (Ó Ríordáin and Hunt 1942, 62). The two buildings excavated were part of a complex of twelve houses, associated with a hollow way and set within rectangular enclosures or tofts. However, other houses seem to have existed in the general vicinity of the site and there was a strong local tradition that the settlement was once much larger. The site of a castle exists just to the south-west of the houses (*ibid.,* 38–9, 43–4).

House 1 was the larger and earlier of the two houses investigated at Caherguillamore. It was rectangular and had stone-built walls with rounded corners externally. It had internal dimensions of *c.* 12m east/west by *c.* 4.4–4.8m north/south and seems to have had a thatched roof. The external faces of its stone walls were originally covered with a wattle-reinforced clay rendering. The ash from a hearth centrally placed within the house suggests that turf was the main fuel. The western third or so of the house was screened off by a wooden partition. This room originally had its own doorway, located at the westernmost end of the south wall of the house, which was blocked up at a later date (Ó Ríordáin and Hunt 1942, 44–7).

House II was clearly later than House I. It lay just to the south of the latter building and was roughly parallel to it. House II's internal dimensions were *c.* 8.4m east/west by *c.* 3.8m north/south, and its stone walls were not as well built as those of House I. It had a northern doorway and a central hearth which also yielded evidence for the use of turf. There was no sign of an internal wooden partition or second doorway (Ó Ríordáin and Hunt 1942, 47–9).

The finds from these houses and their environs included a silver penny of Edward I, assorted iron knives, shears, a rowel-spur, various doorkeys, spindle-whorls, a bobbin for weaving, quernstones, whetstones, glazed pottery and bone pins (Ó Ríordáin and

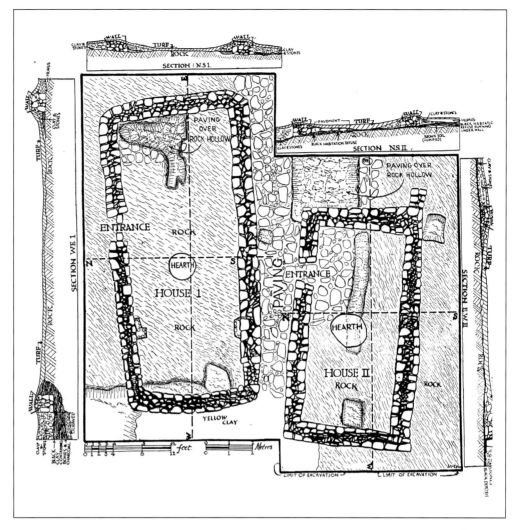

Fig. 13—*Plan of the excavated medieval houses at Caherguillamore, Co. Limerick* (Ó Ríordáin and Hunt 1942).

Hunt 1942, 49–60). Animal bones included those of cattle, pig, sheep and goat. Horse, dog and rabbit bones also occurred at the site. There was also evidence for 'fowl' (hens?) and geese (*ibid.*, 60). The artefacts from the site suggest that these two houses were occupied in the period from *c.* 1300 into the sixteenth century (*ibid.*, 61; Barry 1987, 73). They certainly suggest a thriving agricultural community located at an unimportant Anglo-Norman manorial centre—well capable of supporting itself and producing a surplus (as hinted at by the presence of the silver coin). The finds and houses are very similar to those that turn up on excavations of medieval villages in England (Barry 1987, 73–4). Therefore the excavation at Caherguillamore allows an insight into the material culture and way of life of peasants apparently of English descent in rural medieval Limerick.

Jerpoint Church, Co. Kilkenny
The excavation of another medieval settlement at Jerpoint Church townland, Co. Kilkenny, was carried out in 1973 by Claire Foley for the OPW. This site was built on an artificial platform of alluvial mud beside the River Nore and unfortunately much of it had been bulldozed before excavation. The site appeared as a low, scrub-covered rise before bulldozing and excavation, and there were no indications of any house remains there (Foley 1989, 72–5). It is generally held that this site lay either on the very edge of or just immediately outside the rural borough of Newtown Jerpoint (Barry 1987, 75–6; Foley 1989, 124). Two well-defined buildings were uncovered by the excavation, with further evidence for a third structure to their south off the mud platform.

The earliest recognisable building on the site (there was occupation pre-dating this structure) consisted of a rectangular peasant house, Structure 1, built of mud walls placed on low stone footings. This mud-floored house had an internal width of *c.* 5.4m north/south and was at least 10m in length east/west, probably considerably more. It had a central hearth and clay chimney. Its doorway lay along the south wall. It appears that Structure 1 was divided into two rooms by a mud partition wall. It was argued that the easternmost room here was a byre, as there was evidence for tethering posts and feed pens. There seems to have been a timber-framed, lean-to structure tacked onto the northern side of the house. Finds from Structure 1 include iron horseshoes, nails, a ring and a hook, along with some sherds of Ham Green ware and a bone point. A spindle-whorl, an iron pin and two sherds of Ham Green and Saintonge green-glazed ware were associated with the lean-to building (Foley 1989, 80–6). It appears that this house was then rebuilt at some stage. The walls of this second phase were also of mud on stone footings. The central hearth continued in use. The finds from this period include a bronze box-lid, iron nails and knives, along with sherds of green-glazed Saintonge and Ham Green ware (*ibid.*, 86–7). Cattle and sheep bones predominated on the site, while pigs, poultry, domestic geese and horses were also evident (*ibid.*, 123). The house was then abandoned for a period.

The next phase of activity at the site saw the construction of Structure 2, a substantial mortared stone building of at least two storeys, over what had been the western end of the primary peasant house. This new stone building had an internal width of *c.* 5m north/south. Its exact length is unknown, but it seems to have been well over 10m. This building was entered through a doorway in its eastern gable wall which led into an entrance lobby. Another doorway led into the ground floor of the building on the entrance lobby's western side. A stone stairway, leading to the first floor of the building, occurred on the northern side of this feature. The only finds from this building consisted of an iron horseshoe, a bronze tailor's pin, two sherds of Spanish Merida ware and one sherd of English ware (Foley 1989, 88–90).

A circular, drystone-lined pit, *c.* 1.7m deep, probably contemporary with this two-storeyed masonry building, occurred on the northern side of the excavated area. This was interpreted either as a well or as a cold storage area for hanging carcasses of meat and fowl. An iron wood-wedge, nails, various fragments of iron and a sandstone hone were found in the fill of this well (Foley 1989, 91–3).

Two shallow parallel trenches, oriented east/west, were found on the southern side of the excavated area off the mud platform. They seem to represent the foundation trenches of a timber-framed building erected on horizontally laid sill-beams. The exact stratigraphical relationship between this structure and the rest of the site is uncertain. The finds associated with this building include a sandstone hone, some locally produced coarse and glazed ware sherds, a sherd of imported ware from England and three sherds of Merida ware (Foley 1989, 90–1).

This medieval settlement site at Jerpoint Church is clearly very important. It was argued by the excavator that the site was occupied from the mid- to late thirteenth century, possibly into the early fourteenth century (Foley 1989, 73, 125). It is noticeable that the occupation of Structure 1, the peasant longhouse, was associated with Ham Green ware in both its phases (*ibid.*, 125). This point led Sandes (1993, 3) to argue that the occupation of this building began in the early thirteenth century and not *c.* 1250, based on new research into the dating of Ham Green ware. Therefore it appears that the settlement site excavated by Foley at Jerpoint Church townland was first occupied at some stage in the early thirteenth century and continued in use for 100 years or so. Structure 1 is similar in its layout and range of finds to House 1 at Caherguillamore. It is clearly a peasant longhouse, occupied by a self-supporting farming family apparently of English descent or even origin.

Structure 2 is far more difficult to understand. It is a very substantial stone building and consequently it has been suggested that it represents the remains of a manor house (Barry 1987, 76; Foley 1989, 125). Yet few finds were found associated with this struc-

Pl. 20—*The remains of the rural borough of Newtown Jerpoint, Co. Kilkenny, from the air.* (Photo: Cambridge University Committee for Aerial Photography.)

ture and it has also been postulated that it functioned as a barn (Foley 1989, 125). The excavation of the stone-built medieval barn at Kebister, Shetland, indicated that this structure was also two storeys in height (Yeoman 1995, 119–20).

It is clear that a roadway once skirted the site at Jerpoint Church, linking it to the known rural borough of Newtown Jerpoint, 200–300m to the east (Pl. 20; Foley 1989, 124). This makes it possible to suggest that the site represents the westernmost edge of this rural borough, which was strung out along this roadway, during the thirteenth century. It could have been the earliest part of the settlement to be abandoned owing to the vicissitudes of the fourteenth century. The settlement continued to shrink eastwards until it was finally abandoned in the seventeenth century. This model would see the village remains marked on the first edition of the Ordnance Survey map for the area as representing the settlement around the time of its final desertion, with the strong possibility that earlier medieval peasant houses lie in the flat fields between it and the site of Foley's excavation, along the line of the old roadway.

Bourchier's Castle, Lough Gur, Co. Limerick
A rescue excavation at Bourchier's Castle, Lough Gur, Co. Limerick, in 1977–8, carried out in advance of the construction of a carpark, produced evidence for two medieval houses of general thirteenth- and early fourteenth-century date (Cleary 1982; 1983). There was no sign of these houses prior to excavation. Indeed, the area had been intensively cultivated up to the 1950s (Cleary 1982, 77; 1983, 77). These two houses lay about 130m due north of Bourchier's Castle, a later tower-house. It has been suggested that they represent the remains of part of a village that clustered around the thirteenth-century Fitzgerald castle or undefended manor house which is believed to lie under Bourchier's Castle (Barry 1987, 81).

The first house excavated at the site was subrectangular in plan, with rounded east-

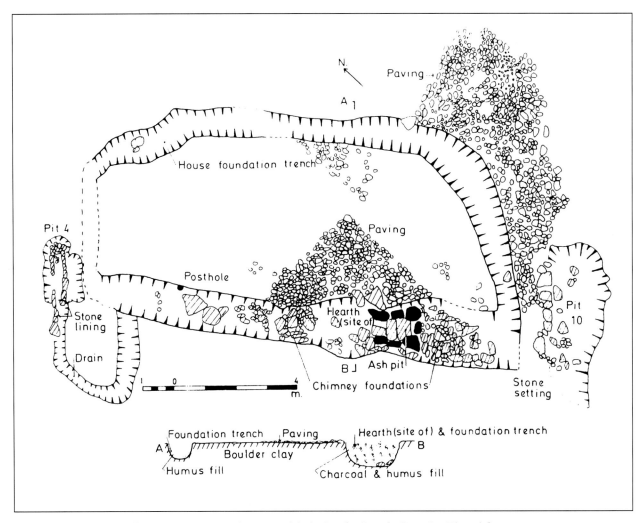

Fig. 14—*Plan of the first house excavated at Bourchier's Castle, Lough Gur, Co. Limerick* (after Cleary 1982; 1983).

ern and northern corners (Figs 14–15). Its walls were seemingly made of a post-and-wattle frame liberally covered with mud. The house had external dimensions of 14.5m south-east/north-west by 7.6m north-east/south-west. Its hipped roof was originally thatched. A hearth with a stone chimney was located in its original south-western wall. A stone-lined, box-like ash pit was located beside it. Small cobblestones paved the floor of the house in front of this fire, while the rest of the building just had a clay floor (Cleary 1982, 78–80). The excavator maintained that there was no real evidence for an internal partition within the house, despite the fact that she believed that the north-western end of the house acted as a byre (*ibid.*, 84). A drain to take animal waste led from the western corner of the house into a large pit outside the north-western wall (*ibid.*, 80, 84). A storage pit, which was later turned into a cesspit, was located by the external face of the south-eastern wall (*ibid.*, 80–1, 84–5). The finds associated with the construction and habitation of this house include iron furnace bottoms, nails, a knife fragment, sherds of locally produced unglazed cooking ware and glazed jugs. The charred seeds of oats, barley and wheat were found in the ash pit (*ibid.*, 79–80).

The second house at Bourchier's Castle was basically an inverted L-shape in plan. It was divided into two rooms and a drystone-built annexe leaned against its southern end. The house itself seems to have been a mud-walled structure, with a thatched roof supported on rafters which lay directly on top of the walls. Room 1 was rectangular in plan, with internal dimensions of 8.6m by 5m. The main entrance to the house lay on the western side of this room. Room 1 was divided internally into two parts and there was no evidence for a hearth (Cleary 1983, 51–3). Room 2 lay to the east of the first

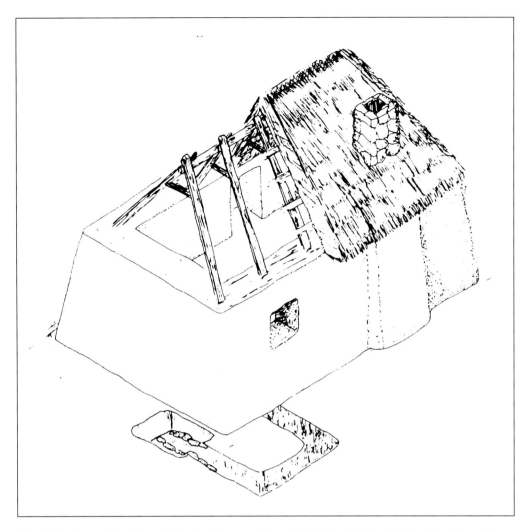

Fig. 15—*Reconstruction of the first house at Bourchier's Castle, Lough Gur, Co. Limerick* (after Cleary 1982; 1983).

room. Indeed, it shared its western wall with Room 1. Room 2 had internal dimensions of *c.* 7.5m north/south in width and at least 14.5m east/west in length. There was no evidence again for an original hearth site (*ibid.*, 53–4). The drystone annexe was built up against the southern gable of Room 1. This structure was open on its southern side and a trough-like feature occupied its north-eastern corner. This led the excavator to suggest that the lean-to building was a byre (*ibid.*, 54). This second house had an attached yard which contained a corn-drying kiln and a stone-built hearth site (*ibid.*, 64–70). The finds from this house included iron slag, nails, knives, keys, horse trappings, hooks, horseshoes, a bronze stick-pin, a bone comb, sherds of locally produced unglazed cooking ware, sherds of local green-glazed pottery and a few sherds of Saintonge green-glazed ware. Cattle, sheep and pig bones occurred in profusion as well (*ibid.*, 55–61). The stratigraphy of the site suggests that this second house at Bourchier's Castle was a generation or so later than the first house there (Cleary 1982, 85; 1983, 77–8). The first house seems to have been constructed and used during the first half of the thirteenth century (Cleary 1982, 85; 1983, 77). The second house was built in the later part of the same century, and was occupied into the early fourteenth century (*ibid.*).

Piperstown, Co. Louth

The site at Piperstown, Co. Louth, consisted before excavation of a series of house platforms, linear banks marking rectangular areas, a hollow way and a low motte. It is the only place in Louth where deserted village remains are visible today (Fig. 16; Barry

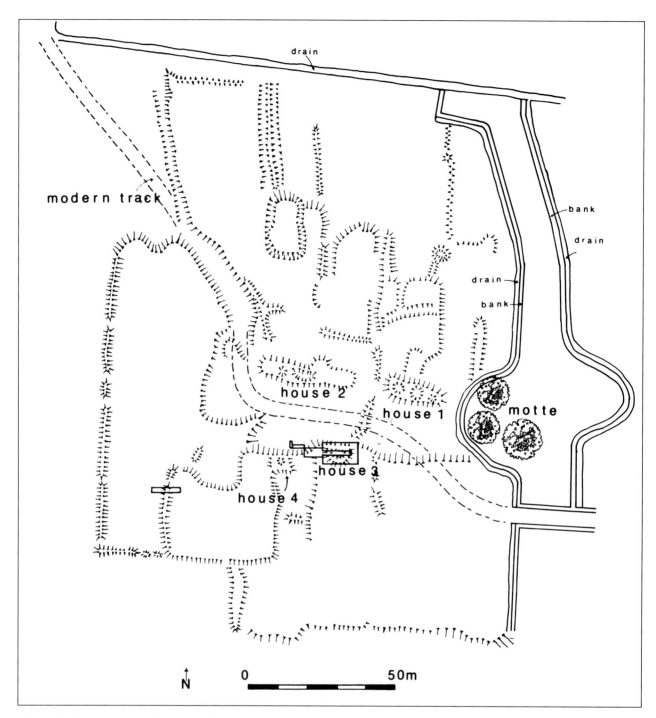

Fig. 16—*Plan of the earthworks and excavated areas at Piperstown, Co. Louth* (after Barry 1996).

1987, 22; 1996, 136; Buckley and Sweetman 1991, 300). In 1316 fourteen houses were destroyed by the Irish at *Pippardestown* or Piperstown (Barry 1996, 136). It was excavated in 1987 over a four-week period, with excavation concentrating on one house site. This house had external dimensions of 8m east/west by 5.6m north/south. Its walls seem to have been constructed of sill-beams laid horizontally into bedding trenches, into which timber uprights or timber framing would have been placed. The doorway into the house lay along its southern wall. There was also an internal partition dividing the house in two, with the hearth located in the western room. A doorway connected the rooms. The easternmost room contained a stone-covered drain. This led the excavator to suggest that this room was used for keeping livestock, with human habitation occurring in the western one (Barry 1996, 137)—showing the house to be a medieval longhouse. The artefactual evidence suggests a complex occupational sequence. The vast majority of artefacts were clearly post-medieval in date and it seems that the house was deserted in the very early years of the eighteenth century. However, the primary occupation of the house *seems* to be associated with general thirteenth-century material (Barry 1997, 137). It is certainly possible that a house could be occupied for such a long time, as its various timbers and panels could be replaced individually as they decayed at different rates over time. It must also be remembered that the two houses at Caherguillamore seem to have been occupied for two to three centuries (Ó Ríordáin and Hunt 1942, 61).

Dunmanoge, Co. Kildare

Dunmanoge, Co. Kildare, was clearly an important early Anglo-Norman manorial centre within the territory of Ardree, which was granted by Strongbow to Thomas le Fleming before 1176 (*Song,* lines 3112–13; O'Conor 1993, 713, 759–60; Otway-Ruthven 1961, 169). A rural borough was founded here before 1199 by either the latter or his successor, Milo de Stanton (Bradley 1986, 168–9). It seems that the *caput* of the cantred of Ardree was transferred to Dunmanoge in the very early thirteenth century (Otway-Ruthven 1961, 169). There was a small excavation here in 1984, in a totally flat field about 100m to the north of the medieval parish church, in the townland of Blackcastle, as the site lay along the route of the Cork–Dublin pipeline. The excavation produced evidence for what appears to be a rectangular peasant farmstead of general thirteenth/early fourteenth-century date, a yard and a series of pits and drains. The finds include locally produced unglazed cooking ware (including Leinster cooking ware), glazed jugs (which are copies of French and English imports), 'animal bones', iron nails, an iron doorkey and an iron ring. It is noticeable that there was no evidence for stone footings or post-holes associated with the house. Spreads of redeposited boulder clay, stones and a trench defined the outline of the structure (Sleeman and Hurley 1987). This seems to suggest that the house here was some form of timber-framed structure whose uprights were fitted into large wooden sill-beams which lay directly on the flat ground surface or were bedded into the trench. This form of building can leave little archaeological trace if the sill-beams are merely laid on the ground (Barry 1987, 89; Greene 1983, 85–6; Higham and Barker 1992, 338; O'Conor 1993, 371–7). This house was clearly part of the borough settlement at Dunmanoge, which was effectively never larger than an agricultural village. Presumably, future excavation at the site will uncover evidence for more houses in the flat fields around the medieval parish church there (Bradley 1986, 174–5). The finds from Blackcastle are very similar in their range to those found in association with the peasant houses excavated at other Anglo-Norman manorial centres.

Duleek, Co. Meath, and Ballymore Eustace, Co. Kildare

The manor of Duleek, Co. Meath, was held during the medieval period by the Augustinian houses of Llanthony Prima and Secunda (A. Simms 1988b). A recent small rescue excavation at Duleek uncovered evidence for two rectangular structures, associated with finds of general thirteenth/fourteenth-century date. There was no indication of these buildings before excavation (C. MacSporran, pers. comm.). The remains of medieval peasant houses have also recently turned up under a completely flat field within the bounds of what was once the medieval rural borough of Ballymore Eustace, Co. Kildare (A. Hayden, pers. comm.).

Phosphate analysis has been successfully used twice in Ireland to locate the sites of medieval nucleated settlements. Phosphate deposits in soil increase in places where there has been intensive human habitation. This method was used to find the original site of the rural borough of Oughterard, Co. Kildare, in a completely flat field (Hall *et al.* 1985, 22). The technique also indicated the focus of medieval occupation at the site of the rural borough at Newcastle Lyons, Co. Dublin (Edwards *et al.* 1983, 365–74).

Summary

This review of the excavated evidence for what appear to be the houses of manorial tenants of English origin indicates a number of important things. The very limited amount of excavation carried out at the sites of Anglo-Norman manorial centres certainly suggests that nucleated settlements did occur at such places in the parts of Ireland that saw large-scale English immigration during either the late twelfth or the early thirteenth century. Most importantly, these investigations have shown that house sites of medieval peasants can occur at places where there were no surface indications prior to excavation.

These excavations have also thrown some light on the material culture of these peasants. The finds give an overall picture of self-sufficiency in terms of food, clothing and, apparently, tools. The silver penny of Edward I from the house at Cahirguillamore and the imported pottery from the earliest house at Jerpoint Church suggest that these peasants also produced an agricultural surplus and were part of a market economy. Furthermore, the occurrence of locally produced cooking ware and glazed jugs hints at the existence of rural industries and specialist crafts at these sites—a subject about which little is known in Ireland. For example, the excavation of the rural borough of Rattray, Buchan, in Scotland produced evidence for a pottery and a smithy in this essentially agricultural community (Murray and Murray 1993).

These excavations of peasant dwellings indicate what house types were lived in by these manorial tenants. The materials used to build the walls of the houses could vary—stone, mud, timber or a combination of these. Presumably this depended on what was available locally, as well as the skills of the builders. House II at Caherguillamore was a simple one-roomed affair. Such houses were common in medieval England (Glasscock 1987, 229). The house at Blackcastle/Dunmanoge was only partially excavated and hence little can be said about it, other than that it was rectangular and probably timber-framed. Yet it can be argued that the plans of the other excavated peasant houses show a certain degree of conformity. Structure 1 at Jerpoint Church and the house at Piperstown are relatively long, rectangular buildings which were divided into two rooms. One room at both houses, which had a hearth, was used for human habitation. The other room functioned as a byre. Basically these two houses were a variation of the longhouse—a medieval house type seen across the British Isles. House I at Caherguillamore seems to have had a similar design: it also was a two-roomed structure, and the fact that the westernmost room originally had its own doorway suggests that it may have functioned as a byre. The excavator of the earliest house at Bourchier's Castle believed that it was a one-roomed, unpartitioned structure whose north-western end functioned as a byre. However, the existence of a post-hole along the building's south-western wall to the north-west of the fireplace could well indicate an internal partition (Cleary 1982, 80). The original plan of the house may have looked very similar to what seems to have existed at Piperstown, Structure 1 at Jerpoint Church, and House I at Caherguillamore.

Lastly, the later house at Bourchier's Castle needs to be discussed. At first glance, its excavated plan shows it to be a unique building of two largish rooms and an annexe. The long easternmost room at right angles to the western one cannot be paralleled elsewhere in Ireland. The excavator presumed that this room was part of the living quarters of the house, yet there was absolutely no evidence for a doorway linking both rooms. A corn-drying kiln existed outside in the attached yard close to this easternmost room. Corn-drying kilns often occur in association with barns, according to the written sources (N. Brady, pers. comm.). Indeed, one existed beside the barn within the moated site at Kilferagh, Co. Kilkenny (Hurley 1987, 90–1). This may suggest that the eastern room of the second house at Bourchier's Castle is in fact an attached barn, entered by a doorway at its eastern end—an entranceway which remains to be uncovered by excavation. This would explain why there appears to be no means of communication between the two main rooms of this house. If this reinterpretation is correct, the westernmost room here (called Room 1 in the excavation report), with its own internal partitioning, is quite similar in plan to the other medieval peasant houses so far excavated in Ireland.

Therefore, the available evidence so far gleaned from excavation suggests that the typical house of the manorial tenant of English origin in medieval Ireland consisted of a two-roomed structure, with one end functioning as a byre and the other as a living area. This byre, which sometimes had a drain, was generally entered from the room used for human habitation. There seems to have been no separation of these two areas by a cross-passage with opposite doorways as seen in many peasant longhouses in England. Nor is there any evidence from medieval Ireland for the peasant farm complex where the dwelling-house and the byre were two distinct buildings, one at right angles to the other in a courtyard effect. This was a common form of medieval peasant house in England (Glasscock 1987, 229).

Clearly, excavation does provide some insight into the material culture and house types of peasants of probable English origin living in what appear to be villages at Anglo-Norman manorial centres. Yet only five of these probable villages or rural boroughs have seen some excavation to date (excluding the ongoing small-scale rescue excavations at Duleek or Ballymore Eustace). Only seven peasant houses (again not including those that have just turned up on the latter digs) at these manorial centres have been excavated out of the many thousands of dwellings that must have existed in the countryside of medieval Ireland. Clearly, more information is needed about the nature of the English peasant house in medieval Ireland.

3.3—Dispersed English peasant settlement on Anglo-Norman manors in Ireland

3.3a—General theories

As noted above, historical geographers believe that at least some English free tenants lived out in separate pieces of land in townlands of their own within the geographical boundaries of Anglo-Norman manors (section 3.2a). The question amongst these scholars is whether or not this phenomenon dates to the earliest period of Anglo-Norman settlement in Ireland. What archaeological evidence is there to help resolve this question of exactly when English free tenants set up in townlands of their own? What monument types or settlement forms did these people inhabit during the medieval period?

3.3b—Undefended isolated farmsteads or house clusters

The archaeological evidence for undefended dispersed settlement within the bounds of Anglo-Norman manors is at present scanty. In 1935 Seán Ó Ríordáin very briefly excavated one of a number of conjoined rectangular enclosures at Ballynamona townland in east County Limerick, close to the Tipperary border. Some sherds of green-glazed thirteenth/fourteenth-century pottery, calf, oxen and pig bones, and a fragment of a decorated disc-quern were found in the few cuttings made across this enclosure (Ó Ríordáin 1936, 181–2). It has been argued that this site represents the remains of a moated site (Barry 1977, 88; 1987, 87). An analysis of the plan of the earthworks provided by Ó Ríordáin indicates that the site consisted of eight or nine conjoined rectangular enclosures. These may be the tofts of a cluster of medieval houses located away from the manorial centre, and possibly represent the remains of houses and yards belonging to free tenants of English origin living in Ballynamona townland during the medieval period. However, as noted, it is believed that betaghs, native Irish tenants on Anglo-Norman manors, also lived out in house clusters in townlands away from manorial centres. It is possible that the earthworks at Ballynamona are the remnants of a Gaelic betagh settlement rather than an English one. More research and excavation are needed at this site before its true function and nature are fully understood.

Nevertheless, its existence indicates that house clusters in townlands away from manorial centres did occur during the medieval period. This discussion also reveals the difficulty of actually identifying the ethnicity of any given peasant settlement from artefacts alone.

There is barely any archaeological evidence for isolated undefended farmsteads either. In 1988 a rescue excavation, in advance of the gas pipeline link between Dublin and Belfast, uncovered evidence for what appears to be an isolated medieval farmyard associated with sherds of Leinster cooking ware and glazed pottery at Saucerstown, Co. Dublin (Halpin 1989).

So the archaeological evidence for isolated, undefended medieval farmsteads and house clusters away from known Anglo-Norman manorial centres is small. However, this cannot at present be taken as evidence that there was little English peasant habitation away from these centres, scattered out in townlands within the bounds of any given manor. The lack of archaeological evidence may be due to other reasons—mainly because there has been no real attempt up to now to find these places, and partly because today these sites are located deep in the countryside, well away from the places that are likely to be developed at present. It has already been noted that most work on the medieval period in Ireland so far has taken place in urban areas (section 1.2f). Conversely, the construction of cross-country gas pipelines has allowed archaeologists to investigate a number of rural sites, well away from modern villages and towns. It is noteworthy that this essentially rural, large-scale project has turned up evidence for one isolated medieval farmstead, hinting that intensive future research will discover other such sites. Another reason for the lack of archaeological evidence for isolated medieval farmsteads may simply be that they occur under modern ones. A good place for habitation today may also have been so in the past. The site of any given modern farmstead may have been occupied since the medieval period (Aston 1985, 82; Barry 1977, 125). For example, archaeologists have never checked what lies under apparently eighteenth-century farmsteads in places like south Tipperary or Kilkenny. There simply has not been enough work done to make categorical archaeological statements about whether or not isolated houses or house clusters lived in by English-speaking peasants were common on Anglo-Norman manors in eastern Ireland.

3.3c—Moated sites: defended, isolated medieval homesteads

Archaeologists have long realised that moated sites represent the remains of isolated, semi-defended homesteads in medieval Ireland. There has been little attempt to fit this settlement form into the different models of manorial settlement proposed by various historical geographers over the last fifteen years (section 3.2a). Archaeologists have been left to try to understand the nature, date and function of this monument type during the medieval period.

Moated sites mostly appear today as rectangular earthworks bounded by banks and ditches (Pls 8, 21–3; Fig. 17). Sometimes these surrounding ditches are water-filled, but not always (Barry 1977, 111–12; 1987, 84). Occasionally moated sites are circular (Moore 1996, 95). A few wedge-shaped examples occur too, such as those at Ballyroan and Rathaspick, Co. Laois (Fig. 18). The majority of moated sites in Ireland occur in certain southern and eastern counties, such as Wexford, Kilkenny, Tipperary, mid-Cork and Limerick (Fig. 19; Glasscock 1970, 162–6)—some of the areas that were heavily colonised by English peasants in the late twelfth and early thirteenth centuries (section 3.1). It is also clear that other regions that saw heavy English settlement, such as the present counties of Meath, Dublin and Louth, contain almost no moated sites. These latter counties really constitute the core of the Anglo-Norman colony in Ireland. Very few moated sites occur in the heartlands of Gaelic-controlled areas of medieval Ireland either (Barry 1987, 85). It has therefore been argued that the distribution of moated sites in Ireland indicates that very often they are concentrated along what were the border areas of the Anglo-Norman colony in Ireland, where the settlers would appear from the documentary evidence to have come under increasing pressure from the neigh-

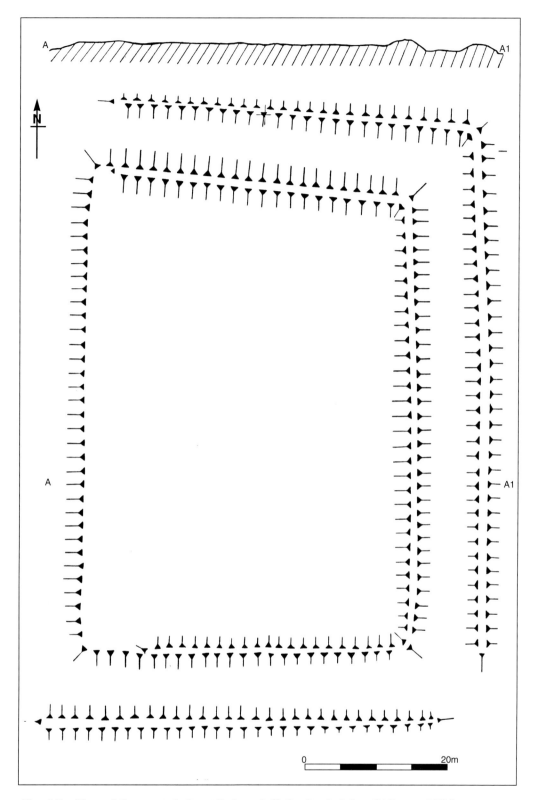

Fig. 17—*Plan of the moated site at Raheenduff, Co. Laois* (after O'Conor 1986).

bouring Irish from the second half of the thirteenth century onwards. Moated sites were needed in such districts as a protection against lawlessness, cattle-raiding and petty larceny (Barry 1977, 176; 1981; 1987, 84–5).

It has been postulated that moated sites in Ireland mostly functioned as the defended manor houses and farms of minor Anglo-Norman gentry in the thirteenth and fourteenth centuries (Barry 1977, 101–2; 1996, 137). Specifically, it has been argued in a detailed historical examination of the medieval cantred of Knocktopher, Co. Kilkenny, that they seem to represent a secondary phase of Anglo-Norman settlement in Ireland

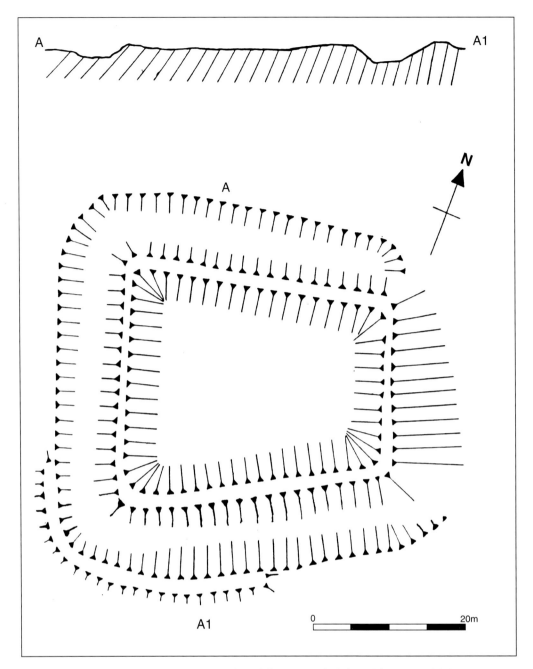

Fig. 18—*Plan of the moated site at Rathaspick, Co. Laois* (after O'Conor 1986).

and belong to the period 1225–1325. This hypothesis was based on two observations. Firstly, moated sites within this cantred were located on slightly less productive soils than the soils located around known manorial centres in the region and therefore reflect a movement away from these primary centres of Anglo-Norman settlement. Secondly, it was argued that because moated sites were not usually located at the sites of medieval parish churches, this meant that they date from after the establishment of the parochial system in the area—a process apparently finished by *c.* 1200–25 (Empey 1982, 335).

Two main points arise from this discussion of work carried out in the past on moated sites in Ireland. Firstly, they have been regarded as representing the homes and farmsteads of relatively unimportant Anglo-Norman knights. They have traditionally been seen as minor lordly sites. Secondly, they are not believed to have been built during the primary phase of Anglo-Norman settlement, belonging instead to a later period associated with the movement onto more marginal lands—which in some cases were close to the territories of the Irish.

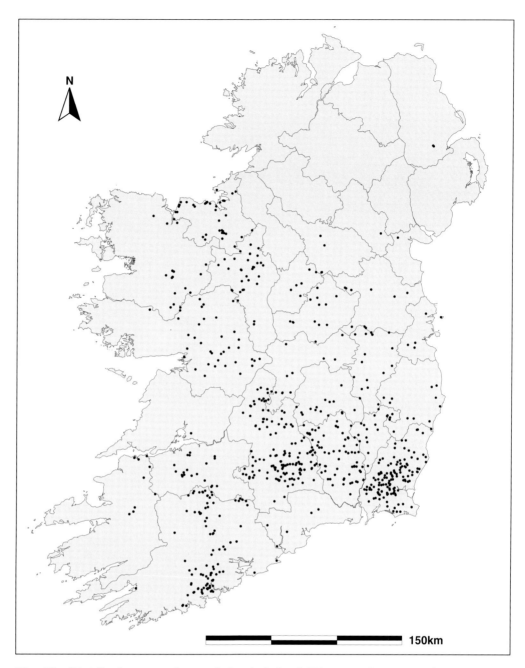

Fig. 19—*Distribution map of moated sites in Ireland* (Discovery Programme).

More recent work is beginning to challenge some of these assumptions. It will be argued below that at least some moated sites in Ireland were built and constructed by the Gaelic Irish (section 4.2b). Some moated sites must be the remains of monastic granges located on the scattered estates of the many medieval monasteries (Graham 1985b, 22). It is also possible that a few moated sites in Ireland may represent the remains of hunting lodges, as elsewhere in the British Isles—especially those on very marginal land (J. Knight, pers. comm.). Furthermore, since moated sites rarely occur at the sites of the *capita* of Anglo-Norman manors in Ireland, it has been suggested that they represent the farmsteads of assarting free tenants (McNeill 1997, 148–9).

The view that at least some moated sites in Ireland were the defended farmsteads of free tenants of English origin as opposed to the manor houses of minor Anglo-Norman gentry has much to recommend it, although the idea has not been developed. Certainly, many of the moated sites constructed in thirteenth- and early fourteenth-century England were built by peasants clearing new land in what had previously been forest. The ditches and banks around these isolated farmsteads gave them a measure of

61

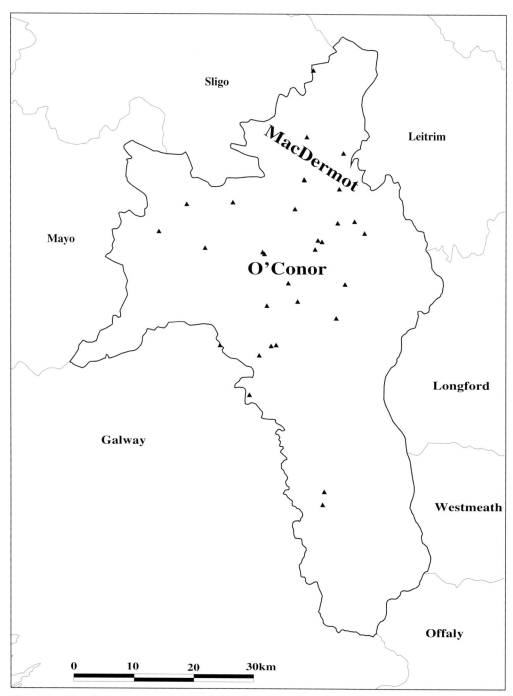

Fig. 20—*Distribution map of moated sites in County Roscommon* (Discovery Programme).

protection against the general lawlessness of such districts (Emery 1962, 385–6; Roberts 1962; 1968, 109; Platt 1978, 11). Therefore, while moated sites in England were initially constructed as defended manor houses in the twelfth century, peasants also began to build them in the thirteenth century, especially its latter half (Platt 1978, 111–15). Moated sites in England were not solely a lordly phenomenon. This suggests that in medieval Ireland free tenants, largely well-to-do peasants mostly of English origin, living out in townlands that made up Anglo-Norman manors, could have constructed moated sites, especially in districts that bordered on regions controlled by native Irish lords. This would certainly explain why moated sites are rarely located at the *capite* of Anglo-Norman manors. It would also account for the fact that moated sites are hardly ever mentioned in the historical sources. As noted, documentary sources such as inquisitions and extents rarely describe the dwellings of manorial tenants (section 3.2a).

It has been suggested that about 750 moated sites existed in medieval Ireland (Glasscock 1970, 164). However, the ongoing work of the Archaeological Survey of Ireland is increasing this figure annually. For example, it was once thought that 118 moated sites occurred in County Wexford (Barry 1987, 85), but recent fieldwork has suggested that at least 130 once existed in the county, and probably more (Moore 1996, 95, 110). Similarly, thirteen moated sites were once believed to have occurred in Roscommon, but the work of the Survey indicates that the figure is about 30 for this county (Fig. 20). These increasing numbers suggest that the final total of moated sites existing in the Irish countryside will be between 900 and 1000.

It was noted above that the site at Ballynamona, Co. Limerick, was not a moated site (section 3.3b). Therefore only five definite moated sites and one possible example have been excavated in Ireland to date, and two of these are not relevant to the discussion in this chapter. It will be argued below that the earthwork excavated at Tildarg, Co. Antrim, is a moated site originally constructed by the Irish (section 4.2b). Furthermore, the suspiciously small, rectangular, ditched and banked enclosure excavated at Carnaghliss, Co. Antrim, does not really seem to be a medieval moated site. The pottery found underneath its bank and within its interior dates from the late sixteenth to the early eighteenth century (Yates 1983), suggesting that the site is not medieval in date. This means that only four moated site excavations are of relevance here. Can these four excavations tell us anything about the status of the people who built these sites? Furthermore, do these investigations indicate when these moated sites were first built?

Kilmagoura, Co. Cork

The excavation (as yet not fully published) of a moated site at Kilmagoura, Co. Cork, took place in 1967. Three main phases of occupation on the site were uncovered. Phase 1 saw the building of the moated site. There were no indications of a pre-existing house or farmyard at the site prior to the erection of the earthwork. Phase II saw the raising of the interior of the moated site by the spreading of a 30cm-deep layer of soil over it. A well-used stone pathway was associated with this phase, although the excavator could find no evidence for buildings dating to this second period of occupation. Phase III saw the centre of the moated site being raised even further to provide the foundations for what was interpreted as a stone building, presumably a house. Other fragmentary stone foundations found within the site were seen as representing the remains of farm outbuildings associated with this house. There were no signs of a palisade on top of the site's earthen bank in either Phase II or Phase III. No precisely datable finds were associated with the different periods of occupation at the site. They included a disc-quern fragment, many oyster shells and some iron nails. A piece of a wooden dish was found in the ditch. A late sixteenth-century rowel-spur and four sherds of post-medieval pottery were found at the site, but these were deposited later than the main periods of occupation there. The foundation timbers of a causeway/entranceway across the ditch were found on the western side (Glasscock 1968, 196–7). An uncalibrated radiocarbon date of AD 1225–70 was obtained from a sample taken from these timbers (Barry 1987, 89–90). Consequently, it was stated that the site dated from the late thirteenth or early fourteenth century. It was argued that the lack of finds meant that the site had only actually been occupied for a short length of time (Glasscock 1968, 196–7).

Yet the excavated evidence from the site can be interpreted somewhat differently. Firstly, the radiocarbon date from Kilmagoura is meaningless, suggesting merely that the site was built and occupied at some stage between 1163 and 1393, when it is properly calibrated. Radiocarbon dates are simply not specific enough for medieval sites. Secondly, it has been argued that perhaps no structures were found associated with the Phase II occupation at the site because the building methods used leave little archaeological trace. Timber-framed buildings resting on large wooden sill-beams, which lay directly on the flattened ground surface, could have been built during this period of habitation (Barry 1987, 89). It might also be added that the stone foundations

Pl. 21—*Moated site at Mylerspark, Co. Wexford.* (Photo: *Dúchas*, The Heritage Service.)

Pl. 22—*Moated site at Ballymoon, Co. Carlow.* (Photo: *Dúchas*, The Heritage Service.)

Pl. 23—*Moated site at Aughclare, Co. Wexford.* (Photo: *Dúchas*, The Heritage Service.)

of buildings associated with Phase III may not actually be the surviving bases of masonry houses and outbuildings. It is just as likely that these foundations represent the dwarf walls of buildings whose superstructures were of timber. In all, the structures associated with Phases II and III at Kilmagoura were probably more complex than the excavator allowed for in his brief post-excavation report. Thirdly, as noted, the excavator suggested that the lack of finds from Kilmagoura indicated that the site was inhabited only for a very short while, despite the fact that two periods of occupation were recognised. The number of finds from the site is not actually stated. Certainly the range of finds from Kilmagoura is broadly similar to those found during the excavations of English peasant houses at Anglo-Norman manorial centres, outlined above (section 3.2c). Presumably the number and range of artefacts found on any given site are directly related to the material culture and status of that place's original builders. The relative lack of finds at Kilmagoura may be a hint that this site was occupied by substantial free tenants rather than minor lords. Furthermore, it might be added that many medieval farming sites that were inhabited for long periods do not produce much in the way of finds. This is partly because household rubbish was very often collected and used for manuring surrounding fields (e.g. Wrathmell 1989, 31–3; M. Gardner, pers. comm.). It may also be an indication that many of the everyday objects used on medieval farms were made of organic materials. A lack of finds from any given medieval site cannot, therefore, be taken as evidence that the place was only inhabited for a short while.

What can be deduced from the evidence at Kilmagoura? Firstly, there is no real evidence to date the construction of the moated site to the late thirteenth or early fourteenth century. It could equally well date from *c.* 1200. Secondly, as noted, the finds are remarkably simple and do not really suggest the home of a minor Anglo-Norman knight, being more reminiscent of the material culture associated with the peasant houses excavated to date in Ireland (section 3.2c).

Rigsdale, Co. Cork

The moated site at Rigsdale, Co. Cork, was excavated in 1977 prior to the building of a new Garda station. Much of the site had been damaged prior to excavation. The main features uncovered consisted of what was interpreted as a large, unfinished, rectangular stone-built hall (whose internal dimensions were *c.* 18m east/west by *c.* 8m north/south), which had a garderobe attached onto its north-eastern corner, and the plinth of an apparently unfinished gatehouse (Sweetman 1981, 195–7). The construction of the site was securely dated to the late thirteenth/early fourteenth century on the basis of an Edward I penny found at the base of the moated site's bank, close to the old ground surface. Other finds, such as three sherds of Saintonge polychrome ware and a late thirteenth-century form of horseshoe, also suggest that the site was built around 1300. Nails, some sherds of Saintonge green-glazed ware, spindle-whorls, net-weights, stone hones, an adze or mattock, knives and a silver penny of Edward I were also found on the site (*ibid.*, 200–13).

It was suggested that this site was only temporarily occupied and never completed by its builders, probably owing to pressure from the Irish. A number of reasons were given for this argument. Firstly, the lack of collapsed, good-quality building stone beside the low foundations of the hall was taken as evidence that this building was never finished (Sweetman 1981, 195). Secondly, there was no evidence for a palisade on the bank around the site, and this was seen as proof that the site was never completed (*ibid.*, 204). Thirdly, the excavator believed that the relatively few artefacts found on the site in comparison to the many found on castle excavations indicated only a brief occupation (*ibid.*, 205).

More recent work carried out on medieval sites in both Britain and Ireland has made it possible to reinterpret the excavated evidence from Rigsdale. Firstly, the reasons why relatively few finds can turn up on medieval farming sites occupied over a long period were discussed above. Anyway, the artefacts from Rigsdale are as numerous as those found on most of the other moated site excavations in Ireland. A lack of finds can no longer be taken as firm proof of short occupation at any given site. Secondly, the fact that there is no indication today of a palisade on any given earthwork's bank should not be taken as evidence that one did not exist during that site's period of use. Methods of palisade construction could have been used at Rigsdale that leave little archaeological trace (e.g. Higham and Barker 1992, 338). Thirdly, very little collapsed stone may have been found around the low foundations of the hall because the original superstructure of this building was made of wood or timber framing. Therefore there is reason to suggest that the occupation of Rigsdale was more intensive and prolonged than its excavator argued for in the excavation report.

It is difficult to know how to interpret Rigsdale. The large, hall-like structure uncovered by Sweetman is certainly indicative of high status. The preponderance of imported Saintonge ware at the site might support this view of lordly ownership, suggesting the possibility that Rigsdale was built and occupied by a minor Anglo-Norman gentry family. The importance of Sweetman's excavation here lies in the fact that he firmly dated the construction of the site to the late thirteenth/early fourteenth century on coin evidence.

Kilferagh, Co. Kilkenny

The moated site at Kilferagh, Co. Kilkenny, was partially excavated in 1982 as it lay along the route of the Cork/Dublin pipeline. The main features uncovered consisted of the remains of a stone-built, keyhole-shaped corn-drying kiln, the foundations of the western end of a small outbuilding, and what was interpreted as a barn. The walls of the latter building were originally built of wattle and daub, and it seems to have been eventually destroyed by fire. The fragmentary remains of the western end of a small house were found on the western side of the excavated area. Much of this building was destroyed prior to excavation. Again, it was argued by the excavator that the low surviving stone foundations of this house suggested that it was originally built of masonry (Hurley 1987, 88–93). However, as noted above, the superstructure of such a building could have been of timber. This small house seems to have had internal dimensions of 3m by 2m (*ibid.*, 92). This makes it really too small for a dwelling and it must represent the remains of an outbuilding, used either for storage or for sheltering animals.

The finds from Kilferagh include iron nails, small sheep shears, a barrel-padlock, iron slag, a bronze pin, a bronze needle and a stone hone. Quite an amount of locally produced pottery was found on the site, including green-glazed jugs (which seem to be copies of Ham Green and Saintonge green-glazed jugs) and glazed and unglazed cooking ware (including Leinster cooking ware). Two sherds of Saintonge green-glazed ware were found in the rakings from the kiln (Hurley 1987, 93–6). The crop and plant remains included wheat, oats, barley, rye, peas and beans. The bone assemblage included evidence for cattle, sheep, pig, horse and rabbit. Oyster shells were also found (*ibid.*, 99–100).

Hurley (1987, 96–7) dated the occupation and construction of Kilferagh to the late thirteenth and early fourteenth centuries on the basis of the pottery from the site. Yet almost nothing is known about the origin and chronology of these indigenous wares that were made in imitation of imported English and French pottery (Barry 1987, 96). Furthermore, Leinster cooking ware first appears in the late twelfth century (C. Sandes, pers. comm.). Indeed, the present writer has found Leinster cooking ware in what appears to be a pre-1210 context at Carlow Castle (O'Conor 1997, 16). The two sherds of Saintonge green-glazed ware could also just as well be very early thirteenth-century in date—possibly even earlier (C. Sandes, pers. comm.). All that can be said is that the moated site at Kilferagh was built at some time in the thirteenth century and was occupied into the next century.

The site appears to have been occupied permanently (Hurley 1987, 96). The finds and buildings uncovered, which are predominantly associated with agriculture, strongly suggest that the moated site here was inhabited by a self-sufficient farming family. The manor of Kilferagh was held by the Avenell family, who seem to have come to Ireland from south Wales around 1200, in the thirteenth and fourteenth centuries (Brooks 1950, 164, 254). The *caput* of this manor was situated on a ridge overlooking the Nore about a mile from the site. A later tower-house marks the site today (Hurley 1987, 88). Surely the most logical way to interpret the moated site at Kilferagh is to see it as the semi-defended homestead of a well-to do peasant—a free tenant who held his land of the Avenell family.

Ballyveelish, Co. Tipperary
A moated site at Ballyveelish, Co. Tipperary, was also partially excavated in 1982 as it too lay on the line of the Cork/Dublin pipeline. The remains of what appear to have been four buildings occurred within the excavated part of the site. Structure A, which seems to represent the remains of a dwelling-house, was square, with dimensions of *c.* 5m by *c.* 5m. Its walls were wattle-built and it is unclear how it was originally roofed. It seems to have been eventually destroyed by fire (Doody 1987, 74–6).

Structure B lay to the south of Structure A and its shape was defined by the remains of shallow trenches. It seems to have had overall measurements of *c.* 8.7m north/ south by *c.* 5m east/west. The shallow trenches seem to have held sleeper-beams which supported a timber superstructure. Structure B was apparently divided into three and may have functioned as an animal shelter (Doody 1987, 76–7).

Structure C lay to the south of Structure B. It was only partially excavated and may originally have been built of stone or timber and stone. It contained a hearth and seems to have been divided in two by a wattle partition. It seems to have also functioned as a dwelling-house and was eventually destroyed by fire (Doody 1987, 77–8). Structure D, which lay on the south-western part of the moated site's interior, seems to represent the remains of a small, stone-built building (*ibid.*, 78–9).

The finds from the occupation associated with these buildings include two sherds of locally made green-glazed ware of general thirteenth- to fourteenth-century date, about twenty sherds of locally made unglazed cooking ware (including Leinster cooking ware), fourteen disc-quern fragments, a stone hone, twenty nails, an iron knife fragment, hooks, a punch, a horseshoe, a bone peg and a bronze stick-pin (Doody 1987, 81–2). The bones of cattle, sheep and horse were also found (*ibid.*, 85–6), along with the charred remains of rye, wheat, oats and barley. Evidence for the growing of peas was also uncovered during the course of the excavation (*ibid.*).

No artefacts were found at Ballyveelish that could be used specifically to date the construction of the site. As noted, little is known about the chronology of local wares in medieval Ireland, although Leinster cooking ware starts to be produced in the second half of the twelfth century (C. Sandes, pers. comm.). All the finds from the site suggest that it was built some time in the thirteenth century and occupied into the fourteenth century (Doody 1987, 83–4; Barry 1987, 91). Like Kilmagoura and Kilferagh, the finds from Ballyveelish suggest that this moated site was occupied by a self-sufficient farming family. Again, the artefacts from the site are very similar in their range and number to those found during the excavations of undefended peasant houses in eastern Ireland (sections 3.2c, 3.3a). It is probably best to interpret Ballyveelish as the home of a substantial free tenant.

In conclusion, it appears that the function of moated sites in medieval Ireland was more complex than once thought by Irish archaeologists. It will be noted in Chapter 4 that some moated sites appear to have been built by the Irish, while others must mark the locations of granges on scattered monastic estates (section 4.2b). Quite a number may well have been the homes of minor Anglo-Norman gentry, such as perhaps the moated site at Rigsdale, Co. Cork. However, the best way to interpret the excavated evidence from the moated sites at Ballyveelish, Kilmagoura and Kilferagh may be to see them as the defended farmsteads of well-to-do peasants of English origin, working their land away from their manorial centres. The numbers and range of artefacts found on these three sites are remarkably similar to the finds recovered from the excavations of undefended medieval peasant houses located beside manorial centres (section 3.2c).

What was the process behind the construction of moated sites by these free tenants? The moated site at Ballyconnor/Mylerspark cost a full £13 11s. 6d. to build, approximately 12% of the annual income of the manor of Ross (Colfer 1996, 17). This would be far too expensive for even a substantial peasant farmer, capable of producing a surplus. It must be remembered that the site was an outfarm located on demesne land belonging to the Bigod manor of Ross. The largest expenses here were the payments for the very substantial gates (£9 15s.) and the wages of the workmen (*ibid.*, 17–19). It is also a very large moated site (Pl. 21; *ibid.*, 19). Leaving aside the expense of the gate, the actual cost of the materials used at Ballyconnor/Mylerspark was a paltry 4s. 8d. Arguably, a far simpler moated site would have been quite affordable for a well-to-do free tenant, provided that he used his own labour and that of his family and neighbours. He in turn could have repaid his neighbours by working for them on their own projects. Such informal reciprocal arrangements between farmers were common in rural Ireland until recently, and certainly still occur in parts of the west.

At what date did free tenants begin to construct moated sites away from manorial centres? Rigsdale, the one firmly dated moated site so far excavated in Ireland, was built around 1300. This date ties in well with the only surviving detailed account of the building of a moated site. This was the site of 'Ballyconnor', identified on the ground today as the moated site at Mylerspark, Co. Wexford, which was constructed in 1282–4 (Hore 1900–11, i, 26–31; Barry 1987, 87; Colfer 1996, 17–19). It could be argued that the dating evidence from Rigsdale and Mylerspark suggests that moated sites in Ireland were constructed in the late thirteenth or early fourteenth century, either as a result of assarting or as a security measure against the depredations of the resurgent Irish. This in turn could be seen as supporting Graham's (1985a, 6–10, 13; 1985b, 6–17; 1993, 74) view that dispersed peasant settlement on manors in eastern Ireland is not a phenomenon associated with the primary period of Anglo-Norman control in the country but instead dates to a far later stage of activity. Therefore the dating of both Rigsdale and Mylerspark/Ballyconnor could be taken as refuting the theory of A. Simms (1983) and Edwards *et al.* (1983) that dispersed English settlement was always a feature of Anglo-Norman manors in Ireland.

The present writer believes, however, that nothing precise can be said about the exact dating of moated sites in Ireland. Rigsdale and Mylerspark/Ballyconnor are only two out of a possible thousand moated sites in the country. They represent too small a sample to make definite statements about the nature and dating of this widespread monument type. Indeed, both sites may be untypical as both seem to be associated with lordship. As noted, the dating of the other three excavated moated sites is not so precise, partly owing to the fact that little is known about the chronology of the locally made pottery found on these sites. It is possible that one or all three of these sites could date from the early thirteenth century. This uncertainty means that at present the moated site series in Ireland can contribute little to the ongoing debate concerning the exact appearance of dispersed English peasant settlement within Anglo-Norman manors in eastern Ireland. However, since it was argued in this section that many moated sites seem to have been the homes of free tenants, the present writer believes that future excavation and research at other moated sites will help to provide at least part of the answer to this question.

3.4—Field systems on Anglo-Norman manors

Irish medieval field systems have received very little academic attention (Graham 1985b, 23). It is still held that open-field farming, practising a three-crop rotation, with peasant holdings divided into strips of land scattered throughout large common fields, was introduced into eastern Ireland by English settlers. Many parts of Leinster and Munster must have had large stretches of open arable land, especially during the thirteenth century (Barry 1993a, 117; Duffy 1997, 111–12; Edwards *et al.* 1983, 352, 356–7, 360–1, 363–4; Glasscock 1987, 211; Graham 1993, 74–6; Hall *et al.* 1985, 16–20, 22; Leister 1976; A. Simms 1983, 138, 146).

The historical, pictorial and paltry archaeological evidence suggests that the open fields under strip cultivation in these parts of eastern Ireland were far smaller than those of the English midlands. For example, the open fields in the medieval county of Dublin were only a quarter the size of English fields of the same type. This is because the original size of these open fields in eastern Ireland was determined by pre-existing townland boundaries, which invariably made them smaller than those outside Ireland (Edwards *et al.* 1983, 364; Hall *et al.* 1985, 20; A. Simms 1983, 146–7). However, it must be added that manorial documents of late thirteenth- and early fourteenth-century date suggest that free tenants living out in townlands of their own had compact, consolidated, possibly enclosed holdings not unlike modern farms (Glasscock 1987, 211; Graham 1985b, 23; 1993, 74–5; Otway-Ruthven 1951, 2–3). Again, as before, owing to the late nature of the documentary sources, it is not certain whether these compact holdings were created in the early days of the colony, existing side by side with large open fields, or whether they evolved during the course of the thirteenth century because of such things as clearance of new land by individuals or agreed exchanges of arable strips amongst free tenants. This consolidation of holdings into compact farms continued to occur throughout the rest of the medieval period. Almost all originally open-field land in eastern Ireland had been enclosed and consolidated into compact farms by the seventeenth century (Glasscock 1987, 211). This decline in the use of large open fields may be due to a movement away from arable towards stock-rearing and pasture in fourteenth-century Ireland (Barry 1993a, 100–1; Glasscock 1987, 206–9; Graham 1993, 76).

Ridge-and-furrow attributable to the medieval period does not occur in Ireland, where flat ploughing was apparently preferred, and its absence makes it difficult to identify medieval fields on the ground. Flat ploughing, however, does leave plough headlands, often along furlong boundaries. Traces of a medieval open-field system associated with the manors of Oughterard and Castlewarden were identified in County Kildare by plotting the earthworks of these headlands and furlongs in the modern landscape (Hall *et al.* 1985, 19–20). Medieval toft or garden boundaries and common grazing land were also recognised at Newcastle Lyons, Co. Dublin (A. Simms 1983, 141, 143).

3.5—Conclusions

3.5a—English peasant settlement on Anglo-Norman manors—current state of knowledge

What, then, is the current state of knowledge regarding the existence of nucleated villages in Anglo-Norman Ireland? In summary, McNeill's work in Ulster has shown that nucleated villages as a settlement form did not occur in large parts of Anglo-Norman-controlled Ireland. The available evidence suggests that this was largely because there was little colonisation of these areas by English peasant cultivators. The manors in these areas were inhabited and worked by mainly Irish tenants, who lived out in the townlands that made up the manors. The fact that Anglo-Norman lords did not carry out demesne farming in Ulster, and apparently other border districts, also militated against the formation of villages in these areas (section 3.2a). Villages do seem to have occurred in the parts of eastern Ireland that saw large-scale immigration of peasants from western Britain. However, even in the most Anglicised parts of eastern Ireland, one model proposed by A. Simms and others postulated that the pre-existing Irish townland system meant that English free tenants always lived away from these villages, rural boroughs and manorial centres in farmsteads scattered throughout the landscape. Therefore this view holds that manorial villages were never very large in Anglo-Norman Ireland (section 3.2a). A somewhat different model put forward by Graham was that much larger villages of English style could well have been a feature of the initial phase of Anglo-Norman settlement in Ireland, say during the period 1169–1230. He believes that any dispersed settlement within manors in eastern Ireland, historically attested in late sources, belongs to a secondary movement of English peasants out from these villages during the course of the thirteenth and fourteenth centuries (section 3.2a). This discussion shows that there is a general agreement amongst historical geographers and historians that villages of some sort (many of which had borough status or at least burgesses living in them) occurred at most Anglo-Norman manorial centres in eastern Ireland. The present debate amongst these scholars is really about the size and development of these settlements over time.

The discipline of archaeology has contributed little so far to the understanding of the villages and rural boroughs inhabited by English peasants at Anglo-Norman manorial centres in eastern Ireland. The earthworks of deserted villages do not occur at most of these places, perhaps because these settlements were deserted in the fourteenth century. The relatively few Anglo-Norman centres that do have village earthworks at them today seem to have been deserted in the main during the seventeenth century (section 3.2b). Very few excavations, all small-scale, have been carried out at these places. Nevertheless, these investigations have produced interesting results. The artefacts present a picture of self-sufficient peasants mainly of English origin growing their own food and making their own clothes and possibly tools. Certain finds indicate that these peasants also produced an agricultural surplus for sale and seem to have been part of a market economy. Excavation has also shown that medieval houses can occur underneath what are now flat fields at sites where no remains of deserted village earthworks are visible today (section 3.2c).

The question of dispersed English peasant settlement within Anglo-Norman manors was also addressed in this chapter. Very few undefended isolated farmsteads belonging to tenants of English origin have been recognised in eastern Ireland, probably because there has been no real attempt to date by archaeologists to find such places. It is highly likely that intensive future research will find more examples of this medieval settlement type (section 3.3b). Moated sites were clearly built for a number of different reasons in medieval Ireland (sections 3.3c, 4.2b). However, it was suggested that many moated sites in border areas of the colony were in fact built by free tenants of English descent or even origin and were not an exclusively lordly phenomenon. Only five out of a possible thousand moated sites have been excavated to date in this country. Three of these seem to have been the homes of substantial peasants of English origin. The excavated evidence from these three sites again suggests self-sufficiency, with a surplus being produced for sale (section 3.3c).

At present, because there have been so few excavations, it is not known exactly when dispersed English settlement became a feature of the manorial landscape in the heavily colonised parts of eastern Ireland. Certainly, the moated sites at Rigsdale and Ballyconnor/Mylerspark date from the late thirteenth century (section 3.3c). Yet these two sites are not necessarily typical as they seem to be associated with lordship. The other moated sites excavated are not so precisely datable. They could have been built long before the late thirteenth century, and may even be part of the primary English peasant settlement of any given area in the first years of the thirteenth century (section 3.3c).

3.5b—English peasant settlement on Anglo-Norman manors—priorities for future research

The whole question of how English peasant settlement developed and declined within the geographical boundaries of Anglo-Norman manors is clearly a major priority for future research into rural settlement in medieval Ireland. Perhaps this question can be put more simply. Is the model of relatively small nucleated villages at manorial centres, with free tenants living contemporaneously in townlands away from these places, a feature of the primary period of Anglo-Norman settlement in Ireland, or is it related to a later phase of activity? A large amount of fieldwork, excavation and historical research needs to be done to answer this question. It should include an excavation of a deserted village at a manorial centre in eastern Ireland, which would provide information about the foundation, size, function and decline of these nucleated settlements. This excavation would also provide an insight into the nature of any pre-Norman settlement at such a site.

This future research should also include the excavation of a moated site located away from the manorial centre but within the bounds of the same manor. Such an excavation would test the hypothesis that many moated sites in eastern Ireland were occupied by substantial peasants of English origin or descent. It would be important for this excavation to date the initial construction of the moated site. If it was first built in the earliest years of the thirteenth century, it would provide a strong hint that dispersed English peasant settlement occurred within the bounds of well-settled Anglo-Norman manors from the outset of the colonisation process. This would be seen as further proof that the Irish townland system militated against the formation of large English midland-style villages at Anglo-Norman manorial centres, and that its existence encouraged many incoming English peasants to live in dispersed settlements from the start (sections 3.2a–b, 3.3a–b).

Such excavations and integrated research would also provide information on the material culture and house types of these peasants, and would give an insight into their methods of agricultural production. The lack of excavation at rural settlement sites means that these aspects of medieval life are little understood by scholars today.

4. SETTLEMENT AND SOCIETY IN MEDIEVAL GAELIC IRELAND

4.1—Introduction

This chapter looks at Gaelic settlement and society in medieval Ireland, which was overwhelmingly rural in nature. It has already been noted that Gaelic peasant cultivators, normally called 'betaghs' in the colonial sources, were an important and large element of the population within the bounds of Anglo-Norman manors in eastern Ireland (section 3.1). It must also be remembered that the arrival of the Anglo-Normans in Ireland in the late twelfth century was not like the conquest of England by William the Conqueror in 1066. In Ireland individual Anglo-Norman lords had carved out territories for themselves in the late twelfth and thirteenth centuries. There had been a strong tendency amongst these lords to leave regions and districts of economically more marginal land to Irish lords and lineage groups. These Gaelic-dominated regions included most of Ulster west of the Bann, much of Connacht, west Munster and the bogland and mountain zones of the Anglo-Norman lordships of Meath and Leinster. The relationship between the Gaelic lords in these regions and the Anglo-Normans and colonial government varied considerably from virtual independence in some areas to the status of rent-paying tenants in others (Down 1987, 443; Frame 1981, 71–2; Glasscock 1987, 225–6; Nicholls 1972, 13; 1987; Smyth 1982, 104–12; Watt 1987a, 311–12). The settlement forms and material culture associated with these areas of Gaelic lordship from the late twelfth century onwards are the main focus of this chapter. Much of the discussion is also of some relevance to the settlement history and material culture of Ireland during the century prior to the arrival of the Anglo-Normans in 1169.

Very little is known about the material culture and settlement patterns of Gaelic Ireland throughout the medieval period (Barry 1987, 51, 200). This is partly due to the fact that relatively little archaeological work has been done in Ireland on the period in general over much of this century (section 1.3a). Another reason is the nature of the surviving evidence. Historical sources containing economic and social information about Gaelic Ireland are virtually non-existent for the thirteenth, fourteenth and fifteenth centuries, the largest number coming from the sixteenth and seventeenth centuries (Nicholls 1987, 398). This is partly because Gaelic lords did not produce administrative and economic records in the same quantity as elsewhere in medieval western Europe (Nicholls 1987, 398; Watt 1987b, 314). It has also been argued that the overwhelming majority of those records that were produced by thirteenth- and fourteenth-century Gaelic lords were either destroyed in the endemic warfare that characterised Ireland into the seventeenth century or lost through simple archival neglect over the last 800 years (Nicholls 1987, 398). However, a great mass of annalistic material, poetry and literature from medieval Gaelic Ireland does survive, although most of these sources have been under-studied by modern historians (Duffy 1997, 3–4). The medieval Irish annals, with their notoriously laconic entries, are really the major source of information as yet for Gaelic Ireland up to the sixteenth century, especially in areas well away from regions controlled by the Anglo-Normans (Barry 1987, 9).

This lack of surviving documentary records and the underexploitation of existing sources for medieval Gaelic Ireland also have implications for archaeology. For example, at the beginning of this century Goddard Orpen used the available colonial sources of late twelfth-, thirteenth- and fourteenth-century date, which are far more extensive than those for contemporary Gaelic society, to argue for the medieval and ultimately Anglo-Norman origins of motte castles (Orpen 1906a, 435–8; 1907b; 1907c, 133;

1909d, 313; 1911–20, i, 341; ii, 344). Conversely, the lack of detailed socio-economic documentation for medieval Gaelic society, such as the non-existence of the equivalent of manorial extents or inquisitions, along with the limited work carried out on the available literary sources, means that it is difficult at present to recognise Irish secular settlement sites of pre-tower-house date in the modern landscape in comparison to Anglo-Norman centres. This difficulty has probably contributed to the lack of archae-ological work on medieval Gaelic Ireland: it is far easier to study recognisable Anglo-Norman monuments.

Anglo-Norman, English and even western European chroniclers and observers during the whole medieval period, such as Giraldus Cambrensis, Stephen of Lexington and Jean Froissart, clearly believed that native Irish society was barbarous, undeveloped and uncivilised by the standards of the time (e.g. *Topographia*, 100–3, 106–10; *Froissart*, 430–3; Nicholls 1987, 397; Watt 1987b, 318). This attitude of contempt was to continue amongst some English writers into the seventeenth century and beyond (Ellis 1985, 33; Watt 1987a, 310). The view that the medieval Irish were a primitive people seems to be due to the contrasts between Gaelic Ireland and the truly feudalised lands of contemporary England and western Europe (Nicholls 1987, 397). This statement has to be qualified, as it is clear that Gaelic society had taken on facets of contemporary European 'feudal' culture well before 1169, although it was never to experience feudalism in its classical form (e.g. Flanagan 1989; Doherty 1980; 1985; Duffy 1997, 46–8; Ó Corráin 1972; 1978; 1989, 47–52; Ó Cróinín 1995, 291–2). Certain aspects of Gaelic political and military life continued to develop along general European lines throughout the medieval period and into early modern times (K. Simms 1987). Furthermore, as argued in the last chapter, the organisation of settlement and the economy in certain parts of Anglo-Norman Ireland, such as the earldom of Ulster and in border regions of the colony, were not very different to what occurred in Gaelic parts of the country (section 3.2a). Overall, medieval writers such as Giraldus Cambrensis and modern historians such as Goddard Orpen seem to have over-emphasised the differences between Anglo-Norman and Gaelic Ireland (Duffy 1997, 1–6; Flanagan 1989, 1–3).

Yet there were contrasts between the economy, society and political life of medieval Gaelic Ireland and the feudal world of England and most of western Europe. Medieval Gaelic society was what social anthropologists call a clan or lineage-based society (Nicholls 1972, 8–12; 1987, 397–8). It continued to manifest characteristics that foreign observers at least would have interpreted as being archaic. The economy remained largely pastoral, and barter, especially in cattle, was the most frequent method of business transaction. Large nucleated villages did not exist and settlements were for the most part dispersed, either in isolated farmsteads or in house clusters. Transhumance or booleying appears to have played a large part in the yearly agricultural strategy. There is no real evidence of true urbanisation outside possibly a few ecclesiastical centres such as episcopal sees (Nicholls 1987, 397). Marriage and divorce remained lay affairs governed by secular law, which seems to have drawn no distinction between the legitimate and the illegitimate for the purpose of inheritance. Primogeniture was not the firmly established method of succession to lordship, although there are examples of eldest sons succeeding their fathers within the Gaelic system. This led to a multiplicity of heirs in matters of land and lordship, which in turn gave rise at times to political instability within the whole Gaelic polity, but it also meant that there was always a male heir to a lordship or kingdom. The formal rite of kingly inauguration contained strong pagan and secular elements. Poets and subchiefs, as well as clergy, played a major role in these proceedings, which did not take place in churches but at sites associated with the mythological past of the lineage groups to which the kings belonged (Nicholls 1972, 3; 1987, 397–8, 423–4; Richter 1988, 1812; K. Simms 1987, 21–89; Watt 1987b, 315, 319–22). Brehon law, rather than common law, with its somewhat archaic but nonetheless evolving features of joint family responsibility, private distress and failure to recognise any real form of criminal law, was the legal system of Gaelic Ireland until the seventeenth century. Theft, homicide and arson were regarded as simple torts to be resolved by the payment of damages or compensation to the injured party, his kin and, increasingly, his lord. It is clear that this legal system did take some concepts from common law over the course of time but still remained remarkably different from it (Nicholls 1972, 44–57; 1987, 427–9).

The system of inheritance to land was by what became known as 'Irish gavelkind'. The unit of ownership was not the individual, or even his nuclear family, but the whole patrilineal family group. Land appears to have been held in allodial ownership by this group and was periodically redistributed amongst members of the kin group in systems that varied from region to region. This does not mean that land was never alienated from the family group, either by straightforward purchase or by pledge. Indeed, land regularly changed hands in this manner. Therefore privately owned land did exist in Gaelic Ireland. This was the way expanding lineage groups gained power at the expense of weaker, declining kindreds (Nicholls 1972, 10–12, 37–8, 57–64; 1987, 430–3). Other relatively archaic institutions, such as fosterage and hostage-taking, were used to cement alliances and enforce agreements (Watt 1987b, 319). The general appearance of the Irish, in terms of dress and weaponry, was also different to the Anglo-Norman and English world (*Topographia*, 101–3, 107–8; Dunlevy 1989, 27–64).

Recent work certainly suggests that in many ways medieval Gaelic society from the eleventh century onwards was developing along similar lines to much of western Europe. Yet the available historical sources also indicate that medieval Gaelic society had features that were very different to the truly feudalised lands of France, Germany or England (Nicholls 1987, 397; Richter 1988, 189–93). It could be argued, therefore, that the hostility shown towards Ireland in certain texts was based on an unfamiliarity and lack of sympathy with medieval Gaelic culture. As noted above, the specific aim of this chapter is to examine the settlement forms and material culture associated with Gaelic Ireland during the medieval period, especially from the late twelfth century through to when the native Irish began to build tower-houses in the fifteenth century. This chapter will also attempt to show that while the culture of medieval Gaelic Ireland was different in many ways to classical Anglo-Norman society, this does not necessarily mean that it was underdeveloped and backward-looking. It will be argued that many of the traits of medieval Gaelic society that manifest themselves in the archaeological record today were efficient, practical and ultimately sensible responses to the landscape and politics of the time, as well as to their economic organisation. Indeed, many features of Gaelic society came to be adopted by the Anglo-Normans from the fourteenth century onwards as part of the Gaelicisation of large parts of the colony.

4.2—Gaelic high-status sites, *c.* 1100–1400

4.2a—Gaelic castles, *c.* 1169–1400
It was shown in Chapter 2 that most castles were the centres of rural estates and administration and not just military strongholds (sections 2.1, 2.2). It was also noted above that there have been few attempts by archaeologists and others to locate medieval Irish habitation sites in the modern landscape (section 4.1). Obviously one possible way of identifying the centres of medieval Gaelic estates and rural administration is to look at the field evidence for high-status Irish habitation sites in the modern landscape.

Irish lords began to build tower-houses in the early fifteenth century, just after 1400 (Cairns 1987, 9). Clearly castles are high-status sites as they were usually lordly residences (section 2.2). What is the evidence for castles in Gaelic Ireland before 1400? Certainly, the Welsh and the Highland Scots erected castles during the twelfth, thirteenth and fourteenth centuries (Dunbar 1981; King 1988, 130–46). Orpen (1907c, 134) stated that some motte castles must have been erected by the Irish, although he seemed unable to find specific examples. Glasscock (1975, 101) also maintained that a few mottes may have been built by Gaelic Irish lords. McNeill (1980, 102–3; 1997a,

158) has argued that a dozen mottes in mid-Antrim were erected by the O'Flynns of Uí Tuirtre. Furthermore, he suggests that the sparse scatter of mottes to the west of the medieval earldom, over most of the modern province, were Gaelic-built, since most of this huge area was never colonised by the Anglo-Normans. Specifically, he has recently suggested that the motte at Crown Mound, Newry, Co. Down, was erected by the Magennis lords of Iveagh, and that the motte at Managh Beg, Co. Derry, was put up by the O'Cahans (McNeill 1997, 73, 158). The motte at Coney Island may have been put up by a Gaelic archbishop of Armagh some time in the thirteenth century (*ibid.*, 73). It has been suggested that the mottes at Monally and Srahan, Co. Laois, located way up in the Slieve Blooms, were built by the Gaelic Irish (O'Conor 1992, 9–10; 1993, 209). Graham (1988a, 25–6; 1988b, 110–11, 115–17, 126) has suggested that the mottes at Sheaunbeg and Cloonburren, Co. Roscommon, *might* have been native-built, in an argument criticising the tendency of Irish archaeologists and historians this century to classify monuments of the medieval period ethnically. He also argued that the earthwork at Rathdooney More, Co. Sligo, was an Irish-built motte castle (1988b, 121–6). This site has been reclassified as a raised rath by the Archaeological Survey of Ireland (Mon. No. SL033-087). However, the overall evidence suggests that most motte and ringwork castles, defined here as earthen fortresses surmounted by well-built, elaborate and complex timber defences (section 2.1), as opposed to other, less defensive earthwork fortifications, were built by the Anglo-Normans (Orpen 1907c, 134; Glasscock 1975, 99–101; McNeill 1997, 72–4; O'Conor 1992, 8–10; 1993, 188–95, 204–37; forthcoming).

Some masonry castles have been postulated in the past as having been built by Gaelic kings and lords during the thirteenth and fourteenth centuries. More recent work has suggested that some of these castles were in fact erected by the Anglo-Normans. For example, it has been stated that the keepless castle at Ballintober, Co. Roscommon, built around 1300, was an O'Conor copy of nearby Roscommon Castle (Pl. 24; Leask 1941, 69; Glasscock 1987, 221). However, both the historical and the architectural evidence suggests that this large stone castle was actually built by Richard de Burgh in the first years of the fourteenth century (Barry 1995, 218; Claffey 1974–5; McNeill 1997, 101–3). Again, some others of these Irish castles should not really be classified as such as they lacked the defensive features of true examples. For example, Hags Castle or *Caislen na Caillige,* Co. Mayo, which may have been built by the O'Conors in the late twelfth or early thirteenth century (McNeill 1997, 161; O'Conor 1993, 229–30), is located on a small, possibly artificial island in Lough Mask and consists of a circular enclosure defined by a thick mortared stone wall, whose internal diameter is 32m (Mon. No. MO117-003). Overall, it looks a remarkably simple structure and is similar to a cashel in its morphology, as opposed to a contemporary masonry castle, which would have carried far more complex defences. Again, it has been suggested that the MacDermots had a masonry castle on Castle Island, Lough Key, Co. Roscommon (Graham 1988a, 33; Lynn 1985–6, 104; McNeill 1997, 160), but the surface remains on this natural island today consist of a nineteenth-century folly, within which are the remains of a late medieval tower-house. There is certainly no visible evidence for a thirteenth-century masonry castle (Mon. No. RO006-046). This site is never called a castle in the sources—always *Carraic Loch Ce* or the Rock of Lough Key (O'Conor 1993, 227–8). A 1235 reference to fireboats being sent against the island suggests that its defences were of timber at this date at least (*ALC; AC*). It is probably best to classify the site as a natural island fortress during the thirteenth and fourteenth centuries, whose artificial defences were not as formidable as those of true castles. It will be shown below that such fortresses on natural islands were common in many parts of medieval Gaelic Ireland (section 4.2b).

It would seem that certain sites have been wrongly identified as Irish masonry castles of thirteenth- or fourteenth-century date. Some of these were in fact erected by Anglo-Norman lords, while others do not seem to have carried the same complexity of defences as true castles.

76

Pl. 24—*Ballintober Castle, Co. Roscommon, built by Richard de Burgh in the first years of the fourteenth century.* (Photo: Kieran O'Conor.)

However, there are some masonry castles of thirteenth- or fourteenth-century date that appear to have been built by the native Irish. These include the polygonal enclosure castles of general thirteenth-century date at Connor and Doonbought, Co. Antrim. These two castles lack mural towers or gatehouses and are extremely simple in plan. Connor seems to have been the centre of the O'Flynn lordship of Uí Tuirtre (McNeill 1977; 1980, 102–3; 1997, 158–60). Another Irish-built castle of thirteenth-century date may be Castle Kirke, Co. Galway, which is located on a small natural island on Lough Corrib (Gosling 1993, 162; Lynn 1985–6, 102–3; McNeill 1997, 162–3). Two further examples are Elagh, Co. Donegal, and Harry Avery's Castle, Co. Tyrone, both in western Ulster (McNeill 1980, 114; 1997, 163–4). Yet, overall, Gaelic masonry castles of pre-tower-house date are few in number. The general impression from both fieldwork and the historical sources is that the overwhelming majority of stone castles of pre-1400 date were built by Anglo-Norman lords or the colonial government (McNeill 1997, 157–64; O'Conor 1992, 8–10; 1993, 204–37). This lack of field evidence for conventional castles of pre-tower-house date in Gaelic parts of medieval Ireland is confirmed by statements made by Giraldus Cambrensis in the 1180s and Stephen of Lexington about 40–50 years later that the Irish of their time did not build castles (*Topographia*, 119; *Lexington*, 112; Stalley 1987, 9).

4.2b—Crannogs, natural island fortresses, moated sites and cashels
While the evidence suggests that remarkably few earthwork and masonry castles were built by native Irish lords before *c.* 1400, when tower-houses began to be built in Gaelic areas (section 4.2a), there are a large number of references in the surviving sources to fortified Gaelic lordly residences that do not appear to have been masonry or motte castles. These fortifications are not referred to as *caislen*, *caistel* or *castellum* in these pre-1400 sources. It was argued above that even earthwork castles had serious defences, such as wooden mural towers offering flanking defence and palisades looped for archery, during their period of use, and that this is why they were referred to as castles in the sources (sections 2.2, 2.3). This suggests that annalists and chroniclers did not call these defended Gaelic sites castles because they were not regarded as defensive enough to be termed such.

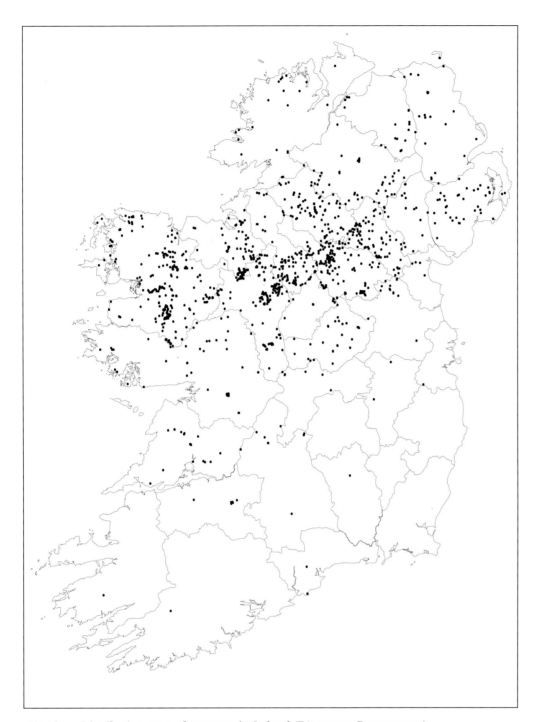

Fig. 21—*Distribution map of crannogs in Ireland* (Discovery Programme).

These references to pre-1400 Gaelic fortifications are mainly to places in Connacht, western Ulster and Clare. This is simply because many of the medieval historical sources relating to Gaelic Ireland that are extant today, or at least those that have been edited by modern historians, originated in these areas. As always, there is a certain difficulty in identifying places mentioned in historical documents with surviving monuments. Nevertheless, recent fieldwork, especially by the Archaeological Survey, has allowed at least some of these historically attested late twelfth-, thirteenth- and fourteenth-century Gaelic sites to be recognised in the modern landscape. Apart from the odd Irish castle, the Gaelic lordly residences mentioned in the surviving sources are mostly referred to in three different ways: the *crannóg*, the *inis* or 'island' site and, lastly, the *longphort* or 'stronghold' site. The aim of this section is to attempt to identify some of these sites on the ground today and to discuss their morphology.

Crannogs

A crannog can be defined as an artificially constructed island in a lake (Pls 25–8; Fig. 21). They were made by dumping layers of stone, soil, timber, peat, brushwood and even domestic rubbish onto some shallow area of a lough to create an occupation platform (Ó Ríordáin 1979, 89; Lynn 1983, 50–1). While there is considerable debate about their actual origins, it is clear that palisaded, defended crannogs flourished in the Early Christian period from about the sixth century onwards (Lynn 1983, 50–1). The occupation of crannogs during the medieval and post-medieval periods has also long been noted but never dealt with thoroughly (Barry 1987, 19; Hayes-McCoy 1964, 9–10; Ó Ríordáin 1979, 93; Wood-Martin 1886, 146–56, 236–8). Occupation at Lough Faughan crannog, Co. Down, continued into the thirteenth century (Collins 1955). The crannog of Island MacHugh, Co. Tyrone, produced evidence of considerable habitation in the thirteenth century and apparently in the fourteenth century, although it was constructed at a much earlier date (Davies 1950, 45–56, 92; Ivens *et al.* 1986). The site continued to be inhabited throughout the fifteenth and sixteenth centuries. A tower-house was built on it during the early part of the latter century (Davies 1950, 56–85; Ivens *et al.* 1986, 99). The small test excavation of a probable crannog at Lough Atrain, Co. Cavan, suggested that the site was occupied in the thirteenth and fourteenth centuries (Davies 1946, 32–4).

It was noted above that there has been little Irish interest in medieval archaeology over much of this century (sections 1.2, 1.3). Little attention has also been paid to the large numbers of stray finds of general medieval date found on many crannogs, now housed in various museums throughout Ireland (Ó Floinn, forthcoming, 111–12). For example, ring brooches of general thirteenth–fifteenth-century date have turned up as stray finds on a number of crannogs (Deevy 1998, 35–7). The occurrence of so many stray finds of medieval date on many unexcavated crannogs suggests that at least some of these sites were inhabited in the thirteenth or fourteenth century and later. The recent recognition by the Archaeological Survey of the foundations of rectangular mortared stone houses on certain Roscommon crannogs suggests that these sites were occupied at some stage after *c.* 1200 (Mon. Nos RO005-015, 017-090, 025-004). Therefore there is archaeological evidence for the occupation of crannogs in the medieval period.

Pl. 25—*Crannog on Lough Talt, Co. Sligo.* (Photo: Kieran O'Conor.)

Pl. 26—*Crannog on Fenagh Lough, Co. Leitrim.* (Photo: *Dúchas*, The Heritage Service.)

Pl. 27—*Crannog on Gortinty Lough, Co. Leitrim.* (Photo: *Dúchas*, The Heritage Service.)

The direct use of the word *crannóg* itself only appears in the sources after *c.* 1200. A crannog belonging to the O'Reillys on Lough Oughter, Co. Cavan, was attacked by Walter de Lacy, lord of Meath, in 1220 (*ALC*). William Gorm de Lacy built the crannog of Inis Laodhachain in 1223. Shortly after its erection, it was attacked by Connachtmen (*ibid.*). Turlough MacAedh O'Conor escaped from the crannog of Lough Leisi (Kilglass Lough, Co. Roscommon) in 1246 (*AC; ALC*). This crannog is mentioned again in 1456, when Loughlin Oge O'Hanly, lord of the Cinel Dobhtha, was slain there in a succession dispute. Miles Costello garrisoned the crannog of Claenlough (Belhavel Lough, Co. Leitrim) in 1247, having captured it from the MacRannells. The latter then retook it with the help of Turlough and Aedh O'Conor (*AC; ALC; AFM*). The crannog of Lough Laoghaire, Co. Tyrone, is directly mentioned in a dispute between different branches of the O'Neills in 1436 (*AC*). A poem lamenting the death of Brian O'Neill, king of Tír Eogain, at the Battle of Downpatrick in 1260 describes the latter as *Briain Locha Laoghaire* or 'Brian of Lough Laoghaire' (*Mac Con Midhe*, 151). Another O'Neill dynast

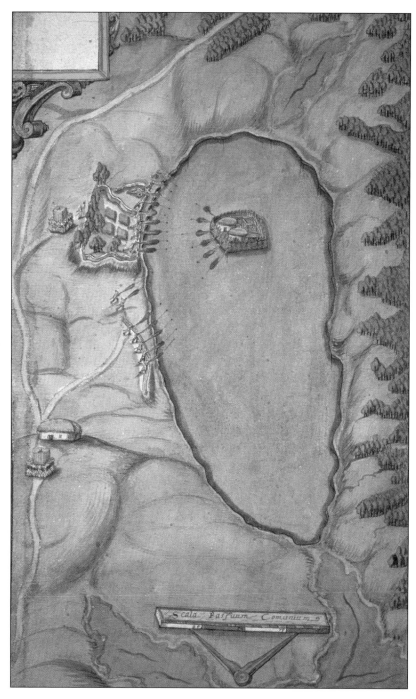

Pl. 28—*Contemporary depiction of a crannog under attack in Ulster, c. 1600* (Bartlett map; see Hayes-McCoy 1964). *The palisade around the edges of the crannog consists of nothing more than a post-and-wattle fence.*

died at Lough Laoghaire in 1325 (Wood-Martin 1886, 155–6, 179). These seem to be indirect references to the use of the crannog as a kingly residence in the thirteenth and fourteenth centuries. It has been suggested that the crannog at Island MacHugh can be equated with Loch Laoghaire (Davies 1950, 57). MacClancy's crannog on Lough Melvin is mentioned in 1455, when it was taken by Turlough Maguire (*AFM*). This site, while not specifically mentioned, appears to have been attacked by Cathal O'Rourke and his sons in 1419 (*AFM*). In 1477 a great storm demolished 'many stone and wooden buildings and crannogs and ricks all over Ireland' (*AC*), suggesting that crannogs were a common feature of medieval lakeland Ireland. The crannog of Lough Bethach (Lough Veagh, Co. Donegal), the residence of Niall Garb O'Donnell, was burned by Eogan O'Donnell in 1524 (*AC*). Caffar O'Donnell lived in this crannog in 1559 (*AFM*). It is probably the site indirectly mentioned in 1258, when there is a reference to O'Donnell lying 'on his deathbed on Lough Beathach', having been wounded in action at the Battle of Credran Cille (*AFM*). There are many more direct references to crannogs, as well as contemporary depictions of them, in the provinces of Connacht and Ulster throughout the sixteenth and early seventeenth centuries (Pl. 28; Wood-Martin 1886, 146–54, 236–8; Hayes-McCoy 1964, 9–10, 16, 20). There are also references to crannogs being attacked in Ulster during the 1640s (Wood-Martin 1886, 148–9). There are even hints that some crannogs may have been occupied as late as the 1690s in Ireland (Hayes-McCoy 1964, 20). Davies (1946, 29) believed that the crannog at Deredis Upper, Co. Cavan, was occupied into the early eighteenth century.

Inis or 'island' sites

Many crannogs are simply referred to as *inis* or 'island' sites in the various sources up to the seventeenth century. For example, Giraldus Cambrensis, writing in the 1180s, stated that Irish lords very often lived on islands in lakes, using them as 'places of safety and refuge, as well as of habitation' (*Topographia,* 37), again suggesting that crannogs were a common feature of lakeland Ireland in the late twelfth century. There is a reference to a recently built 'island' called Inislachain 'upon Loch Ruidhe' in 1170 *(AU)*. The 'island' of Lough Cairrgin (Ardakillen Lough, Co. Roscommon) is frequently referred to in the sources. In 1293 Magnus O'Conor, king of Connacht, died of sickness here *(AC)*. Donell O'Conor burnt the 'island' of Lough Cairrgin in 1388 *(AU)*. The 'islands' of Lough Cairrgin or Ardnakillen Lough were captured by O'Conor Don in 1467 *(AC)*. The sites of six crannogs can be recognised around the partly drained lake today (Mon. Nos RO028-102-7). The 'island' of Inchiquin is mentioned in 1313 (*Caithreim Thoirdhealbaigh*, i, 70; ii, 63), and a large crannog is visible on Lough Inchiquin, Co. Clare, today (Mon. No. CL017-05901). Donnell O'Coffey and his two sons were slain in their house on Cro-Inis, 'an island on Loch Ainninn Mic Neimhidth', in 1446 *(AC; AFM)*. This site has been identified as a crannog on the north-western side of Lough Ennell, Co. Westmeath, which was apparently a kingly residence in the eleventh century as well (Farrell and Buckley 1984). Overall, there are many references to 'fortified islands' during the sixteenth and early seventeenth centuries in Ulster and Connacht, and presumably most of these sites were crannogs (Wood-Martin 1886, 146–8).

Nevertheless, some of these *inis* sites appear to refer to defensive earthworks on completely natural islands. For example, O'Donnell plundered *Eo-inis* in 1231 *(AFM)*. Eonish is a long, natural drumlin island in Lough Oughter, Co. Cavan. A univallate ringfort about 54m in diameter, a graveyard (presumably marking the site of a medieval church) and a holy well occur on this island today (O'Donovan 1995, 92, 215, 219). Farrell Mac Tagadain was slain on Inishfree in 1245 *(AFM)*. This is a small natural island at the eastern end of Lough Gill, Co. Sligo (Mon. No. SL015-097). The MacDermot fortress on a small natural island in Lough Key, Co. Roscommon, was mentioned above (section 4.2a). Derbhail, daughter of Aedh O'Donnell, visited Conor MacDermot, lord of Moylurg, on *Inis-Doighre* in 1343. She became ill and died on the island, and was buried at Boyle Abbey *(ALC; AFM)*. Cathal MacDermot drowned off *Inis-Doighre* in 1393 *(AU; ALC)*. *Inis-Doighre* can be identified with Inishatirra Island, a large drumlin island in Drumharlow Lough, Co. Roscommon, just over 23 acres in extent (O'Conor 1998), which lay within the MacDermot territory of Moylurg throughout the medieval period. It was an area of Roscommon that never saw any Anglo-Norman settlement (Graham 1988a, 30; MacDermot 1996, 435–42). The island was still in MacDermot hands in the early seventeenth century (MacDermot 1996, 88, 446, 469), and the evidence suggests that it was always under their control throughout the whole medieval period. Furthermore, there appears to have been a lordly residence on the island for at least part of this time. This is important, as the archaeological remains on the island today consist of an almost square moated site with a large oval enclosure attached to its north-eastern side (Mon. No. RO007-084). This moated site seems to have been built by the MacDermots, lords of Moylurg, as one of their residences (O'Conor 1998).

A few *inis* sites are clearly riverine. A praise-poem in honour of Godfraidh O'Donnell, king of Tír Conaill, written before 1257, mentions his fortress on *Inis Saimhear* (*Mac Con Midhe*, 57, 275). This can be equated with the small natural island of Inis Samer, located in the estuary of the Erne at Ballyshannon, Co. Donegal (Pl. 29;

Pl. 29—*This natural island in the Erne estuary at Ballyshannon, Co. Donegal, was the site of the medieval O'Donnell fortress of Inis Samer. Presumably these natural island fortresses functioned in much the same way as crannogs.* (Photo: Kieran O'Conor.)

Mon. No. DG107-055). Cathal O'Farrell, lord of Annaly, died on Inis Cuan in the 'river of Cluain Lis Becc Mic Mac Conla' in 1282 (*AC*; *AFM*).

Many other general references to '*inis*' or 'island' sites exist in the sources. Only future fieldwork and historical research will determine whether these are natural islands, riverine sites or artificial crannogs, although it is predicted that the majority will turn out to belong to the latter monument type. An Anglo-Norman force was expelled from the 'island' of Uí Finntain in 1194 (*AU*). Aedh O'Farrell was burned on the 'island' of Lough Cuile (presumably somewhere in modern County Longford) by the sons of Aedh Ciabrach O'Farrell in 1232 (*ALC*; *AC*). O'Gara was slain by his own kinsmen on Inis Bolg, 'an island in Loch Techet', in 1435 (*AFM*). Brian O'Farrell was killed in 1443 as he was trying to escape by force from the 'island of Port-an-Ghuirtan', where he had been held prisoner for two and a half years by Donnell Boy O'Farrell (*AFM*). The island of Loch Iamhrugain is mentioned in 1450 (*AU*).

There are also references to raids on lakes or residences on lakes, indirectly suggesting that there were inhabited natural islands or crannogs on them. It is probable that the majority of these implied fortresses were crannogs. For example, there is a reference to MacDermot, lord of Moylurg, dying 'in his own mansion (*ina tigh fein*) on Claenlough' (*AFM*). Aedh O'Neill pillaged 'Loch Nea', bringing all 'the treasures' of O'Conor out of it in 1225 (*AU*). This lake seems to have been located in the vicinity of Roscommon town. A lake, with a crannog (Mon. No. RO039-042) in it, once existed in the townland of Loughnaneane, just to the west of Roscommon Castle. Certainly, Roscommon seems to have been an important O'Conor centre prior to the building of Roscommon Castle by the Dublin government after *c*. 1269. The monastery of Roscommon was clearly very rich prior to the coming of the Anglo-Normans, producing high-quality metalwork for Turlough O'Conor and other O'Conor dynasts (Edwards 1990, 147). There also appears to have been an important thirteenth-century O'Conor centre here. This would explain why Felim O'Conor founded a Dominican priory at Roscommon in 1253 (Gwynn and Hadcock 1970, 229). Dominican and Franciscan friaries in Gaelic Ireland were invariably located close to the strongholds of

Irish kings and lords throughout the medieval period (Leask 1955–60, iii, 89). It is postulated that the crannog at Loughnaneane was occupied during the thirteenth century and was an O'Conor residence. In 1367 the Clann Muircertagh pillaged Lough Berraigh (*AU*). 'Loch Farbach' or Lough Arrow on the Sligo/Roscommon border was captured by Rory MacDermot in 1398 (*AC*). While there are a couple of natural islands in this lake, at least fourteen crannogs have also been recognised by the Archaeological Survey here (Mon. Nos SL034-199, 215, 219; SL040-048, 116–18, 120, 166, 168, 173, 178–9). A tower-house dating from *c.* 1600 occurs at Drumdoe, Co. Roscommon, on the shores of Lough Arrow. A crannog lies just offshore from it (Mon. Nos RO003-011, -012). The juxtaposition of these two monuments is a strong hint that the latter site was occupied throughout the medieval period.

Crannogs and natural islands shared one common defensive feature: they were all surrounded by water. Militarily, this would have made them quite difficult to capture. This does not necessarily mean that their peripheral defences were complex or strong. The crannogs depicted on maps of Ulster around 1600 are merely defended by post-and-wattle fences (Pl. 28; Hayes McCoy 1964, 20). At least one late sixteenth-century crannog was merely defended by a hedge, albeit with sharpened stakes in it (Wood-Martin 1886, 147–8). Simple plank palisades are seen too. A collapsed palisade of oak planks, now waterlogged, is visible on the substantial, largely stone-built crannog at the eastern end of Lough Meelagh, Keadue, Co. Roscommon, very close to the medieval parish church at Kilronan (Mon. No. RO004-004). There is much historical evidence to suggest that the O'Duignans had a centre at Kilronan during the medieval period (MacDermot 1996, 205–6), and it is possible that this crannog represents the site of their main residence. It would be simple to verify this by obtaining a dendrochronological date from one of the planks.

The longphort *or 'stronghold' site*
Another type of defended Irish residential site mentioned in the various surviving Gaelic historical sources of the thirteenth and fourteenth centuries is the *longphort* (also spelt *longport, longpurt* and *longpuirt* in the sources), normally translated into modern English by historians as 'fortress' and 'stronghold'. The annalists and chroniclers who use the word *longphort* during the medieval period appear to be making a distinction between these sites and castles. Furthermore, unlike crannogs and natural island fortresses, most *longphort* sites seem to have been located on dry land.

It has been argued that the term *longphort* was used in the medieval Irish sources to describe temporary fortified camps erected during the course of campaigns or sieges (Graham 1988b, 125). Certainly, this word is occasionally used in the sources to describe such temporary fortresses. For example, a *longphort* was clearly being used as a temporary fortified camp in Clare in 1314 (*Caithreim Thoirdhealbaigh*, i, 78; ii, 71). The available historical evidence suggests that the word often also meant a permanent defended settlement of some sort, from about 1200 onwards at least. A 'palace (*pailiss*)' and 'houses (*tigib*)' are mentioned in 1306 as being located within Aedh O'Conor's *longpurt* at Cloonfree, Co. Roscommon (*AC; ALC*). 'Houses (*tigib*)' are described as being within the *longpuirt* of Cathal O'Conor at Fasa Choillidh, Co. Sligo, in 1318 (*ALC*). Rory O'Conor's 'house' in his *longport* of Ardnakillen, Co. Roscommon, is referred to in 1368 (*AC; ALC*). These are all clearly strongholds within O'Conor lands in Roscommon and Sligo, and appear to be have been permanently occupied lordly sites. Natural deaths are also recorded at these places. Mahon O'Brien, *tigearna Tuadmuman*, died 'in his own stronghold (*ina longpurt fein*)' in 1314 (*AFM*). Cathal MacDonagh died 'in his own stronghold (*ina longpurt fein*)' at Portinch, Co. Sligo, in 1404 (*ALC*). Some sites are mentioned more than once in the sources, hinting that they were occupied over a long period. Conor O'Brien is described as having built 'a stronghold with earthworks (*longport comnaide*)' at Clonroad, Ennis, Co. Clare, around *c.* 1260 (*Caithreim Thoirdhealbaigh*, i, 4; ii, 5). The site is mentioned again in 1276 or 1277, 1284 and 1317 (*Caithreim Thoirdhealbaigh*, i, 5–8, 24, 132; ii, 6–7, 26, 116). The *longport* of MacMahon at Rath

Tulach in Oriel was mentioned in 1345, 1365 and 1368 (*AU*; *AFM*). Tadg, son of Magnus O'Conor, was taken prisoner by Rory O'Conor in the *longpurt* of Ardnakillen in 1368 (*AC*; *ALC*; *AFM*). The site was burned again by Donnell O'Conor in 1388 (*AFM*). MacDermot's *longport* (apparently located on Longford Hill, Rockingham Demesne, Co. Roscommon) is first mentioned in 1342 and again in 1348 and 1385 (*AC*; *AFM*). Overall, the sources indicate that these 'strongholds' were mainly permanently occupied sites.

Other references to *longphort* sites include the O'Flaherty example on Iniscreamha (a small natural island on Lough Corrib, Co. Galway), which surrendered to Hugh O'Conor in 1221 (*AFM*). The *longport* of Conor O'Kelly was burned by some of Aedh O'Conor's followers in 1260 (*AC*). Aedh O'Conor's *longport* at Snam Muiredaig (Drumsna on the Roscommon/Leitrim border) was burned by the men of Breifne in 1261 (*AC*). Felim O'Conor's *longport* at Cloonsellan, Co. Roscommon, was burned in this year too (*AC*). The 'great stronghold (*morlongport*)' of Cumea Mac Conmara of Clanncullen is mentioned in 1278 (*Caithreim Thoirdhealbaigh*, i, 11; ii, 12). The *longport* of O'Brien is mentioned in 1308 (*Caithreim Thoirdhealbaigh*, i, 37; ii, 37). The *longport* of Rory O'Conor was taken by William Burke in 1309 (*AFM*). The *longport* of Murtough O'Brien, lord of Thomond, was attacked by Dermot O'Brien and the de Clares in 1311 (*Caithreim Thoirdhealbaigh*, i, 50; ii, 48). Dermot O'Brien retired to 'his own fortress (*da longport fein*)' after the Battle of the Abbey in 1317 (*Caithreim Thoirdhealbaigh*, i, 132; ii, 116). In 1388 John O'Toole was slain by a clown in his *longport* (*AFM*). Presumably this site lay somewhere in modern Wicklow. The famous Art MacMurrough died 'in his own stronghold (*ina longport fein*)' in either 1414 (*AC*) or 1417 (*ALC*). Murchad O'Conor Faly died 'in his own stronghold (*ina longpurt fein*)' in 1421 (*ALC*).

What is the archaeological evidence today for these medieval Gaelic sites? Many of them cannot be located in the field at present. However, certain observations can be made from the available evidence. None of these sites can be identified with classic motte or masonry castles. This tallies with the observation, noted above, that medieval Gaelic annalists and chroniclers made a distinction between castles and *longphort* sites. Arguably, this negative evidence is also further proof that few conventional castles were built by Gaelic lords before *c.* 1400. Certainly, the standing monuments that can be equated with pre-1400 *longphort* sites are not castles. As noted, the O'Flaherty *longphort* of Iniscreamha is mentioned in 1221. This site consists of a small natural island containing a massive cashel, surrounded by a deep, rock-cut ditch (M. Gibbons, pers. comm.). Indeed, it is very similar in its morphology and siting to Hag's Castle or *Caislen na Caillige*, mentioned above, also located in Lough Corrib (section 4.2a). Cashels can be described as usually circular enclosures defined by substantial drystone-built walls, and were certainly common as a settlement form during the Early Christian period. They were basically the drystone-walled equivalent of earthen ringforts, and seem to have also functioned as semi-defended farmsteads. Only a very small number of cashels have ever been excavated (Edwards 1990, 14). Certainly, very little has been written about their post-1169 usage. However, apart from the evidence from Iniscreamha, there is a certain amount of evidence to suggest their continued use into post-medieval times.

The innermost enclosure at the hillfort of Rathgall, Co. Wicklow, which is more or less circular with an internal diameter of *c.* 40m, seems to have been a purpose-built medieval cashel (Pl. 30), probably erected by one of the local O'Byrnes. There was certainly substantial occupation of this central enclosure during this period, as up to 2000 sherds of medieval pottery were found during the course of the excavation there. This pottery included Leinster cooking ware and locally produced glazed jugs. Two silver coins of late thirteenth- and fourteenth-century date were found in association with this pottery. The remains of a rectangular house of medieval date were found outside the central enclosure. It seems to have been of wattle-and-daub construction, the walls apparently built of horizontal layers of wattle woven around upright posts with a mud coating, and to have had a thatched roof (Long 1994, 238–42; Raftery 1970). Again, the

Pl. 30—*The hilltop at Rathgall, Co. Wicklow. The innermost stone-walled enclosure seems to have been a purpose-built medieval cashel.* (Photo: *Dúchas*, The Heritage Service.)

evidence from ongoing excavation of the cashel at Ballynaveenoragh, Co. Kerry, seems to suggest that this site had a thirteenth-century phase (E. Gibbons, pers. comm.). Historical and fieldwork evidence also suggests that cashels continued in use until the late seventeenth century. The cashel at Cahirmacnaghten, Co. Clare, seems to have been occupied by the O'Davorens up to the seventeenth century. A large house and kitchen are described as within it in a will and deed of partition made by Gillanaeve O'Davoren in 1675 (Westropp 1897, 121; 1902, 640). The cashel is described in the will as a 'keannait' or *cenn ait,* which can be directly translated as meaning a 'chief or head-place'. It has been argued that this word was used, amongst others, to describe a forti-fied enclosure in late medieval and post-medieval Gaelic Ireland (Nicholls 1987, 405). The cashel is *c.* 30m in diameter and the foundations of rectangular buildings can be seen in the interior. The ground level within the site is far higher than that of the sur-rounding terrain, which has been taken as evidence of long occupation (Harbison 1975a, 38; MacNamara 1912). Fieldwork in the Burren by the Discovery Programme has suggested that a number of cashels were occupied in the late medieval period, including the cashels at Cashlauan Gearr, Cahirmore and Cahirmoyle (Mon. Nos CL010-057, 005-09402, 005-056). Only excavation will properly determine whether these sites were occupied continuously from the Early Christian period into late medieval times. However, thirteenth- and fourteenth-century coins turn up as stray finds on some Burren cashels, as well as on Aran. This seems to be a strong indication that some of these sites were occupied in the period *c.* 1200–1400 as well (C. Cotter, pers. comm.). Tower-houses also occur within a few cashels, such as the one on Inishere, Co. Galway, and at Cahercullaun, Co. Kerry (Westropp 1902, 631). This may also be an indication that such cashels were inhabited continuously until these small castles were built within them during the fifteenth or sixteenth century.

Therefore, while the subject has never been properly researched, there is a certain amount of evidence to suggest that some cashels remained in use throughout the medieval period and into the seventeenth century. Furthermore, the evidence from Iniscreamha suggests that at least some pre-1400 *longphort* sites were well-defended cashels. It is postulated that future excavation will turn up many examples of cashels with medieval phases.

It was noted above that the *longpurt* of Cloonfree is mentioned in 1306 (*AC*; *ALC*). Today this *longphort* can be associated with the moated site at Cloonfree, Co. Roscommon (Mon. No. RO029-009; Quiggin 1913, 334; Graham 1988a, 30–1; O'Conor 1998). It was also noted above that a site called *longport Meic Diarmaida* was mentioned in 1342, 1348 and 1385, and seems to have been located somewhere on Longford Hill, Rockingham Demesne, Co. Roscommon, close to the main MacDermot fortress of *Carraic Locha Ce* (*AC*; *AFM*). Where is this site exactly? Certainly, a small, unimpressive ringfort exists on the southern slopes of Longford Hill (Mon. No. RO006-048). However, at the base of Longford Hill, beside Lough Key, near the spot marked 'landing stage' on the first edition of the OS map for the area, are the remains of a partly levelled moated site, which is not marked on the original SMR map. Presumably this is the best candidate for MacDermot's *longphort*. Indeed, its location might suggest it to be associated with *Carraic Locha Ce* or the 'Rock of Lough Key'. This moated site presumably acted as the *de facto* farm centre of MacDermot lands in the immediate vicinity, with farm buildings and stables within it. Obviously such functions could not be carried out from the 'Rock' itself, as it was located far out in the lough. It might be added that the moated site at Knockalough, Co. Sligo (Mon. No. SL032-199), is located on the shores of Cloonacleigha Lough, near Ballymote. A crannog lies just offshore from this site (Mon. No. SL032-198). This moated site may also be the service site associated with the crannog. The juxtaposition of a moated site with a crannog at Knockalough suggests that the latter monument was occupied during the medieval period as well.

Moated sites

It was noted above that moated sites have traditionally been regarded as a settlement form solely associated with the Anglo-Normans (section 3.3c). However, the historical sources indicate that the moated sites at Cloonfree and Longford Hill, Rockingham Demesne, as well as the one on Inishatirra Island, were built and occupied by Gaelic lords, notably the O'Conors and MacDermots. These three sites are all located in north Roscommon. The Anglo-Normans never made any real attempt to settle this region and it always remained in Irish hands (Graham 1988a, 30; MacDermot 1996, 435–42). Indeed, for this reason it has already been argued by one writer that a series of moated sites in the vicinity of the modern village of Strokestown were built by the Gaelic Irish (Graham 1988a, 30–1). In all, approximately 30 moated sites occur in Roscommon (Fig. 20). It is probable that most, if not all, of these sites in the main part of the county north of Roscommon town were erected by native Irish lords. For example, Dungar (modern Frenchpark, Co. Roscommon) was part of the medieval territory of a junior and subordinate branch of the MacDermots (MacDermot 1996, 299–300). A Dominican priory was founded at nearby Cloonshanville in 1385, hinting that Dungar was an important medieval centre (Gwynn and Hadcock 1970, 223; MacDermot 1996, 300–1). A fine moated site exists to the north of the modern village of Frenchpark in the townland of Frenchpark Demesne (Mon. No. RO015-008), presumably another MacDermot residence during the medieval period.

Another probable example of a Gaelic-built moated site occurs in the neighbouring county of Leitrim, another area that saw little or no Anglo-Norman settlement. Only one definite moated site exists in this county (M. Moore, pers. comm.). This site, which has a later tower-house built across its northern edges, is located on a peninsula jutting out into the northern part of Lough Allen in the townland of Corry. The later tower-house is marked 'Forde's Castle (in ruins)' on the OS six-inch map of the area (Mon. No. LE018-036). In 1530 a 'wooden house' belonging to MacConsnava (the Irish for Forde) was burned by O'Donnell on Lough Allen (*AFM*). As no crannogs seem to exist in this part of Lough Allen, it has been suggested to the present writer that this is a reference to the moated site at Corry. The tower-house seems to have been built after 1530 (M. Moore, pers. comm.), suggesting the strong possibility that this moated site represents the centre of the MacConsnava lordship of Muintir-Kenny during the medieval period.

Therefore there is good evidence for Gaelic-built moated sites in Roscommon and for one in Leitrim. This suggests that other moated sites in Ireland, especially in parts of the west, could have been built by the Irish. For example, the moated site at Knockalough, Co. Sligo, was probably built by an Irish lord as it is associated with a crannog. In all, the Archaeological Survey have identified 33 moated sites in modern County Sligo. Effective Anglo-Norman movement into parts of Connacht took place from the mid-1230s onwards under Richard de Burgh, who, while maintaining direct control of south Galway, apportioned large blocks of north Galway, east and north Mayo and Sligo to various well-established colonial families such as the de Berminghams, Cogans, Fitzgeralds, de Lacys and Barretts. Anglo-Norman control took a different form here to the more settled areas of eastern Ireland, discussed above (sections 3.1, 3.2, 3.3). Manorial and burgess settlements were far rarer in Connacht than in Leinster or Meath, and occurred only beside or near established castles. There was little English peasant immigration into the parts of the province taken over by the Anglo-Normans. The majority of Gaelic lords in these areas were not dispossessed of their lands. The de Burghs and their chief tenants merely acted as overlords, often absentee at that, accepting tribute from these Irish lords (Frame 1981, 38–45; Glasscock 1987, 217; Lydon 1987a, 165; Watt 1987a, 312). This suggests that there was little English or Anglo-Norman settlement on the ground in medieval Sligo. Given the evidence for Irish-built moated sites in adjacent Roscommon, it is possible that at least some of the moated site series in Sligo, besides Knockalough, were Gaelic-built. This is probably the case in other parts of Ireland that saw the survival of Irish lords alongside Anglo-Norman knights, or in districts that lay on the borders between Anglo-Norman and Gaelic lordships. Some of the moated sites in these regions must have been built by Irishmen.

Another observation concerns the status of the builders of the moated sites at Cloonfree, Longford Hill, Rockingham Demesne, Corry and on Inishatirra Island. It was argued that in Anglo-Norman parts of eastern Ireland moated sites seem to have been built by men of relatively low status—either free tenants or minor manorial lords (section 3.3c). Important Anglo-Norman lords built and lived in castles of some form, or at least had one on their scattered estates (section 2.1). However, the evidence from the Roscommon sites indicates that Gaelic kings and lords of the first rank built and inhabited moated sites during the thirteenth and fourteenth centuries, at least in parts of the west.

Clearly, some *longphort* sites were moated sites. Yet many areas of medieval Gaelic Ireland did not really contain moated sites—for example, this monument type hardly exists across Ulster. This might be the place to discuss the site at Tildarg, Co. Antrim, excavated by Brannon in 1983. This earthwork, which seems to have been occupied in the thirteenth century and contains three house platforms, is located on the side of a mountain near Ballyclare, at a height of 900ft. The excavator argued that the site was Gaelic-built and suggested that it was associated with transhumance practices (Brannon 1984). The earthwork itself consists of a rectangular enclosure with internal dimensions of *c.* 65m north-north-west/south-south-east by *c.* 36m west-south-west/east-north-east, defined by a 5–6m-wide earthen bank and a fosse of similar width. It was argued that this earthwork could not be classified as a moated site simply because it was located at too great a height (*ibid.*, 170). However, its morphology really does suggest that it should be classified as one. It might be added that some moated sites in south-east Ireland are found in similar locations on the sides of hills and mountains (Barry 1977, 93–4, 176). Therefore Tildarg seems to be a moated site built by the Irish some time in the thirteenth or even early fourteenth century. However, there are very few moated sites in Ulster. Again, as noted above, the modern county of Leitrim in Connacht contains only one definite moated site, and only one example has been identified in the modern county of Clare (Mon. No. CL051-083). Regional differences therefore seem to have existed within Gaelic-controlled parts of medieval Ireland, with Irish lords in some areas choosing to build moated sites.

The fact that Clare contains only one moated site is important. The only extant prose narrative from medieval Gaelic Ireland, the *Caithreim Thoirdhealbaigh* or 'The Triumphs of Turlough', which is interspersed with long poems, comes from this county. Apparently written around the mid-fourteenth century, it deals primarily with a bloody internecine struggle between different branches of the O'Briens for the lordship of Thomond (modern County Clare) during the late thirteenth and early fourteenth centuries. The *Caithreim Thoirdhealbaigh* is highly partisan towards the Clan Turlough More, one of the two opposing O'Brien factions, and is also very hostile towards the Anglo-Norman settlers in the region (Westropp 1903, 139; Orpen 1911–20, iv, 67; Watt 1987b, 316). It is full of references to Gaelic-held *longphort* sites. As mentioned above, some of these may have been well-defended cashels. However, over much of Clare, including areas mentioned in the *Caithreim Thoirdhealbaigh*, the earthen ringfort is the ubiquitous field monument today. Were some of these medieval Gaelic *longphort* sites ringforts? Put slightly differently, what is the evidence for the use of ringforts during the thirteenth and fourteenth centuries in Ireland, either in Clare or elsewhere?

4.2c—The medieval ringfort—fact or fiction?

There is considerable academic debate as to whether earthen ringforts continued to be occupied and constructed into the medieval period. This controversy is fuelled by conflicting archaeological, historical and field evidence.

What is the excavated evidence for the occupation of ringforts during the thirteenth and fourteenth centuries? The general view amongst archaeologists is that the vast majority of ringforts date from the Early Christian period (Ó Ríordáin 1979, 31–3; Edwards 1990, 18–19; Stout 1997, 22–31). It has been noted that the overwhelming body of excavated evidence places the construction and occupation of ringforts in the period from the sixth to the eleventh century (Lynn 1975a, 45; 1975b). More recently, an analysis of the available dendrochronological and calibrated radiocarbon dates seems to suggest that the majority of ringforts were constructed and occupied from the beginning of the seventh century through to the end of the ninth century (Stout 1997, 24). Despite this, a number of scholars (mainly historical geographers) believe that there is a certain amount of evidence to suggest that the ringfort was a common settlement form in Ireland throughout the medieval period (Proudfoot 1970, 40–5; Barrett and Graham 1975, 34–6). The present writer has critically reviewed the excavated evidence used by these scholars for the postulated medieval ringforts and has found, firstly, that far too much stress has been laid on stray finds of medieval pottery, with the overwhelming majority of sites having no post-1200 occupation layers whatsoever. Secondly, some sites which had been termed medieval ringforts can no longer be classified as such during this period, as they had been transformed *c.* 1200 into straightforward motte castles by the Anglo-Normans (O'Conor 1986, 95–104). The evidence from the final phase of occupation at the raised rath at Ballynarry, Co. Down, which dates mainly from the thirteenth century, suggests that it was no longer in native hands, being the residence of an Anglo-Norman or English bailiff for St Patrick's Priory at Downpatrick (Davison 1961–2; Edwards 1990, 19). Certainly, the secondary occupation of the raised rath at Ballyfounder, Co. Down, ended in the thirteenth century (Waterman 1958a), but the area around Ballyfounder was the region most heavily settled by the Anglo-Normans in Down, with the Savages retaining control there until the early seventeenth century (McNeill 1980, 120–1). Perhaps this site, too, was taken over by Anglo-Norman or English settlers *c.* 1200. This all suggests that much of the excavated evidence for the continued occupation and construction of earthen ringforts after *c.* 1200 is slight and has tended to be overemphasised.

Both Glasscock (1987, 227) and Edwards (1990, 8–9) have noted that the vast majority of ringfort excavations to date have taken place in eastern Ireland, mostly in the modern counties of Down and Antrim (Stout 1997, 24). Conversely, there have been very few excavations of ringforts in the western half of Ireland, in regions that remained under strongest Gaelic control up to the seventeenth century. This means that the dating evidence for ringforts gained from past excavations cannot be safely used in the debate about whether or not this monument type continued in use during the medieval period. This evidence is not balanced enough as yet and more excavations of ringforts in the west of Ireland are needed.

The existing excavated evidence from ringforts can also be looked at more critically. Conventional theory at present places the occupation and construction of most ringforts in the centuries between *c.* 500 and *c.* 1000. However, while many ringforts may have been deserted by this date, this does not mean that this monument type went out of use. The well-defended ringfort at Beal Boru, Co. Clare, was apparently built in the early eleventh century and remained in use until the first years of the twelfth century (O'Kelly 1962). More importantly, the County Down excavations of Lismahon (Waterman 1959a), Castleskreen (Dickinson and Waterman 1959), Duneight (Waterman 1963) and Rathmullan (Lynn 1981–2) all indicate that these sites were, or appear to have been, occupied as raised raths or 'flat' ringforts until their takeover by the Anglo-Normans at some time after the conquest of the area by John de Courcy in 1177, when they were turned into motte castles. It would therefore appear that the original Irish occupants of these apparently quite well-defended sites abandoned them for political reasons and not because they regarded raised raths or 'flat' ringforts as being out of date at this period.

Furthermore, it must be more than coincidental, given that the majority of datable excavated sites have been dated to before *c.* 1000, that most of the archaeological evidence for the eleventh- and twelfth-century occupation of sites in the ringfort tradition comes from sites that later functioned as Anglo-Norman mottes. It is hardly surprising, given the freebooting nature of the first Anglo-Norman colonists, that they wanted to utilise existing centres in their desire for quick profits. Historians have also noted the propensity of the first wave of Anglo-Norman settlers to use pre-existing Irish lordly sites as places to build their castles and set up their estate centres (Flanagan 1993, 385–9; Bhreathnach, forthcoming). Fieldwork also suggests that many mottes in eastern Ireland have ringfort precursors—the implication being that at least some of these latter sites were occupied until the mottes were erected by the Anglo-Normans (Ó Ríordáin 1979, 56; O'Conor 1993, 61–3). In essence, the present writer suggests that the lack of archaeological excavations at important Anglo-Norman sites such as motte castles could have ramifications for the dating of ringforts as well. Many sites with eleventh- and twelfth-century occupation layers may lie under mottes or other castle types, as the evidence from the above-mentioned Down sites suggests. Future excavation at early Anglo-Norman sites in eastern Ireland, such as motte castles, could indicate that many sites in the ringfort tradition were occupied, and even built, at far later dates than *c.* 1000.

Excavated evidence from east Ulster and hints from fieldwork elsewhere suggest that some sites in the ringfort tradition in eastern Ireland were abandoned because of political upheavals caused by the arrival of the Anglo-Normans, who very often turned these sites into motte castles. Conversely, this suggests that some sites in the ringfort tradition continued in use in areas of Ireland that remained under Gaelic control during the medieval period, notably but not exclusively in the western half of the country. There was no political reason for these sites to be deserted by their occupants, as these areas were not affected by the arrival of the Anglo-Normans to the same extent as elsewhere. But these medieval ringforts remain largely undiscovered since little excavation of this monument type has taken place in western Ireland, perhaps because the parts of Ireland that were controlled by Gaelic lords during the medieval period are remote from the main areas of modern Irish archaeological research and work.

However, it must be added that there are two excavated ringforts in Clare that seem to show evidence of post-1169 occupation. These are the sites of 'Thady's Fort' and Garrynamona, excavated in advance of work on Shannon Airport (Rynne 1963). The latter site, while in the ringfort tradition, consisted of a raised area surrounded by a low bank and a discontinuous ditch. The habitation associated with this enclosure was basically seventeenth-century in date. The site was not well defended, the bank functioning only as the equivalent of a 'low' wall around a modern farmyard today (Rynne 1963, 258–67). This site, like many excavated Early Christian examples, shows that a large percentage of ringforts had paltry defences and that it is something of a misnomer to call all of them 'forts'.

More relevant to this search for the identification of certain ringforts as medieval *longphort* sites is the excavation of 'Thady's Fort'. Only eight days were available for the investigation of this more defensive-looking bivallate ringfort (Rynne 1963, 245). Little work was done on the site's defences as the excavator concentrated his efforts on the interior of the fort. Rynne (1963, 245–57) uncovered evidence for the foundations of a rectangular house and dated its initial occupation to *c.* 1600. This excavation has not figured prominently in the general debate on the medieval usage of ringforts owing to perceived problems with its interpretation (Glasscock 1987, 228). Edwards (1990, 19) put it more clearly and stated that the finds were only associated with the occupation of the undoubtedly late rectangular house and not with the actual construction of the ringfort's banks. Yet Rynne (1963, 255–6) definitely stated that the ringfort bank here started to erode only at some stage after the house was built, and therefore he believed that they were more or less contemporaneous. Given this evidence and the fact that earlier occupation levels were not found during the course of the excavation, the present writer agrees with Rynne that the rectangular house was built soon after the construction of the ringfort. This is what the archaeological evidence presented in the excavation report suggests and therefore it cannot be lightly ignored. It is also located in precisely an area where medieval and post-medieval ringforts should be expected, being a region of Gaelic lordship up to the seventeenth century which saw little Anglo-Norman settlement. Overall, there is a certain amount of excavated evidence to support the view that some sites in the ringfort tradition continued to be built and used after *c.* 1000 and throughout the medieval period.

What is the distributional evidence for the occupation and construction of earthen ringforts during the thirteenth and fourteenth centuries? Barrett and Graham (1975, 37, 43) noted the general scarcity of ringforts in eastern Ireland in comparison to western regions of the country, where far greater numbers occur in the field. They suggested that the former area should contain far more ringforts, either levelled or standing, because it contains Ireland's best agricultural soils. They also pointed out that eastern Ireland was the region of the country that saw the greatest amount of Anglo-Norman control and settlement, and drew attention to the distinct negative relationship between areas that were thickly settled by the Anglo-Normans and regions that contain high densities of ringforts. These latter areas correspond in a general way to regions of Irish control and survival during the medieval period.

Barrett and Graham (1975, 37–43) use the present county of Meath as a specific example in their argument. Areas of prolonged and intensive Anglo-Norman settlement in the south and east of the county contain far fewer ringforts than more marginal districts of colonial control in the north and north-west of the county. This division is seen by Barrett and Graham as reflecting the later line of the Pale, which was delimited by an act of the Irish parliament in 1495. This they saw as merely an official recognition of a frontier zone, between areas of Gaelic settlement in the far north of the county and the Anglo-Normans in the south, which had already been in existence for a couple of centuries prior to this official act. They suggest that the reason for the high density of ringforts in north Meath is that the indigenous Irish continued to construct and occupy this monument type throughout the medieval period. The ringforts in south Meath were seen as being purely of Early Christian date, with no later additions after 1169, thus explaining their lower numbers (Barrett and Graham 1975, 37–43).

This hypothesis has been developed by further research and fieldwork. Barrett

(1982) noted that in Louth there are far fewer ringforts in areas that experienced strong Anglo-Norman control and settlement during the medieval period. A similar situation exists in County Wexford, with the majority of ringforts occurring in the northern half of the county, an area that saw a high degree of Gaelic lordly survival during the medieval period (Bennett 1989b, 53; Moore 1996, 28). Therefore, on distributional grounds at least, there is a certain amount of evidence to suggest that ringforts continued to be built and occupied after *c.* 1200.

What is the historical and cartographic evidence for the construction and use of ringforts throughout the medieval period and beyond? Donnchad O'Brien built 'a circular hold and princely residence of earth (*dorigne foirgnemh agus flaithisdad circallda no comchruinn comnaide)*' at some time before 1242 at Clonroad, Co. Clare (*Caithreim Thoirdhealbaigh*, i, 2; ii, 2). This has been taken by various scholars to refer to the construction of a ringfort (Westropp 1902, 625; Cairns 1987, 6; Watt 1987b, 333). The words *rath* and *lios* were used in the Early Christian sources to describe sites that are now classified as earthen ringforts (Edwards 1990, 12). Both words are rarely used in the surviving sources of the medieval period. For example, it is stated that after the Battle of the Abbey (Corcomroe Abbey, Co. Clare) in 1317 '*gach ri ina riglongport* (every king in his stronghold?), *gach ollam ina raith* (every judge in his *rath*) and *gach laoch ina laios* (every layman in his *lios*)', amongst others, remained calm (*Caithreim Thoirdhealbaigh*, i, 134; ii, 117). This has been taken to mean that ringforts were in common use in Clare during the medieval period (Rynne 1963, 271). Again, a poem written after the death of Tomas Mag Shamhradhan in 1343 mentions his *lios* (*Book of Magauran*, 74–5). Cartographic evidence from Irish maps of *c.* 1600 appears to show scores of ringforts in Ulster (Belmore 1903, 16–20). Cairns (1987, 6) states that it is unlikely that these were included for antiquarian interest, as these maps were created for military and economic reasons. He believes, therefore, that ringforts were occupied,

Pl. 31—*A ringfort containing houses at Tullahogue, Co. Tyrone, around 1600* (Bartlett map; see Hayes McCoy 1964).

in Gaelic Ulster at least, until the seventeenth century. Furthermore, there is a depiction, also dated to *c*. 1600, of what appears to be an occupied ringfort at Tullahogue, Co. Tyrone (Pl. 31). It shows a circular area surrounded by a bank and ditch, containing two inhabited thatched houses. No palisade is depicted on the bank of the ringfort; instead, trees can be seen growing on it, although the enclosure is entered through two substantial wooden gateways in the bank (Hayes-McCoy 1964, 8–9). It has recently been argued that the sixteenth-century O'Byrne residence at Ballinacor, Glenmalure, Co. Wicklow, was a ringfort (Long 1994, 242–8). A poem of around 1580 refers to it as a *lios* (*ibid.*, 245).

Overall, there are very few direct historical references to ringforts in use during the medieval period up to the seventeenth century. It was argued by the present writer that the lack of excavated evidence for medieval ringforts is really due to the nature of modern Irish archaeological research and work, which have been concentrated in eastern parts of Ireland, rather than to the complete desertion of this monument type by *c*. 1000. More credence should be given to the cartographic, pictorial and distributional evidence which suggests that ringforts continued in use until the seventeenth century in areas dominated by the Irish. There is a certain amount of excavated evidence to support this, which has perhaps been too harshly criticised in the past. Furthermore, it was argued above that there is evidence for the use of cashels after *c*. 1200 (section 4.2b). Cashels are really nothing more than the stone-walled equivalent of earthen ringforts. They mostly occur in rocky country where suitable stone was available for building and where it would be difficult to erect ringforts. The fact that they seem to continue in use during the medieval period should be taken as further evidence that ringforts did as well. It is therefore felt that future excavation at specifically targeted sites will yield evidence for the use of ringforts up until the seventeenth century.

It was shown above that some *longphort* sites were defensive-looking cashels or moated sites. Furthermore, while the occasional *longphort* mentioned in the sources seems to have been either a natural island fortress or a crannog, the overall evidence suggests that most of these sites were located on dry land (section 4.2b). As noted, the earthen ringfort is the ubiquitous field monument in areas suggested by the sources to contain *longphort* sites, such as parts of Clare. The corollary to this is that some sites in the ringfort tradition in these areas must be *longphort* sites. Again, this statement has to be qualified. The excavated evidence from Garrynamona and many Early Christian sites, along with the pictorial evidence from Tullahogue, shows that many, if not the majority, of ringforts were nothing more than enclosed farmsteads, with very paltry defences. This type of ringfort was not a *longphort*. Clearly, however, some sites in the ringfort tradition were always quite defensive-looking. The immediately pre-Anglo-Norman phase at Lismahon, Co. Down, Phase II, had substantial defences (Waterman 1959a, 141–6). Phase 2 at Castleskreen, Co. Down, again immediately pre-Anglo-Norman, saw the bank of the site being defended by a stout palisade. The entranceway through this earthen bank was defended by a substantial, heavy wooden gate (Dickinson and Waterman 1959, 70–1). The defences of the pre-Norman phase at Duneight, Co. Down, were also quite substantial (Waterman 1963, 59–61, 76). The present writer feels that it was this type of well-defended ringfort that was called *longphort* in the sources. This statement needs to be explained further. Certain scholars of the medieval period might suggest that a well-defended medieval ringfort or even raised rath should be called either a ringwork or motte castle. Mottes and ringwork castles, generically called earthwork castles by modern archaeology, had very substantial and impressive timber defences during their period of use, which is why they were called castles in both the colonial and the Gaelic sources (sections 2.1, 2.2). The fact that *longphort* sites are not called castles is an indication that their defences were not considered strong enough to warrant the term. Therefore a medieval ringfort or raised rath, even if defended by a stout palisade, heavy gateway, deep ditch and steep bank, should continue to be classified as such.

One ringfort that is a good candidate for a medieval *longphort* site is the impressive-

Pl. 32—*The ringfort at Tulsk, Co. Roscommon.* (Photo: Kieran O'Conor.)

looking example at Tulsk, Co. Roscommon (Pl. 32; Mon. No. RO022-114). It is located just to the south-east of the remains of a tower-house (Mon. No. RO022-114) and across the road from a Dominican priory (Mon. No. RO022-114). The tower-house was constructed in 1405 by O'Conor Roe (*ALC*), and the priory was founded in 1446 or 1448 (Gwynn and Hadcock 1970, 230–1; O'Conor *et al.* 1996). It was clearly a very important medieval Gaelic centre. It is possible that the ringfort there represents the site of a pre-tower-house O'Conor residence. It might also be added that another moated site (Mon. No. RO028-014) occurs at Ogulla, beside the site of a medieval church and holy well (which is still visited), about 1.5km west-south-west of Tulsk. This presumably represents the remains of another medieval O'Conor centre.

4.3—Houses, lack of castles, and military tactics in Gaelic Ireland during the medieval period

It was argued above that Gaelic Irish lords rarely built castles prior to *c.* 1400 (section 4.2a). It was shown in the last two sections, however, that Gaelic lords of the late twelfth, thirteenth and fourteenth centuries did possess fortifications, although these sites were not as defensive as true castles in the European sense (sections 4.2b, 4.2c). These settlement forms in Gaelic-dominated areas included moated sites, cashels, crannogs, natural island fortresses and, less clearly, earthen ringforts. It is the aim of this section to explain why so few conventional castles were built by Gaelic lords in the latter period.

It is difficult at first glance to understand why the Irish did not build castles in any numbers during the thirteenth and fourteenth centuries. There are numerous refer-

Pl. 33—*Oval-shaped, one-roomed, windowless 'creats' can be seen beside the ruined churches in this depiction of Armagh around 1600* (Bartlett map; see Hayes McCoy 1964).

ences in the sources to Gaelic lords successfully besieging and capturing even the most complex and well-garrisoned Anglo-Norman masonry castle, suggesting that they had the necessary military ability and resources to seize these castles. An example of this point is the description of the siege of the de Clare castle of Bunratty in modern County Clare by Turlough O'Brien in 1305, during the course of which he built a *foslongport* or temporary camp. He even blocked the river with some form of fortified wooden plank bridge or barrier in order to prevent seaborne supplies and reinforcements reaching the castle (*Caithreim Thoirdhealbaigh*, i, 29; ii, 31). Clearly, O'Brien and other Irish lords understood the art of siege warfare in much the same way as any contemporary Anglo-Norman magnate.

It seems that the Gaelic house, even the dwellings of the upper echelons of society, tended to be of an insubstantial nature, generally consisting of nothing more than relatively small houses of wattle, clay, earth and branches until the seventeenth century and beyond (Nicholls 1987, 403). Little is known about the physical appearance of the dwellings of peasants in Gaelic-dominated parts of medieval Ireland, partly because few have been excavated since their locations are hard to recognise in the modern landscape. It has been argued on pictorial evidence from around 1600 that at least two types of peasant houses existed in Gaelic Ulster at that date.

The first type of Gaelic dwelling recognisable at this time was the 'creat'—a small, one-roomed, windowless house of circular or oval plan. It seems to have been very simply constructed of post-and-wattle, covered with sods. The hearth was centrally placed in the middle of the house and it seems that smoke escaped through a simple hole in the thatched roof (Pl. 33; Gailey 1987, 88–9; Robinson 1979, 1–3; Williams and Robinson 1983, 37). It has been argued that this type of house was associated with 'booleying', the seasonal migration of people and cattle to upland, woodland or bogland summer pastures, noted above as being a feature of the Gaelic economy right through the medieval period up to the seventeenth century (Robinson 1979, 3; Williams and Robinson 1983, 37). Yet the pictorial evidence from around 1600 also suggests that these simple 'creats' occurred in well-settled lowland areas as well, often on the edge of existing nucleated settlements such as Armagh, Newry and Carrickfergus. While 'creats' are definitely associated with booleying, their location at the latter places also suggests that they may represent the dwellings of the poorest people in Gaelic society in permanently settled areas, at least in the late sixteenth and seventeenth centuries. Unfortunately no example of this house type has been excavated to date, presumably because their originally flimsy nature makes them difficult to trace archaeologically. Therefore it cannot be said with absolute certainty that this type of dwelling existed in Gaelic-dominated areas before *c.* 1500. However, the simplicity of its plan suggests that this is likely and that 'creats' represent the dwelling-houses of the poorest people in medieval Gaelic society, being associated with both booleying and more permanent settlements.

This evidence from Ulster around 1600 also indicates that there was another, more substantial type of house in Gaelic Ireland. This type of dwelling was subrectangular in plan with very definite rounded corners. Its walls were low and were constructed of clay or sods or post-and-wattle covered with clay. Its thatched roof was apparently supported on cruck-trusses which lay either directly on the ground or on stone pads rather than on the clay or sod walls. The hearth was also central in this type of house, with the smoke escaping through a hole in the roof. Apparently there were no internal partitions in this type of dwelling, which sometimes had opposing doorways (Gailey 1987, 89; Robinson 1979, 7, 13; Williams and Robinson 1983, 30–7). It is clear that such houses were common throughout Gaelic Ulster *c.* 1600. Excavations at Glenmakeeran and Goodlands, however, which are located in mountainous areas of north County Antrim, along with the house within the upland enclosure at Tildarg, Co. Antrim, show that this type of house can date from the thirteenth, fourteenth and fifteenth centuries too, as the primary occupation of these sites was associated with everted-rim ware. These particular houses were connected with booleying, although it was felt that this house type, owing to its relative sophistication, represented a common form of peasant dwelling across all of medieval Gaelic Ulster (Williams and Robinson 1983, 30–7; Brannon 1984, 167–9). The Glenmakeeran and Goodland houses each had an additional annexe attached onto them. This extra room was apparently used to store dairy produce, as the production of cheese and butter was a feature of booleying (Williams and Robinson 1983, 36, 38). It might be added that booleying continued in parts of western Ireland until recent times. For example, in Achill, Co. Mayo, this economic custom continued until the 1940s (Estyn-Evans 1942, 51–5; McDonald 1997, 225–6). Indeed, fieldwork has suggested that oval medieval booley huts exist on Achill too (McDonald 1997, 225), and that many medieval and post-medieval booley huts are extant in upland areas of Down and Antrim (Williams and Robinson 1983, 34–5, 37). Presumably intensive walking of other parts of Ireland will turn up further examples of medieval booley houses. It was this custom of transhumance, which is seen in other parts of Europe, that presumably led post-medieval observers to believe wrongly that the Gaelic Irish were nomads (Estyn-Evans 1942, 55). It would be interesting for any future project on medieval rural settlement to establish whether booleying was also part of the yearly economic strategy on Anglo-Norman manors during the thirteenth and fourteenth centuries.

Therefore two types of peasant house can be tentatively identified as being in use in medieval Gaelic Ireland. Certainly, the second house type mentioned above is not very different in size and shape to the medieval houses excavated at Anglo-Norman manorial centres (section 3.2c). The fact that Gaelic lords seem to have often lived in such dwellings aroused the contempt of outside observers and fuelled claims that medieval Gaelic society was backward and underdeveloped in comparison to most of the rest of western Europe. For example, in 1228 Stephen of Lexington stated that Gaelic kings and lords did not live in stone halls or substantial timber houses but instead dwelt in 'huts of wattle, such as birds are accustomed to build when moulting' (*Lexington*, 112; Stalley 1987, 9). Yet there were good reasons for this form of simple aristocratic abode. Nicholls (1972, 60–3; 1987, 403) has argued that this lack of complex secular lordly dwellings in Gaelic Ireland was partly, if not wholly, due to the Irish custom, mentioned above, of periodically redistributing lands belonging to the kindred group amongst its various male members. This custom must have varied in exact detail from region to region, but in some cases, for example amongst the O'Dempseys of Laois/Offaly, it was an annual event. The actual historical references to this custom (which seems to be based on the view that individual wealth in Gaelic society was related more to the ownership of cattle and flocks rather than the sole possession of any given tract of land) come from sixteenth- and seventeenth-century sources. On the evidence presently available, however, it would appear that this custom occurred throughout the medieval period as well. It must be presumed, therefore, that this did not encourage the investment of labour and material resources in the construction of large dwelling-houses such as two-storey stone or wooden halls. In this cultural scenario, relatively insubstantial dwellings were a far better option even for Gaelic lords. The apparently common use of cruck-trusses in house construction in medieval and post-medieval Gaelic society may be a physical reflection of this custom of periodic land redistribution. They were clearly the most important and costly structural element in many medieval Gaelic houses, but could easily be taken down, moved to a new location and quickly re-erected. It must be remembered that in medieval Gaelic Ireland a lord's wealth really lay in cattle and the men who lived under his protection rather than in land and large houses (K. Simms 1975–6, 99–100, 102). Therefore it was social and economic custom, not innate backwardness, that militated against Gaelic lords building large, complex houses.

While this helps to show why virtually no non-defensive pre-1700 houses exist in the Irish landscape today, it does not explain why Gaelic lords did not build conventional castles and mottes before 1400. It has already been noted that the various references to specific Gaelic fortifications before the latter date, such as crannogs, moated sites, cashels and possibly ringforts, suggest that most of these sites were permanently occupied (sections 4.2b, 4.2c; Nicholls 1987, 404). Tower-houses were built in large numbers in many Gaelic areas during the fifteenth and sixteenth centuries (Barry 1993b, 211; Cairns 1987, 9). It must be presumed, therefore, that such strongholds operated outside this system of periodic land redistribution. This custom does not explain why relatively coherent Gaelic septs, welded together at least for a time under a strong leader, did not usually erect castles at strategic locations for the defence of their territories. Certainly, efficient lay masons, craftsmen and carpenters existed throughout Gaelic parts of medieval Ireland who were eminently capable of building complex masonry castles and elaborate timber castles (Stalley 1987, 42; O'Conor 1993, 269–71).

A conventional view amongst modern European castle specialists is that one of the main functions of a medieval castle, whether of stone or earth and timber, was as a major instrument of defence against full-scale invasion. Its main duty in a defensive war was to hold and deny territory to a large attacking force. This defensive function was extremely important politically as it insured its owner's hold on his land, which invading forces would find hard to break (e.g. Brown 1963, 68; 1976, 24; 1985, 5–7; King 1988, 7; Pounds 1990, 44). An overall review of the sections of this chapter dealing with the historical references to Gaelic medieval fortifications such as crannogs, natural island fortresses and *longphort* sites shows that these places are mainly mentioned in connection with succession disputes within kindred groups, small-scale raids and obits (section 4.2b). They seem to be associated with small-scale warfare that really should be described as feuding. There are remarkably few references to what might be considered serious sieges of these sites by large bodies of men. It would appear, therefore, that medieval Gaelic lords did not use these fortifications in the defence of their lands against large-scale attack and invasion. Indeed, the evidence suggests that they actually deserted these settlements upon the approach of a large, hostile force. For example, in 1276 or 1277 Brian O'Brien, king of Thomond, evacuated his *longphort* of Clonroad, Co. Clare, upon the approach of a powerful force of O'Deas and MacNamaras, under the leadership of his rival Turlough O'Brien, and fled across the Shannon into modern Limerick or Clare (*Caithreim Thoirdhealbaigh*, i, 5; ii, 6). The same source indicates that in 1311 Murtough O'Brien, lord of Thomond, abandoned his *longphort* in the face of an attack by a large force (*Caithreim Thoirdhealbaigh*, i, 50; ii, 48). In 1365 MacMahon fled his *longphort* of Rath Tulach upon the approach of a large army led by Donnell O'Neill (*AFM*). These references again suggest that Gaelic lords used their fortifications only in the context of feuding and succession disputes. They did not use them as strategic weapons in the defence of their territories against larger and more powerful aggressors. It would appear, therefore, that there was a noteworthy difference between Anglo-Norman and Gaelic systems of territorial defence. The fact that the Gaelic fortifications are used mostly in the context of feuding rather than real warfare is another indication that the defences of these sites were far less complex than those on contemporary Anglo-Norman castles.

It is quite clear that during the late twelfth and thirteenth centuries the Anglo-Normans generally settled on the best agricultural land in Ireland for tillage (Mitchell 1986, 174–8; Watt 1987a, 311). Conversely, as noted, it is apparent that Gaelic lordship tended to survive in areas of more marginal agricultural land, such as mountainous and bogland regions, although this has sometimes been overemphasised (section 4.1). The relatively inhospitable nature of the terrain of these Gaelic areas was compounded by the fact that between fifteen and twenty per cent of Ireland was forested during the medieval period. For example, it has been noted that areas of Gaelic lordship and survival in Leinster up to the seventeenth century correspond to bogland and upland regions, which had dense forest cover on their peripheries (Smyth 1982, 101–18).

It appears that, from the eighth century onwards, European warfare came to depend increasingly on mounted warriors. These had evolved by the eleventh century into heavily armoured knights. While foot-soldiers and archers or crossbowmen remained important in any feudal host, it is clear that the knights became the élite force in these armies. It has been argued that no infantry could withstand the shock tactics of their charge, with couched lances held rigidly under their arms, thus concentrating the momentum of horse and rider at one point (Brown 1976, 20, 27–8; 1985, 7–8). Brown (1985, 7) argues that one of the most important features of a medieval castle was that it could not be taken by a cavalry charge, and therefore the warfare of the medieval period was dominated not only by mounted knights but by castles too. He believed that each complemented the other in terms of tactics—that nothing could stand up to a charge of mounted knights except a castle.

There was an alternative way to render heavy cavalry useless, however. Heavily armoured knights were at a grave disadvantage in areas of woodland, bog and mountain as the terrain would have prevented them from charging. It was for this reason that medieval Gaelic lords, whose men rarely wore heavy armour, always tried to bring the Anglo-Normans to battle in such marginal regions and to avoid pitched battles on open plains (Lydon 1963, 143–5; K. Simms 1975–6, 98–9; Richter 1988, 15). The thickly wooded nature of much of medieval Ireland probably reduced the effectiveness of archers and crossbowmen as well, especially in summer (Lydon 1963, 144–5; Otway-Ruthven 1968, 44). The normal tactics of feudal Christendom were unsuitable in the relatively harsh terrain of Gaelic Ireland (K. Simms 1975–6, 98–9).

The most vivid medieval description of contrasting Anglo-Norman and Gaelic methods of warfare comes from Giraldus Cambrensis. He noted, firstly, the similarity between Irish and Welsh military tactics and, secondly, underlined the differences between warfare in Ireland and in France. He stated that heavily armoured knights on large horses, while ideal for warfare on the open plains of France, were useless in the wooded and boggy terrain of much of Ireland when attacked by the light, mobile, unarmoured Irish. He advocated the use of lightly armoured mounted infantry who would be sufficiently quick-moving to catch the highly elusive Irish (*Expugnatio*, 247–8). In another source Giraldus stated, after noting that the Irish did not build castles, that the latter use the woods as their 'forts' and the bogs as their 'trenches' in the defence of their lands (*Topographia*, 119). He also added a cautionary tale about what happened to impetuous young Anglo-Norman knights who pursued the Irish from the open plain into the forest (*Expugnatio*, 137–9). Certainly, Smyth (1982, 104–17) believes that it was largely the protection afforded by this rugged terrain of forest, bog and upland that allowed Gaelic lordships and septs to survive Anglo-Norman and later English attempts at conquest up to the seventeenth century. Further general evidence for this Irish use of the landscape as a military tool and defence against attack comes from Henry Chrysted's account of Ireland and Gaelic warfare to Jean Froissart, the French chronicler, in the late fourteenth century (*Froissart*, 430).

The present writer suggests, therefore, that few castles were built by Gaelic lords before the fifteenth century because the Irish did not employ these monuments in the defence of their territories against large-scale attack. Instead, they used the rugged nature of the landscape as a military tool to prevent or slow down the advance of an invading army. The defended settlement forms that did exist in medieval Gaelic lordships, such as crannogs, moated sites, natural island fortresses, cashels and (probably, in the present writer's opinion) well-defended ringforts/raised raths, were used only in the context of very minor disputes and not in outright large-scale warfare. There is therefore a distinct relationship between Gaelic military tactics and the lack of pre-1400 castles in the regions dominated by them at this time. These Irish military tactics, using the landscape, can be divided into two related types: firstly, an aggressive strategy whereby the terrain was used in direct confrontation with the enemy in battle; secondly and conversely, the use of the landscape to avoid direct conflict with a larger force.

References to the first tactic are numerous. For example, a combined force of Anglo-Normans and Leinster Irish was halted on its initial advance into Ossory in 1169 because the *Osraige* had thrown up trenches and stockades in 'places that were restricted and impassable because of woods and bogs'. After a day of hard fighting, the invaders overran the defences and then proceeded to raid Ossory (*Expugnatio*, 35–6; *Song*, lines 546–99). In 1169 the *Osraige* blocked the pass of Achadh-Ur with earthworks and palisades to stop the advance of Dermot MacMurrough's combined army of Leinstermen and Anglo-Normans (*Song*, lines 1010–40). At a later date, in 1279, when Thomas de Clare hosted against Turlough O'Brien of Thomond, his column of men were ambushed in a wooded marshy place by the local Irish (*Caithreim Thoirdhealbaigh*, i, 15; ii, 16). The same source indicates that a judicious use of fords, woods and ambuscade by the Irish caused the defeat of a large Anglo-Norman force at Dysert O'Dea in 1317 (*Caithreim Thoirdhealbaigh*, i, 140–2; ii, 126–7; Hayes-McCoy 1969, 42–6). Henry Chrysted's late fourteenth-century account of Gaelic tactics included the statement that when the Irish 'know that any man maketh war against them and is entered into their countries, then they draw together to the straits and passages to defend it, so that no man can enter into them' (*Froissart*, 430). Indeed, it must be presumed that many other defeats of colonial armies, tersely recorded in various medieval sources, were occasioned by the use of such tactics by the Irish. For example, Lydon (1987b, 246) believes that the 1274 defeat of a large Anglo-Norman army in the narrow, steep-sided valley of Glenmalure, Co. Wicklow, was due to an inability by the latter to come to terms with these Irish tactics. This type of strategy allowed Gaelic lords to join battle with the Anglo-Normans on their own ground, facing them on rough terrain that was unsuitable for mounted knights. Large battles like Dysert O'Dea and Glenmalure suggest that these tactics were highly effective.

References to the second tactic, whereby the landscape was used to avoid direct battle with a larger, more powerful force, be it Anglo-Norman or Gaelic, are also numerous. For example, upon the advance of Rory O'Conor into Uí Chennselaigh in 1168, Dermot MacMurrough abandoned his capital of Ferns and retreated to an inaccessible place deep in the wooded mountains nearby (*Expugnatio*, 41). Brian O'Brien, aided by Anglo-Norman allies, marched into Thomond in either 1276 or 1277 and attacked his rival, Turlough O'Brien, and his supporters. The MacNamaras, rather than giving direct battle, retreated to the woods of Echte with their herds of cattle (*Caithreim Thoirdhealbaigh*, i, 7–8; ii, 6–7). In 1278 Turlough sought shelter in the woods of Forbar with his supporters, apparently to avoid direct confrontation with the powerful combined army of Brian O'Brien and Thomas de Clare (*Caithreim Thoirdhealbaigh*, i, 11–12; ii, 12). When Dermot O'Brien was devastating Thomond in 1312, the MacNamaras retreated 'to the fastnesses of their country' (*Caithreim Thoirdhealbaigh*, i, 57; ii, 54). The same sept went again to the woods of Echte in 1315, when MacWilliam Burke was raiding through Thomond (*Caithreim Thoirdhealbaigh*, i, 83; ii, 75). In 1365 MacMahon and his followers took themselves and their cattle 'to the fastnesses of his country' (*AFM*).

Jean Creton, a Frenchman who accompanied Richard II on his second expedition to Ireland in 1399, wrote a metrical account of the events leading up to Richard's deposition, starting with the period Richard spent in Ireland (Watt 1987b, 318). His account of the campaign against Art MacMurrough in Leinster provides a valuable insight into Irish military tactics. Richard's army was enormous by any standard, consisting of anything between 8000 and 10,000 men, some of whom were mounted knights (Lydon 1963, 142–3). This impressive army was given no chance to display its power on the battlefield. Creton's account of Richard's march from the Barrow Valley, across the Wicklow Mountains and up the coast to Dublin, in very wet weather, shows how MacMurrough cleverly used the landscape of forest, mountain and bog to avoid direct battle with a force that would have been unbeatable on the plains of France. His men appear to have used guerrilla-style tactics to harass the English column along its line of march, with stragglers being picked off at will by the Leinstermen. It was a famished, sick and demoralised army that eventually reached Dublin (Smyth 1982, 109–11; Webb 1824, 27–45). Richard had been beaten, politically rather than militarily, because he had not broken MacMurrough in open battle, owing to the fact that the latter had used the landscape of his lordship to deny him this possibility. MacMurrough was to remain pre-eminent in Leinster until his death in 1417.

This second type of military tactic allowed smaller, weaker groups and septs to avoid direct battle with larger forces, who would eventually leave the weaker sept's lands, frustrated in their attempts to force their opponents to submit and having been subjected to harrying guerrilla-style tactics. There are scores of other references to Gaelic septs retreating to the wilder parts of their lordships with their cattle upon the approach of a larger army (K. Simms 1975–6, 102–4).

Obviously these two strategies were interchangeable. Chrysted's account states that 'when they see at any encounter that they be overmatched, then they will depart asunder and go and hide themselves in bushes, woods, hedges and caves so that no man shall find them' (*Froissart*, 431). It would appear, therefore, that if Gaelic lords failed to stop an invading army entering into their 'country' by blocking passes through woods, glens and bogs, they had the further option of melting, with their herds, into the landscape.

It would seem, therefore, that few conventional castles were built by Gaelic lords before 1400 because the landscape, rather than fixed permanent fortifications, was the most potent weapon in the defence of any given Irish territory. These tactics were eminently suited to the medieval Gaelic way of life and economy. Certainly, there was some tillage in Gaelic areas. Oats especially were grown in quantity, with a little barley and wheat as well (Nicholls 1987, 411). Flax for linen was also cultivated (*ibid.*). These crops were usually protected by temporary fences of post-and-wattle (*ibid.*). It appears that the medieval Irish ploughed with horses rather than oxen. The plough itself was a cruder type than was used in Anglo-Norman areas, and was pulled by the horse's tail (Lucas 1973; 1974; 1975; Nicholls 1987, 412).

Overall, however, the evidence suggests that medieval Gaelic society was really predominantly pastoral right up to the seventeenth century. It could be argued that a pastoral people, with few real nucleated settlements, living in relatively insubstantial houses in more agriculturally marginal areas, would have less need for large fixed fortifications such as elaborate masonry or timber castles, in comparison to more settled corn-growing areas of western Europe. Nicholls (1987, 410–11) states that in medieval Gaelic Ireland cattle could easily be driven off by their owners in times of trouble and were therefore less vulnerable to attack by enemy forces than, for example, cornfields and granaries. Certainly the evidence outlined above confirms this, with numerous references to cattle being hidden by their owners in remote places during times of unrest. This meant that the landscape was used as both an economic and a military defence in time of war. Upon the withdrawal of an invading force from any given territory, the inhabitants of the district could come out of their hiding places with their main wealth, cattle, intact. Since lordly dwellings and settlements generally were far less substantial than those in Anglo-Norman areas, and because there were relatively few cornfields to burn, it could be argued that the amount of economic damage done to any given medieval Gaelic lordship by an invading force was negligible, provided that they had not captured the cattle of the district.

Presumably the number of cattle in any given area depended on the power of that district's ruling family. It is abundantly clear that large herds of cattle were owned by Irish lords during the whole medieval period (K. Simms 1975–6, 101; Nicholls 1987, 413–15; Lucas 1989). Certainly, the extensive medieval field systems noted in the Carnfree and Rathcroghan areas of County Roscommon suggest large-scale stock-rearing by the O'Conor kings of Connacht in the late twelfth and thirteenth centuries. Individual fields within these systems are generally rectangular, mostly between 170m and 260m wide, and between 250m and 400m long (Herity 1988; 1991, 4, 15–16, 33). It might be added that similar but undated pre-modern field systems exist in the area between Boyle and Ardcarne, Co. Roscommon, in the general vicinity of *Carraic Locha Ce*—the main medieval MacDermot residence on Lough Key, discussed above (sections 4.2a, 4.2b). The large fields in these systems are also rectangular, and occasionally contain the barely visible remains of simple rectangular houses (Mon. Nos RO006- 078, -086, -103, -131, -195). These may be medieval in date, and hopefully future research in the area will verify this. Certainly, cowhides were the main export from Gaelic regions during the whole of the medieval period (Nicholls 1987, 413). It must be presumed that many thousands of cattle existed in any one Gaelic kingdom or lordship.

Obviously it would have been impossible to keep such huge herds of cattle in castles during wartime, owing to the limited space available within any given castle, and also the problem of providing water and fodder during a siege. This point is crucial because the Irish did not make hay during the Early Christian and medieval periods. Instead, certain lands were left ungrazed during the summer, being utilised as winterage for cattle during the leaner months (Kelly 1997, 46–8; Nicholls 1987, 413–15). Therefore, leaving aside the strictly military reasons for Gaelic lords not building conventional castles before *c.* 1400, it was also impractical for them to build large complex fortifications, either of timber or of stone, given their predominantly pastoral economy.

The processes that led Irish lords to eschew the widespread adoption of true castles in the twelfth, thirteenth and fourteenth centuries show how different this society was in many ways to much of contemporary western Europe. This lack of what modern scholars would consider to be typical castles of European type before the fifteenth century was clearly related to the nature of Gaelic society, economy and warfare—not because the Irish were unable to build them. Their methods of territorial and personal defence were a sensible and practical alternative solution, which suited their predominantly pastoral organisation.

4.4—Settlement forms in Gaelic Ireland from *c.* 1400 until the seventeenth century

A review of the first section of this chapter, which briefly analysed medieval Gaelic society and economy up to the seventeenth century, shows that the year 1400 represents no cultural break (section 4.1). Certainly, many of the settlement forms used by the Irish before this date—crannogs, cashels, house types and apparently ringforts—continued in use into the seventeenth century (sections 4.2b, 4.2c, 4.3). This date is used as a division by the present writer because it has been shown that Gaelic lords begin to build tower-houses in the earliest years of the fifteenth century (Pls 15 and 34). This does not mean that there was an immediate and widespread adoption of tower-houses in Gaelic areas of Ireland in the first years of the fifteenth century—most examples date from the late fifteenth and sixteenth centuries and ceased to be built around the mid-seventeenth century (Cairns 1987, 1, 6)—but rather a gradual adoption of tower-houses as a settlement form over a relatively long period. Furthermore, an analysis of the distribution of tower-houses indicates that this castle type was less popular as a settlement form in the northern half of Ireland than in the southern part of the country. Most definite tower-houses occur south of a line from Galway to Dundalk (Fig. 6). For example, only three definite tower-houses exist in the whole county of Cavan (O'Donovan 1995, 234–5), compared to the 410 in Tipperary (Cairns 1987, 3–4). It must be remembered that most of Ireland's lakes occur in *c.* northern half of the country, and one explanation for the smaller numbers of tower-houses over much of Connacht and Ulster may be that many Gaelic lords in these regions continued to live in crannogs (Pl. 28; Fig. 21). In other words, while Irish lords in some areas enthusiastically adopted tower-houses from the fifteenth century onwards, it would appear that this was not universal and varied in intensity from region to region—yet another indication of regional differences in medieval Gaelic Ireland.

Tower-houses, however, do represent the first large-scale evidence of Gaelic Irish lords, at least in some areas, building structures which modern scholars classify as castles. Does this reflect a change in Irish military tactics during the fifteenth and sixteenth centuries?

The available evidence suggests that no new military techniques were adopted. Firstly, Gaelic society remained predominantly pastoral (MacCurtain 1972, 39; Nicholls 1987, 397, 413–15), and it was shown above that this is an important factor in understanding Irish tactics before the fifteenth century (section 4.3). It has been argued that tower-houses first originated in Anglo-Norman areas some time in the fourteenth century (Cairns 1987, 8–10). Yet despite their supposed Anglo-Norman origins, it is clear that, conceptually, tower-houses fitted extremely well into the Gaelic polity. The general consensus amongst scholars is that tower-houses were built as a defence for a lord, his family and retainers against general lawlessness and the mainly small-scale localised warfare that was a common feature of Ireland, as opposed to most of England, right into the seventeenth century. Most of them were not intended to withstand large sieges like the scientifically defended stone castles of earlier periods (Leask 1941, 76; Barry 1987, 186–8; Cairns 1987, 8, 10; Thompson 1987, 22–7; McNeill 1997, 217–21). The dominant factor influencing the siting of most tower-houses seems to be access to good farmland. Defensive and military considerations do not seem to have been taken into account in most cases (Davies and Swan 1939, 178, 184; Cairns, 1987, 11; McNeill 1997, 219–20). Indeed, tower-houses appear mostly to have functioned in much the same way as crannogs, natural island fortresses and *longphort* sites (sections 4.2a–c, 4.3). They may represent the first example of large-scale building in stone amongst Gaelic secular lords, but the ethos behind their construction—protection for an individual, his family and a few retainers against lawlessness and small-scale raiding—can be traced as far back as the beginnings of the Early Christian period.

Tower-houses were not built, therefore, to withstand attack by large bodies of men. It is quite clear that Gaelic lords continued to use the landscape as a defence against

Pl. 34—*A tower-house at Rockfleet, Co. Mayo, probably built by the O'Malleys around 1500.* (Photo: Kieran O'Conor.)

attack by powerful forces after 1400, and right up to the seventeenth century (Ellis 1996, 118; Hayes-McCoy 1940–1; 1969, 87–143, 187; MacCurtain 1972, 39; Nicholls 1987, 404–5; Ó Domhnaill 1946–7; Smyth 1982, 114). The introduction of tower-houses into certain Gaelic areas from the early fifteenth century onwards did nothing to change this practical method of territorial defence, suited as it was to the defensive requirements and economy of Gaelic society. The Irish continued to believe that the landscape, with its woods, bogs, passes, fords and mountains, afforded the best form of defence or offence against a large invading army.

The Gaelicisation of large parts of the Anglo-Norman colony was one of the main features of fourteenth-century Ireland. This movement saw the spread of Irish customs, speech, pastoralism, laws, literature and dress amongst large segments of the colonial population, and the cultural differences between Gaelic and Anglo-Norman areas became increasingly blurred as the century wore on. Apparently, this process also saw the adoption of Irish ways of making war by many families of Anglo-Norman descent (Frame 1981, 132–5; Lydon 1973, 57–61; Richter 1988, 167–71). For example, looking at evidence from sixteenth-century Kerry, one writer has shown that, while tower-houses were used as a defence against general lawlessness, various families of Anglo-Norman descent, such as the Fitzgeralds, evacuated their tower-houses when threatened by a superior force, and hid themselves and their herds in remote places within their lordship (McAuliffe 1991a).

Tower-houses are really an archaeological indication of the cultural uniformity that prevailed across most of Ireland by the fifteenth century (Cairns 1987, 9; K. Simms 1989, 99–101). The fact that they began to be built in certain Gaelic areas after 1400 is an indication that cultural change also affected the native Irish themselves, as a result of intermarriage and contact with neighbouring Anglo-Norman families since the late twelfth century. The ideas and ethos behind the construction of tower-houses represent a mingling of cultures, both Anglo-Norman and Gaelic. Although, as noted, certain moated sites and some few masonry and elaborate timber castles were built in Gaelic Ireland prior to *c.* 1400, the tower-house is really the first secular monument type to demonstrate this fusion of cultures in medieval Ireland—a process which was extremely important for the development of society on this island.

It was also noted above that the settlement pattern across Gaelic-dominated parts of medieval Ireland was generally dispersed (section 4.1). The historical evidence suggests, however, that small, unplanned clusters of peasant houses or huts, mostly 'creats', occurred beside many tower-houses all over sixteenth-century Ireland, including Gaelic and Gaelicised areas (Nicholls 1987, 404; Barry 1993a, 118; W. Smyth 1985, 118–30). Presumably such settlements, like the tower-houses, could be abandoned in times of war (Nicholls 1987, 404). This element of nucleation in sixteenth-century Gaelic Ireland may be a result of the increased warfare of Tudor times, but it is also possible that small clusters of peasant houses always existed beside earlier pre-tower-house Gaelic lordly residences, acting as service settlements for these centres (e.g. O'Keeffe 1996).

4.5—Conclusions

4.5a—Settlement and society in medieval Gaelic Ireland—current state of knowledge

This chapter has dealt mainly with the nature of the settlement forms in Gaelic-dominated parts of medieval Ireland. It was shown that few castles were erected by Irish kings and lords prior to their adoption of tower-houses in the fifteenth century. Masonry castles or earthwork castles surmounted by complex timber defences were rarely built by these men in the twelfth, thirteenth and fourteenth centuries (section 4.2) owing to the nature of their military tactics, which utilised the natural, defensive qualities of the landscape, rather than fixed fortifications, in the defence of their territories against a powerful invading force. This was shown to be a practical strategy for three reasons. Firstly, it nullified the use of armoured knights and, to a certain extent, archers by the Anglo-Normans and allowed the Irish to join battle with technically superior forces on their own terms. Secondly, the wild landscape of parts of their lordships allowed the Irish a line of retreat upon defeat or upon the advance of a hostile force which they felt incapable of directly facing in battle. This opportunity to retreat would have been denied them if they had defended their lands from castles. Thirdly, given the predominantly pastoral nature of Gaelic society, it would have been difficult to feed and protect large herds of cattle in castles during the course of a long siege. It was far more sensible to move these cattle into the forests, bogs or mountains, where they could not be found by the enemy and where feed, in the form of grass, leaves or mast, was available (section 4.3).

It was shown that a number of other settlement forms existed in the countryside of Gaelic-dominated parts of medieval Ireland. Crannogs and fortresses on natural islands were common in lakeland Ireland (which corresponds to most of Connacht and Ulster) during the medieval period and right up to the seventeenth century (section 4.2b). It is clear that some moated sites were built and occupied by Gaelic lords and kings during the thirteenth and fourteenth centuries, especially in parts of north Connacht (*ibid.*). This is an important point, as for many years Irish scholarship has seen moated sites as a purely Anglo-Norman phenomenon (section 3.3c). There is a surprising amount of evidence from various sources to suggest that cashels or stone-walled ringforts, especially defensive-looking ones, continued in use as lordly residences in stony parts of the country throughout the medieval period (section 4.2b). There has been considerable academic debate amongst Irish scholars as to whether earthen ringforts continued to be built and inhabited after *c.* 1000 and up to the seventeenth century.

Again, like cashels, their functional equivalent, there is a body of evidence from various disciplines and sources which suggests that some ringforts continued in use throughout the medieval period (section 4.2c). The bias of the excavated evidence towards a purely Early Christian date for the occupation of ringforts seems to be largely a reflection of the places where modern Irish archaeologists have concentrated their work. There have been few excavations of ringforts in the parts of the country that were controlled by Gaelic lords during the medieval period (section 4.2c). The difficulty of recognising native Irish habitation sites of thirteenth- and fourteenth-century date in the landscape today has been a great impediment to the archaeological study of medieval Gaelic society (section 4.1). Therefore the fact that a series of Gaelic medieval centres of pre-tower-house date were identified in this chapter is extremely important (sections 4.2a–c). Such sites have the potential to yield much information about the material culture and economy of medieval Gaelic Ireland.

Tower-houses start to appear in Gaelic areas of the country at the beginning of the fifteenth century, and are particularly common in the southern half of the country. Indeed, it would seem that in the northern half of Ireland during the fifteenth, sixteenth and seventeenth centuries many Irish lords preferred to live in crannogs (section 4.4). The introduction of tower-houses into certain Gaelic lordships after *c.* 1400 represents the first time that Irish secular lords began to build in stone and to erect fortresses which modern scholars classify as castles. Most tower-houses were not built to withstand attack by a powerful force. This means that Gaelic lords and septs after *c.* 1400 continued to use the landscape of their lordships as the best form of defence against large-scale attack, as their ancestors had done before them (section 4.4).

It was tentatively argued that two types of peasant house seem to have existed in Gaelic areas up to the seventeenth century. The first is the 'creat', a small, windowless, one-roomed circular or oval affair, which seems to have been relatively easy to build in terms of time and materials (section 4.3). It was argued that this was the dwelling of the poorest elements in Gaelic society and not just a house type associated purely with booleying or transhumance (*ibid.*). Small, scattered, unplanned clusters of 'creats' seem to have existed beside late medieval tower-houses, and perhaps beside earlier, pre-tower-house Irish lordly centres as well (section 4.4). The second type was more substantial. Its subrectangular plan shows that it was not very different in size or shape to the houses excavated to date at Anglo-Norman manorial centres (section 3.2c). Yet there seem to have been peculiarities about this type of house that specifically suited medieval Gaelic society. As noted, the main structural elements within this type of house were the cruck-trusses, which were placed directly on the ground surface. Walls were not load-bearing and were therefore built of cheap, relatively flimsy materials such as sods. The important point here is that this type of house was simple to take down and erect elsewhere, as cruck-trusses were easily portable (section 4.3). Given the nature of Gaelic territorial defence, which saw whole population groups melting into the landscape, and their predominantly pastoral society, which saw the movement of cattle and flocks to summer pastures, this house type was an eminently suitable dwelling for native Irish society. The other point about this second type of dwelling is that Gaelic lords also appear to have lived in such houses prior to 1400, and in some parts of the country up to the seventeenth century. The fact that native Irish kings and lords lived in the equivalent of peasant dwellings certainly aroused the contempt of foreign observers. Yet there were cultural reasons for Irish lords living in such comparatively insignificant dwellings. The historically attested custom of periodic land redistribution amongst Gaelic kindred groups seems to have partly created a situation where large houses such as a first-floor hall were not built, simply because occupation could not be guaranteed for long. This may have been another reason why houses with cruck-trusses as their main structural element were preferred by the Irish, as adherence to this custom would have meant a constant rebuilding of houses (sections 4.1, 4.3). Nevertheless, more substantial houses could have been built within permanently occupied sites such as moated sites, cashels or crannogs, and yet this was not done by Gaelic lords. Again, perhaps the best explanation for this is that the military tactics of the Gaelic Irish discouraged the building of large houses, as they would not be defended in outright war. The nature of warfare in Gaelic Ireland, with its emphasis on mobility rather than the defence of fixed fortifications such as castles, militated against the building of substantial dwellings by Irish lords and kings (section 4.3).

It can be seen, therefore, that many of the traits of medieval Gaelic Ireland which often aroused the contempt of contemporary foreign visitors evolved because of the interrelated nature of that society's culture, economy and methods of making war. They were sensible and practical solutions to the conditions of the time.

In conclusion, over much of this chapter the present writer has produced a model of the way Gaelic lords and kings used their fortifications during the medieval period. Basically, it is argued that there was a difference in the scale of the defences used by the Anglo-Normans/later English and the Gaelic Irish on their respective fortifications prior to around 1400, and to a certain extent after this date in certain parts of the country. Logically, however, it is probably best to state that in reality the difference between the defences on Gaelic-occupied crannogs, certain raised raths or 'flat' ringforts and free-standing mottes belonging to minor Anglo-Norman lords is minimal. This may also be true of certain moated sites occupied by Gaelic lords. The present writer knows of at least one moated site in County Sligo which clearly employed flanking defence, possibly in the form of small, square timber towers. This is the moated site at Knockbeg West, Co. Sligo, which also uses the right bank of the Owenmore River in its defences (Mon. No. SL026-018). Possibly the distinction in defensive terms between small timber castles and other forms of medieval fortifications was blurred—all were capable of resisting small-scale attacks. Indeed, on occasion, Gaelic historical sources seem to refer to certain crannogs as castles. A castle (*caislen*) 'on Lough Cairrgin' was burnt by the men of Meath in 1136 (*AT*). It has been suggested that this site was a crannog (Graham 1988a, 21). As noted above, crannogs were clearly in use on this lake throughout the medieval period (section 4.2b). Brian MacMahon's castle (*castrum*) of 'Lochnlach' is mentioned in 1297 (Nicholls 1969–72, 423). This site appears to have been a crannog sited on Ballagh Lough beneath Leck Hill, Co. Monaghan (Brindley 1986, 13; FitzPatrick 1998, 98; J. Smyth 1954, 3–4). Certainly, all these medieval Gaelic lordly centres, such as crannogs, natural islands, moated sites, cashels and ringforts, had many of the attributes of castles in an administrative and economic sense, being the defended residences of Irish lords and kings. It is easy to see why there was a temptation for Gaelic scribes to call some of these sites 'castles', especially if the actual scale of the defences at these places was not very different from those on small mottes erected by minor Anglo-Norman lords. However, it is argued that medieval commentators such as Giraldus Cambrensis or Stephen of Lexington adamantly state that the Irish did not build castles because the latter rarely built the complex timber or masonry castles seen throughout the Anglo-Norman world. Settlement forms such as crannogs or various forms of ringfort, even well-defended ones, belong to a tradition of essentially private fortification that has its origins at the start of the Early Christian period or even earlier (e.g. Edwards 1990, 11–27, 34–40). Mottes or ringworks of the Hen Domen or Stafford type, along with masonry castles in general, have their immediate origins outside Ireland from the tenth century onwards. In all, it is felt that the Anglo-Normans introduced levels of fortification to Ireland during the last decades of the twelfth century and throughout the thirteenth century that had not really been seen before. Morphologically, mottes and ringworks may often look similar to raised raths and ringforts today, but in the main the former types of earthwork castle originally carried more elaborate timber defences than the latter settlement forms during the medieval period. This model of dual traditions of fortification in medieval Ireland certainly explains the archaeological evidence for the lack of classic castles in Gaelic-dominated regions prior to 1400 or so, as well as the historical evidence suggesting that the Irish had fortifications which were not seen by Anglo-Norman observers as castles.

4.5b—Settlement and society in medieval Gaelic Ireland—priorities for future research

Historical sources containing social and economic information about Gaelic Ireland prior to the sixteenth century are rare (section 4.1), and so it is immediately obvious that the discipline of archaeology has a large role to play in any future research on medieval Gaelic Ireland, through excavation and fieldwork. Very little archaeological work, however, has been carried out so far on the settlement, society and economy of Irish-dominated parts of medieval Ireland, which in various ways can be equated with a large part of the island during the whole period (*ibid.*). New ideas about the nature of the settlement forms existing in medieval Gaelic Ireland, especially before *c.* 1400, have been postulated in this chapter (sections 4.2a–c, 4.3). One priority for future research lies in a relatively small-scale project combining historical research and fieldwork to identify and plan Gaelic lordly centres in the parts of Ireland that remained in some way under their control during the medieval period.

There has been little excavation of medieval Gaelic habitation sites, whether lordly centres or peasant houses or settlements. For example, there have been five fully or partly published excavations of what appear to be definite Gaelic sites occupied during the thirteenth and fourteenth centuries (sections 4.2b, 4.3; Brannon 1984; Davies 1950; Long 1994, 238–42; McNeill 1977; Williams and Robinson 1983). There has been only one fully published excavation of a Gaelic tower-house to date—the O'Sullivan Beare tower-house at Dunboy, Co. Cork (Gowen 1978). There has been very little attempt to understand the economic basis of medieval Gaelic society through excavation and fieldwork. Many of the current perceptions about medieval Gaelic society and its economy are really based on historical evidence from the later sixteenth and seventeenth centuries (section 4.1). Clearly, excavation of specifically targeted Gaelic habitation sites is needed to shed more light on the material culture, house types and economy of Irish-dominated parts of medieval Ireland. It is also felt that this series of excavations should be integrated with a campaign of intensive archaeological fieldwork and further historical research to give a better understanding of the development of society and the economy in Gaelic Ireland from the late twelfth century through to the seventeenth century. Such a programme of research should also include an excavation of a specifically targeted ringfort to answer questions about the use of ringforts during the medieval period (section 4.2c).

5. MEDIEVAL RURAL SETTLEMENT IN IRELAND—
AN OVERVIEW

Summaries of the various ideas, conclusions and models proposed in this report have been included at the end of each chapter (sections 1.6, 2.3a, 3.5a, 4.5a). The present writer has also identified what he considers to be the priorities for future research on medieval rural settlement in Ireland, usually at the conclusion of each chapter (section 2.3b, 3.5b, 4.5b, I.1). Various research strategies are outlined in Appendix I. It seems unnecessary to repeat all these conclusions and proposals. Instead, this short chapter will be used to make some general, sometimes abstract, comments about the nature of medieval rural settlement in Ireland.

Medieval Ireland comprised a series of distinct regions, with differences between the settlement patterns of each area. Although this diversity was partly due to the cultural differences between Gaelic and Anglo-Norman Ireland, it was rather more complex than this, at least in the late twelfth, thirteenth and early fourteenth centuries. The overall evidence suggests that there were distinct differences within the rural settlement pattern of Anglo-Norman-dominated parts of medieval Ireland. For example, the dispersed rural settlement pattern of Anglo-Norman east Ulster was clearly different to that of regions like Meath, Leinster or Tipperary, where demesne farming did take place during the thirteenth and early fourteenth centuries, largely carried out from manorial centres which were often located in some form of castle and which had at least some tenants living beside them in nucleated villages or rural boroughs. It must also be said that even in these parts of eastern Ireland, which seem to have been well settled by English peasants in the early thirteenth century, dispersed settlement may always have existed contemporaneously with villages on manors (sections 3.1, 3.2a–c, 3.3a–c, 3.5a). Nevertheless, the settlement pattern of medieval Leinster or Meath, with their villages, rural boroughs, small market towns and open fields, was very different from that of east Ulster and other frontier parts of Anglo-Norman Ireland, where there had been little colonisation by English peasants and where most of the manorial tenants consisted of native Irish farmers living out in the townlands that made up the manor. The Anglo-Normans made far less of an impact on the landscape of these latter regions than on the rich lands of south-east Ireland. Arguably, the settlement patterns and way of life in border areas of Anglo-Norman-dominated parts of medieval Ireland were relatively similar to those of Gaelic Ireland, although it is suggested that in the latter regions few classic European-style timber or masonry castles were built before *c.* 1400—one clear major difference between Gaelic regions and Anglo-Norman areas.

The settlement pattern throughout Gaelic-dominated parts of medieval Ireland seems to have been predominantly dispersed, with most of the population living in scattered farmsteads or small house clusters. The economy was largely pastoral, with transhumance or booleying being practised as part of the yearly agricultural strategy (sections 4.1, 4.3, 4.5). Although native Irish lords did possess fortifications, castles of the types seen elsewhere in western Europe were not common across the landscape of Gaelic Ireland during the twelfth, thirteenth and fourteenth centuries. This began to change when certain Gaelic lords began to build tower-houses after *c.* 1400 (section 4.4). These are just broad generalisations about medieval Gaelic society and there is still much to be learnt. However, it seems that regional diversity was not confined to Anglo-Norman-controlled parts of Ireland. As noted, some Gaelic lords in Roscommon and probably Sligo utilised moated sites as their chief residences, showing themselves willing to adopt what was ultimately an English or Anglo-Norman settlement form (section 4.2b). Yet only one definite moated site has been identified in the adjacent county of Leitrim, and none in Donegal. Indeed, there are few examples of this monument type across Ulster as a whole (*ibid.*). Gaelic lords in these regions up to about 1400 presumably continued to live almost exclusively in crannogs, natural island fortresses, cashels and possibly ringforts—all secular settlement forms that long pre-dated the coming of the Anglo-Normans. Furthermore, the evidence for what appear to be medieval field systems relating to large-scale cattle-rearing in modern north Roscommon is not seen elsewhere (section 4.3). Again, some parts of Gaelic Ireland, such as modern Clare, wholeheartedly adopted tower-houses from the fifteenth century onwards, while other Gaelic-dominated areas, such as much of Ulster, saw little tower-house-building throughout the period (section 4.4). This diversity in settlement forms indicates that regional differences existed across medieval Gaelic Ireland as much as in Anglo-Norman parts of the country. This suggests that rural settlement differed in its exact nature from region to region, even from the fifteenth century onwards, when there was a general cultural uniformity, in terms of things like language and social customs, across the country as a result of the Gaelicisation of many Anglo-Norman families during the fourteenth century.

Another point that emerges from the discussion in the various chapters of this report is that much of the landscape of Ireland has changed since the medieval period. It is clear that much native woodland was cut down in the seventeenth century (Smyth 1982, 116). Yet it is also true that agricultural changes and the growth of new settlements or the expansion of existing ones in recent centuries have masked or destroyed much of the medieval landscape. The popular modern tendency to see the countryside as unchanging is clearly incorrect. Underneath the tranquillity of rural Ireland, the landscape is constantly being changed and remodelled by man as he attempts to gain a living from the soil. Development and change are not solely urban phenomena. The archaeologist's goal is to look at the archaeology of any given area and to understand the changes that have occurred to the landscape and settlement pattern over time. In turn, such a process will allow the settlement, society and landscape of any given period to be reconstructed on paper.

The next point is almost at odds with the last. A comparison of the material culture of medieval peasants in both Gaelic and Anglo-Norman Ireland, as evidenced by the results of the few excavations of their homesteads, suggests that it was really not very different from that of small farmers in more marginal areas of Ireland up to the middle part of this century (e.g. Estyn-Evans 1942; 1957; O'Dowd 1989). A small farmer working his farm around the year 1950 in many parts of the country would have no difficulty in recognising many of the tools, household items, agricultural practices, rural crafts, industries and house types of medieval Ireland. Alternatively, it is suggested that such a farmer would have problems in recognising the technological world his children or grandchildren work in today. This all shows how much rural Ireland has changed over the last 30 or 40 years. For example, rural housing has been completely transformed from two- or three-roomed thatched farmhouses to extensive, fully electrified modern bungalows during these years—a veritable Great Rebuilding (e.g. Aalen *et al.* 1997, 163–4, 240–3). It was stated in the introduction to this report that it is probably best to see the medieval period ending in archaeological terms during the second half of the seventeenth century—long after the calendar date used by historians for the end of the Middle Ages and the beginning of the Early Modern period—but many facets of medieval material culture existed until quite recently in Ireland. This is surely further proof that change is rarely instantaneous and that periods merge with one another for centuries. Therefore, although the events of the sixteenth and seventeenth centuries were crucial in ending the medieval period in Ireland, it could be argued that the final embers of medieval rural life have only been extinguished within living memory. The relatively unchanging nature of much of the material culture of rural Ireland over the centuries suggests that the staff of any future Discovery Programme project on medieval rural settlement should be aware of the work of folk-life specialists, as this may help in the interpretation of their own data. Perhaps a better definition of when the medieval period began and ended in archaeological terms should also be a priority for research in any future project on rural settlement in Ireland.

Lastly, this report suggests ways in which research on medieval rural settlement in Ireland should proceed in the future. It is abundantly clear that the discipline of archaeology could make a huge contribution to the understanding of rural life in medieval Ireland, especially in Gaelic-dominated areas. It is also apparent that a decision by the Discovery Programme to go ahead with a comprehensive programme of research into the whole subject would be warmly welcomed by medieval scholars of different disciplines both in Ireland and elsewhere.

REFERENCES

Abbreviations

AC = A.M. Freeman (ed.), *The Annals of Connacht* (Dublin, 1944).

ACL = D. Murphy (ed.), *The Annals of Clonmacnoise* (Dublin, 1896).

AFM = J. O'Donovan (ed.), *The Annals of the Kingdom of Ireland by the Four Masters* (7 vols) (Dublin, 1848–51).

AI = S. MacAirt (ed.), *The Annals of Inisfallen* (Dublin, 1951).

ALC = W.M. Hennessey (ed.), *The Annals of Loch Ce* (2 vols) (Dublin, 1871).

Archbishop Alen's Reg. = C. McNeill (ed.), *Calendar of Archbishop Alen's Register* (Dublin, 1950).

AT = W. Stokes (ed.), 'The Annals of Tigernach', *Revue Celtique* **18** (1897), 9–95, 150–97, 267–303.

AU = W.M. Hennessey and B. McCarthy (eds), *The Annals of Ulster* (4 vols) (Dublin, 1887–1901).

Book of Magauran = L. McKenna (ed.), *The Book of Magauran* (Dublin, 1947).

Caithreim Thoirdhealbaigh = S.H. O'Grady (ed.), *Caithreim Thoirdhealbaigh* (2 vols) (London, 1929).

Cal. Justic. Rolls Ire. = J. Mills and M.C. Griffith (eds), *Calendar of justiciary rolls, Ireland* (3 vols) (Dublin, 1905–14).

CDI = H.S. Sweetman (ed.), *Calendar of documents relating to Ireland, 1171–1307* (5 vols) (London, 1875–86).

CIPM = [Various editors], *Calendar of inquisitions post mortem* (18 vols) (London, 1904–87).

Clyn's Annals = R. Butler (ed.), *The Annals of Ireland by Friar John Clyn and Thady Dowling* (Dublin, 1849).

Expugnatio = A.B. Scott and F.X. Martin (eds), *Expugnatio Hibernica: The Conquest of Ireland by Giraldus Cambrensis* (Dublin, 1978).

Ext. Ir. Mon. Possessions = N.B. White (ed.), *Extents of Irish monastic possessions, 1540–1* (Dublin, 1943).

Froissart = G.C. Macaulay (ed.), *The Chronicles of Froissart* (London, 1899).

Lexington = B.W. O'Dwyer (ed.), *Stephen of Lexington, Letters from Ireland, 1228–1229* (Kalamazoo, 1982).

Mac Con Midhe = N.J.A. Williams (ed.), *The poems of Gilla Brighde Mac Con Midhe* (London, 1980).

Ormond Deeds = E. Curtis (ed.), *Calendar of Ormond deeds, 1172–1603* (6 vols) (Dublin, 1932–43).

Red Bk. of Kildare = G. MacNiocaill (ed.), *The Red Book of the earls of Kildare* (Dublin, 1964).

Red Bk. Ormond = N.B. White (ed.), *The Red Book of Ormond* (Dublin, 1932).

Song = G.H. Orpen (ed. and trans.), *The Song of Dermot and the Earl* (Oxford, 1892).

Topographia = J.J. O'Meara (ed.), *Topographia Hibernica: The History and Topography of Ireland by Gerald of Wales* (Harmondsworth, 1982).

Aalen, F.H.A., Whelan, K. and Stout, M. 1997 *Atlas of the Irish rural landscape.* Cork.

Addyman, P.W. 1965 Coney Island, Lough Neagh; prehistoric settlement, Anglo-Norman castle and Elizabethan native fortress. *Ulster Journal of Archaeology* **18**, 78–101.

Armitage, E.S. 1912 *Early Norman castles of the British Isles.* London.

Aston, M. 1985 *Interpreting the landscape—landscape archaeology and local history.* London.

Aston, M. (ed.) 1988 *Medieval fish, fisheries and fishponds* (2 vols). Oxford.

Aston, M. 1993 *Monasteries.* London.

Barker, P.A. and Higham, R. 1982 *Hen Domen, Montgomery: a timber castle on the English–Welsh border,* 1. Royal Archaeological Institute.

Barker, P.A. and Higham, R. 1988 *Hen Domen, Montgomery: a timber castle on the English–Welsh border. Excavations 1960–1988: a summary report.* Worcester.

Barrett, G.F. 1982 Ringfort settlement in Co. Louth: sources, patterns and landscape. *Journal of the County Louth Archaeological and Historical Society* **20**, 77–95.

Barrett, G.F. and Graham, B.J. 1975 Some considerations concerning the dating and distribution of ring-forts in Ireland. *Ulster Journal of Archaeology* **38**, 33–45.

Barry, T.B. 1977 *Medieval moated sites of south-east Ireland.* Oxford.

Barry, T.B. 1978 Moated sites in Ireland. In F.A. Aberg (ed.), *Medieval moated sites,* 56–9. London.

Barry, T.B. 1979 The moated sites of Co. Waterford. *Decies* **10**, 32–6.

Barry, T.B. 1981 The shifting frontier: medieval moated sites in counties Cork and Limerick. In F.A. Aberg and A.E. Brown (eds), *Medieval moated sites in north-west Europe,* 71–85. Oxford.

Barry, T.B. 1983 Anglo-Norman ringwork castles: some evidence. In T. Reeves-Smyth and F. Hamond (eds), *Landscape archaeology in Ireland,* 295–314. British Archaeological Reports, British Series 116. Oxford.

Barry, T.B. 1987 *The archaeology of medieval Ireland.* London and New York.

Barry, T.B. 1988 'The people of the country...dwell scattered'; the pattern of rural settlement in Ireland in the Later Middle Ages. In J. Bradley (ed.), *Settlement and society in medieval Ireland,* 345–57. Kilkenny.

Barry, T.B. 1993a Late medieval Ireland: the debate on the social and economic transformation, 1350–1550. In B.J. Graham and L.J. Proudfoot (eds), *A historical geography of Ireland,* 99–122. London.

Barry, T.B. 1993b The archaeology of the tower house in late medieval Ireland. In H. Anderson and T. Wienberg (eds), *The study of medieval archaeology,* 211–17. Stockholm.

Barry, T.B. 1995 The last frontier: defence and settlement in late medieval Ireland. In T.B. Barry, R. Frame and K. Simms (eds), *Colony and frontier in medieval Ireland,* 217–28. Dublin.

Barry, T.B. 1996 Rural settlement in Ireland in the Middle Ages: an overview. *Ruralia* **1**, 134–41.

Barry, T.B., Culleton, E. and Empey, C.A. 1984 The motte at Kells, Co. Kilkenny. *Proceedings of the Royal Irish Academy* **84C**, 157–70.

Bartlett, R. 1993 *The making of Europe. Conquest, colonization and cultural change, 950–1350.* London.

Belmore, Earl of 1903 Ulster maps *c.* 1600. *Ulster Journal of Archaeology* (special volume), 1–23.

Bennett, I. 1984–5 Preliminary archaeological excavations at Ferrycarrig ringwork, Newtown Townland, Co. Wexford. *Journal of the Wexford Historical Society* **10**, 25–43.

Bennett, I. (ed.) 1988 *Excavations 1987—summary accounts of archaeological excavations in Ireland.* Bray.

Bennett, I. (ed.) 1989a *Excavations 1988—summary accounts of archaeological excavations in Ireland.* Bray.

Bennett, I. 1989b The settlement patterns of ringforts in County Wexford. *Journal of the Royal Society of Antiquaries of Ireland* **119**, 50–61.

Bennett, I. (ed.) 1990 *Excavations 1989—summary accounts of archaeological excavations in Ireland*. Bray.

Bennett, I. (ed.) 1991 *Excavations 1990—summary accounts of archaeological excavations in Ireland*. Bray.

Bennett, I. (ed.) 1992 *Excavations 1991—summary accounts of archaeological excavations in Ireland*. Bray.

Bennett, I. (ed.) 1993 *Excavations 1992—summary accounts of archaeological excavations in Ireland*. Bray.

Bennett, I. (ed.) 1994 *Excavations 1993—summary accounts of archaeological excavations in Ireland*. Bray.

Bennett, I. (ed.) 1995 *Excavations 1994—summary accounts of archaeological excavations in Ireland*. Bray.

Bennett, I. (ed.) 1996 *Excavations 1995—summary accounts of archaeological excavations in Ireland*. Bray.

Bennett, I. (ed.) 1997 *Excavations 1996—summary accounts of archaeological excavations in Ireland*. Bray.

Beresford, M.W. and St Joseph, J.K.S. 1979 *Medieval England: an aerial survey* (2nd edn). Cambridge.

Bhreathnach, E. (forthcoming) *Authority and supremacy in Tara and its hinterland c. 950 to 1200*. Discovery Programme Monograph 5.

Bradley, J. 1986 *Urban Archaeological Survey—County Kildare* (4 vols) (limited distribution). Office of Public Works, Dublin.

Bradley, J. 1988 The medieval borough of Bunratty. *North Munster Antiquarian Journal* **30**, 19–25.

Bradley, J. and Dunne, N. 1988a *Urban Archaeological Survey—County Sligo* (limited distribution). Office of Public Works, Dublin.

Bradley, J. and Dunne, N. 1988b *Urban Archaeological Survey—County Roscommon* (limited distribution). Office of Public Works, Dublin.

Bradley, J. and Dunne, N. 1988c *Urban Archaeological Survey—County Leitrim* (limited distribution). Office of Public Works, Dublin.

Bradley, J. and Dunne, N. 1989a *Urban Archaeological Survey—County Monaghan* (limited distribution). Office of Public Works, Dublin.

Bradley, J. and Dunne, N. 1989b *Urban Archaeological Survey—County Cavan* (limited distribution). Office of Public Works, Dublin.

Bradley, J. and Dunne, N. 1989c *Urban Archaeological Survey—County Donegal* (limited distribution). Office of Public Works, Dublin.

Bradley, J. and Dunne, N. 1989d *Urban Archaeological Survey—County Mayo* (limited distribution). Office of Public Works, Dublin.

Bradley, J. and Dunne, N. 1990 *Urban Archaeological Survey—County Galway* (limited distribution). Office of Public Works, Dublin.

Bradley, J. and King, H.A. 1988 *Urban Archaeological Survey—County Dublin* (limited distribution). Office of Public Works, Dublin.

Bradley, J. and King, H.A. 1989a *Urban Archaeological Survey—County Wicklow* (limited distribution). Office of Public Works, Dublin.

Bradley, J. and King, H.A. 1989b *Urban Archaeological Survey—County Carlow* (limited distribution). Office of Public Works, Dublin.

Bradley, J. and King, H.A. 1990 *Urban Archaeological Survey—County Wexford* (limited distribution). Office of Public Works, Dublin.

Bradley, J., Halpin, A. and King, H.A. 1989a *Urban Archaeological Survey—County Waterford* (limited distribution). Office of Public Works, Dublin.

Bradley, J., Halpin, A. and King, H.A. 1989b *Urban Archaeological Survey—County Limerick* (limited distribution). Office of Public Works, Dublin.

Brannon, N.F. 1984 A small excavation in Tildarg townland, near Ballyclare, County

Antrim. *Ulster Journal of Archaeology* **47**, 163–70.

Brindley, A. 1986 *Archaeological Inventory of County Monaghan*. Dublin.

Brindley, A. and Kilfeather, A. 1993 *Archaeological Inventory of County Carlow*. Dublin.

Brooks, E. St J. 1950 *Knights' fees in Counties Wexford, Carlow and Kilkenny (13th to 15th century)*. Dublin.

Brown, R.A. 1963 The Angevin kings 1154–1216. In H.M. Colvin (ed.), *The history of the kings' works*, vol. 1, 51–91. London.

Brown, R.A. 1976 *English castles* (3rd edn). London.

Brown, R.A. 1985 *Castles*. Princes Risborough.

Brown, T. 1981 *Ireland, a social and cultural history, 1922–79*. Glasgow.

Buchanan, R.H. 1970 Rural settlement in Ireland. In N. Stephens and R.E. Glasscock (eds), *Irish geographical studies*, 146–61. Belfast.

Buckley, V.M. 1986 *Archaeological Inventory of County Louth*. Dublin.

Buckley, V.M. and Sweetman, P.D. 1991 *Archaeological Survey of County Louth*. Dublin.

Cairns, C.T. 1987 *Irish tower-houses, a Co. Tipperary case study*. Athlone.

Cairns, C.T. 1991 The Irish tower house—a military view. *Fortress* **11**, 3–13.

Canny, N. 1989 Early Modern Ireland, *c.* 1500–1700. In R.F. Foster (ed.), *The Oxford illustrated history of Ireland*, 104–60. Oxford and New York.

Champneys, A.C. 1910 *Irish ecclesiastical architecture*. London and Dublin.

Childe, V.G. 1938 Doonmore, a castle mound near Fair Head, Co. Antrim. *Ulster Journal of Archaeology* **1**, 122–35.

Childs, W. and O'Neill, T. 1987 Overseas trade. In A. Cosgrove (ed.), *A New History of Ireland, vol. II. Medieval Ireland, 1169–1534*, 439–91. Oxford.

Claffey, J.A. 1974–5 Ballintubber Castle, Co. Roscommon. *Journal of the Old Athlone Society* **1** (4), 218–21.

Clarke, H. 1984 *The archaeology of medieval England*. London.

Clarke, M. 1944 The Black Castle, Wicklow. *Journal of the Royal Society of Antiquaries of Ireland* **74**, 1–22.

Cleary, R.M. 1982 Excavations at Lough Gur, Co. Limerick: Part II. *Journal of the Cork Archaeological and Historical Society* **87**, 77–106.

Cleary, R.M. 1983 Excavations at Lough Gur, Co. Limerick: Part III. *Journal of the Cork Historical and Archaeological Society* **88**, 51–80.

Colfer, W. 1996 In search of the barricade and ditch of Ballyconnor, Co. Wexford. *Archaeology Ireland* **10** (2), 16–19.

Collins, A.E.P. 1955 Excavations in Lough Faughan crannog, Co. Down. *Ulster Journal of Archaeology* **18**, 45–81.

Cooney, G. 1995 Theory and practice in Irish archaeology. In P.J. Ucko (ed.), *Theory in archaeology—a world perspective*, 263–77. London and New York.

Cooney, G. 1997 Building the future on the past: archaeology and the construction of national identity in Ireland. In M. Diaz-Andreu and T. Champion (eds), *Nationalism and archaeology in Europe*, 146–63. London.

Cooney, G. and Grogan, E. 1994 *Irish prehistory—a social perspective*. Dublin.

Cosgrove, A. 1987a England and Ireland. In A. Cosgrove (ed.), *A New History of Ireland, vol. II. Medieval Ireland, 1169–1534*, 525–36. Oxford.

Cosgrove, A. 1987b The emergence of the Pale, 1399–1447. In A. Cosgrave (ed.), *A New History of Ireland, vol. II. Medieval Ireland, 1169–1534*, 533–56. Oxford.

Cosgrove, A. (ed.) 1994 *A New History of Ireland, vol. II. Medieval Ireland 1169–1534* (2nd edn). Oxford.

Cotter, C. 1987 Ferrycarrig, Newtown. In C. Cotter (ed.), *Excavations 1986—summary accounts of archaeological excavations in Ireland*, 37. Dublin.

Cotter, C. 1988 Ferrycarrig, Newtown. In I. Bennett (ed.), *Excavations 1987—summary accounts of archaeological excavations in Ireland*, 30–1. Bray.

Counihan, J. 1990 Ella Armitage, castle studies pioneer. *Fortress* **6**, 51–9.

Counihan, J. 1991 Mottes, Norman or not. *Fortress* **11**, 53–60.

Craig, M. 1982 *The architecture of Ireland from the earliest times to 1880*. London and

Dublin.

Crawford, H.S. 1909 The ruins of Loughmoe Castle, Co. Tipperary. *Journal of the Royal Society of Antiquaries of Ireland* **39**, 234–41.

Crawford, H.S. 1919 The mural paintings and inscriptions at Knockmoy Abbey. *Journal of the Royal Society of Antiquaries of Ireland* **49**, 25–34.

Culleton, E. and Colfer, W. 1974–5 The Norman motte at Old Ross, method of construction. *Journal of the Old Wexford Society* **5**, 22–5.

Cunningham, G. 1987 *The Anglo-Norman advance in the south-west midlands of Ireland, 1185–1221.* Roscrea.

Curtis, E. 1936 Rental of the manor of Lisronagh, 1333, and notes on 'betagh' tenure in medieval Ireland. *Proceedings of the Royal Irish Academy* **43C**, 41–76.

Curtis, E. 1938 *History of medieval Ireland from 1110 to 1513.* London.

Daniels, G. 1950 *A hundred years of archaeology.* London.

Davies, O. 1946 Excavation of a crannog at Deredis Upper in Lough Inchin, Co. Cavan. *Journal of the Royal Society of Antiquaries of Ireland* **74**, 19–34.

Davies, O. 1947 The castles of Co. Cavan. *Ulster Journal of Archaeology* **10**, 78–81.

Davies, O. 1948 The churches of Co. Cavan. *Journal of the Royal Society of Antiquaries of Ireland* **78**, 73–118.

Davies, O. 1950 *Excavations at Island MacHugh.* Belfast.

Davies, O. and Quinn, D.B. (eds) 1941 The Irish pipe roll of 14 John. *Ulster Journal of Archaeology* **4** (supplement).

Davies, O. and Swan, H.P. 1939 The castles of Inishowen. *Ulster Journal of Archaeology* **2**, 178–207.

Davison, B.K. 1961–2 Excavations at Ballynarry, Co. Down. *Ulster Journal of Archaeology* **23**, 39–87.

Deevy, M.B. 1998 *Medieval ring brooches in Ireland. A study of jewellery, dress and society.* Bray.

De Paor, L. 1962 Excavations at Ballyloughan Castle, Co. Carlow. *Journal of the Royal Society of Antiquaries of Ireland* **92**, 1–14.

De Paor, L. 1967 Cormac's Chapel: the beginnings of Irish Romanesque. In E. Rynne (ed.), *North Munster studies*, 133–45. Limerick.

De Paor, L. 1969 Excavations at Mellifont Abbey, Co. Louth. *Proceedings of the Royal Irish Academy* **68C**, 109–64.

Dickinson, C.W. and Waterman, D.M. 1959 Excavations of a rath with motte at Castleskreen, Co. Down. *Ulster Journal of Archaeology* **22**, 67–82.

Doherty, C. 1980 Exchange and trade in early medieval Ireland. *Journal of the Royal Society of Antiquaries of Ireland* **110**, 67–89.

Doherty, C. 1985 The monastic town in early medieval Ireland. In H.B. Clarke and A. Simms (eds), *The comparative history of urban origins in non-Roman Europe*, 45–75. Oxford.

Dolley, M. 1972 *Anglo-Norman Ireland.* Dublin.

Doody, M.G. 1987 Moated site, Ballyveelish I, Co. Tipperary. In R.M. Cleary, M.F. Hurley and E.A. Twohig (eds), *Archaeological excavations on the Cork–Dublin gas pipeline (1981–82)*, 74–87. Cork Archaeological Studies 1.

Down, K. 1987 Colonial society and economy in the High Middle Ages. In A. Cosgrove (ed.), *A New History of Ireland, Vol. II. Medieval Ireland, 1169–1534*, 439–91. Oxford.

Duffy, S. 1997 *Ireland in the Middle Ages.* Dublin.

Dunbar, J. 1981 The medieval architecture of the Scottish Highlands. In L. Maclean (ed.), *The Middle Ages in the Highlands*, 38–61. Inverness.

Dunlevy, M. 1989 *Dress in Ireland.* London.

Eagar, B. 1988 The Cambro-Normans and the lordship of Leinster. In J. Bradley (ed.), *Settlement and society in medieval Ireland*, 193–206. Kilkenny.

Edwards, K.J., Hamond, F.W. and Simms, A. 1983 The medieval settlement of Newcastle Lyons, Co. Dublin: an interdisciplinary approach. *Proceedings of the*

Royal Irish Academy **83C**, 351–76.

Edwards, N. 1990 *The archaeology of early medieval Ireland*. London.

Ellis, S.G. 1985 *Tudor Ireland*. London and New York.

Ellis, S.G. 1996 The Tudors. In T. Bartlett and K. Jeffrey (eds), *A military history of Ireland*, 116–35. Cambridge.

Emery, F.V. 1962 Moated settlements in England. *Geography* **47**, 378–87.

Empey, C.A. 1982 Medieval Knocktopher: a study in manorial settlement—part 1. *Old Kilkenny Review* **2** (4), 329–42.

Empey, C.A. 1983 Medieval Knocktopher: a study in manorial settlement—part 2. *Old Kilkenny Review* **2** (5), 441–52.

Empey, C.A. 1985 The Norman period: 1185–1500. In W. Nolan and T.G. McGrath (eds), *Tipperary: history and society*, 71–91. Dublin.

Empey, C.A. 1988 The Anglo-Norman settlement in the cantred of Eliogarty. In J. Bradley (ed.), *Settlement and society in medieval Ireland*, 207–28. Kilkenny.

Empey, C.A. 1990 County Kilkenny in the Anglo-Norman period. In W. Nolan and K. Whelan (eds), *Kilkenny: history and society*, 75–95, 646–9. Dublin.

Eogan, G. 1997 *The Discovery Programme: initiation, consolidation and development*. Negentiende Kroon-Voordracht, Amsterdam.

Estyn-Evans, E. 1942 *Irish heritage—the landscape, the people and their work*. Dundalk.

Estyn-Evans, E. 1957 *Irish folk-ways*. London.

Fanning, T. 1973–4 Excavation of a ringfort at Pollardstown, Co. Kildare. *Journal of the Kildare Archaeological Society* **15**, 251–61.

Fanning, T. 1975 An Irish medieval tile pavement: recent excavations at Swords Castle, County Dublin. *Journal of the Royal Society of Antiquaries of Ireland* **105**, 47–82.

Fanning, T. 1976 Excavations at Clontuskert Priory, County Galway. *Proceedings of the Royal Irish Academy* **76C**, 97–169.

Farrell, R.T. and Buckley, V.M. 1984 Preliminary examination of the potential of off-shore and underwater sites in Lough Ennell and Analla, Co. Westmeath, Ireland. *International Journal of Nautical Archaeology and Underwater Exploration* **13** (14), 281–5.

Fitzgerald, W. 1896–9 Castle Rheban. *Journal of the County Kildare Archaeological Society* **2**, 167–78.

FitzPatrick, E. 1998 The practice and siting of royal inauguration in medieval Ireland. Unpublished PhD thesis, Trinity College Dublin.

Fitzpatrick, J.E. 1927 Ballymote Castle. *Journal of the Royal Society of Antiquaries of Ireland* **57**, 81–99.

Fitzpatrick, J.E. 1935 Rinndown Castle. *Journal of the Royal Society of Antiquaries of Ireland* **65**, 177–90.

Flanagan, M.T. 1989 *Irish society, Anglo-Norman settlers, Angevin kingship*. Oxford.

Flanagan, M.T. 1993 Anglo-Norman change and continuity: the castle of Telach Cail in Delbna. *Irish Historical Studies* **28**, 385–9.

Fleming, J.S. 1909 Irish and Scottish castles and keeps contrasted. *Journal of the Royal Society of Antiquaries of Ireland* **39**, 174–91.

Foley, C. 1989 Excavation at a medieval settlement site in Jerpoint Church Townland, Co. Kilkenny. *Proceedings of the Royal Irish Academy* **89C**, 71–126.

Frame, R. 1981 *Colonial Ireland, 1169–1369*. Dublin.

Gailey, A. 1987 Changes in Irish rural housing. In P. O'Flanagan, P. Ferguson and K. Whelan (eds), *Rural Ireland—modernisation and change, 1600–1900*, 86–103. Cork.

Glasscock, R. 1968 Kilmagoura. *Medieval Archaeology* **12**, 196–7.

Glasscock, R.E. 1970 Moated sites and deserted boroughs and villages: two neglected aspects of Anglo-Norman settlement in Ireland. In N. Stephens and R.E. Glasscock (eds), *Irish geographical studies*, 162–77. Belfast.

Glasscock, R.E. 1971 The study of deserted medieval settlements in Ireland (to 1969). In M.W. Beresford and J.G. Hurst (eds), *Deserted medieval villages: studies*,

279–301. London.

Glasscock, R.E. 1975 Mottes in Ireland. *Château Gaillard* **7**, 95–110.

Glasscock, R.E. 1987 Land and people, *c.* 1300. In A. Cosgrove (eds), *A New History of Ireland, Vol. II. Medieval Ireland, 1169–1534*, 203–39. Oxford.

Glasscock, R.E. and McNeill, T.E. 1972 Mottes in Ireland: a draft list. *Bulletin of the Group for the Study of Irish Historic Settlement* **3**, 27–51.

Gleeson, D.F. 1936a Drawing of a hunting scene, Urlan Castle, Co. Clare. *Journal of the Royal Society of Antiquaries of Ireland* **66**, 193.

Gleeson, D.F. 1936b The castle and manor of Dromineer, Co. Tipperary. *North Munster Antiquarian Journal* **22–8**, 84.

Gleeson, D.F. and Leask, H.G. 1936 The castle and manor of Nenagh: with a description of the buildings. *Journal of the Royal Society of Antiquaries of Ireland* **66**, 247–69.

Gosling, P. 1993 *Archaeological Inventory of County Galway: Volume 1—West Galway.* Dublin.

Gowen, M. 1978 Dunboy Castle, Co. Cork. *Journal of the Cork Historical and Archaeological Society* **83**, 1–49.

Graham, B.J. 1975 Anglo-Norman settlement in Co. Meath. *Proceedings of the Royal Irish Academy* **75C**, 223–48.

Graham, B.J. 1977a The documentation of medieval Irish boroughs. *Bulletin of the Group for the Study of Irish Historic Settlement* **4**, 9–20.

Graham, B.J. 1977b The towns of medieval Ireland. In R.A. Butlin (ed.), *The development of the Irish town,* 28–60. London.

Graham, B.J. 1978 The documentation of medieval Irish boroughs. *Bulletin of the Group for the Study of Irish Historic Settlement* **5**, 41–5.

Graham, B.J. 1979 The evolution of urbanisation in medieval Ireland. *Journal of Historical Geography* **5**, 111–25.

Graham, B.J. 1980 The mottes of the Norman liberty of Meath. In H. Murtagh (ed.), *Irish midland studies,* 39–56. Athlone.

Graham, B.J. 1985a Anglo-Norman manorial settlement in Ireland: an assessment. *Irish Geography* **18**, 4–15.

Graham, B.J. 1985b *Anglo-Norman settlement in Ireland.* Athlone.

Graham, B.J. 1988a Medieval settlement in Co. Roscommon. *Proceedings of the Royal Irish Academy* **88C**, 19–38.

Graham, B.J. 1988b Timber and earthwork fortifications in western Ireland. *Medieval Archaeology* **32**, 110–29.

Graham, B.J. 1991 Twelfth and thirteenth century earthwork castles in Ireland: an assessment. *Fortress* **9**, 24–34.

Graham, B.J. 1993 The High Middle Ages: *c.* 1100–*c.* 1350. In B.J. Graham and L.J. Proudfoot (eds), *A historical geography of Ireland,* 58–98. London.

Greene, K. 1983 *Archaeology, an introduction.* London.

Grogan, E. 1989 The early prehistory of the Lough Gur region. Unpublished PhD thesis, University College Dublin.

Grogan, E. and Kilfeather, A. 1997 *Archaeological Inventory of County Wicklow.* Dublin.

Gwynn, A. and Hadcock, R.N. 1970 *Medieval religious houses, Ireland.* Dublin.

Haggarty, G. and Tabraham, C. 1982 Excavations of a motte near Roberton, Clydesdale, 1979. *Transactions of the Dumfriesshire and Galloway Natural History and Antiquarian Society* **57**, 51–64.

Hague, D. and Warhurst, C. 1966 Excavations at Sycharth Castle, Denbighshire, 1962–63. *Archaeologia Cambrensis* **115**, 108–27.

Hall, D.N., Hennessey, M. and O'Keeffe, T. 1985 Medieval agriculture and settlement in Oughterward and Castlewarden, Co. Kildare. *Irish Geography* **18**, 16–25.

Halpin, E. 1989 Saucerstown. In I. Bennett (ed.), *Excavations 1988—summary accounts of archaeological excavations in Ireland,* 17–18. Bray.

Harbison, P. 1971 Some medieval Thomond tomb sculpture: lost, found, and imaginary. *North Munster Antiquarian Journal* **14**, 29–36.

Harbison, P. 1973 Some medieval sculpture in Kerry. *Kerry Archaeological Society Journal* **6**, 9–25.

Harbison, P. 1975a *Guide to the national monuments in the Republic of Ireland* (2nd edn). Dublin.

Harbison, P. 1975b Twelfth and thirteenth century Irish stonemasons in Regensburg (Bavaria) and the end of the 'School of the West' in Connacht. *Studies* **64**, 333–46.

Harbison, P. 1977 Some further sculpture in Ennis Priory. *North Munster Antiquarian Journal* **19**, 39–42.

Harbison, P. 1988 *Pre-Christian Ireland*. London.

Hayes-McCoy, G.A. 1940–1 Strategy and tactics in Irish warfare, 1593–1601. *Irish Historical Studies* **2**, 255–79.

Hayes-McCoy, G.A. 1964 *Ulster and other Irish maps, c. 1600*. Dublin.

Hayes-McCoy, G.A. 1969 *Irish battles*. London.

Hennessey, M. 1985 Parochial organisation in medieval Tipperary. In W. Nolan and T.G. McGrath (eds), *Tipperary: history and society*, 60–70. Dublin.

Hennessey, M. 1996 Manorial organisation in early thirteenth-century Tipperary. *Irish Geography* **29**, 116–25.

Henry, F. 1966 Irish Cistercian monasteries and their carved decoration. *Apollo* **84**, 260–7.

Herity, M. 1988 A survey of the royal site of Cruachain in Connacht—IV. Ancient field systems at Rathcroghan and Carnfree. *Journal of the Royal Society of Antiquaries of Ireland* **118**, 67–84.

Herity, M. 1991 *Rathcroghan and Carnfree—Celtic royal sites in Roscommon*. Dublin.

Herity, M. and Eogan, G. 1977 *Ireland in prehistory*. London and Boston.

Higham, R.A. 1989 Timber castles—a reassessment. *Fortress* **1**, 50–60.

Higham, R. and Barker, P. 1992 *Timber castles*. London.

Hodkinson, B. 1995 The Rock of Dunamase. *Archaeology Ireland* **9** (2), 18–21.

Holland, P. 1993–4 The thirteenth-century remains of Cahir Castle, Co. Tipperary. *North Munster Antiquarian Journal* **35**, 62–71.

Holland, P. 1994 Anglo-Norman Galway; rectangular earthworks and moated sites. *Journal of the Galway Archaeological and Historical Society* **46**, 203–11.

Holland, P. 1997 The Anglo-Norman landscape in County Galway: land-holding, castles and settlements. *Journal of the Galway Archaeological and Historical Society* **49**, 159–93.

Hore, H.F. 1900–11 *A history of the town and county of Wexford* (6 vols). London.

Hunt, J. 1946 Clonroad More, Ennis. *Journal of the Royal Society of Antiquaries of Ireland* **76**, 195–209.

Hunt, J. 1950 Rory O'Tunney and the Ossory tomb sculptures. *Journal of the Royal Society of Antiquaries of Ireland* **80**, 22–8.

Hunt, J. 1960 Bunratty Castle. *North Munster Antiquarian Journal* **8** (3), 103–8.

Hunt, J. 1974 *Irish medieval figure sculpture, 1200–1600: a study of Irish tombs, with notes on costume and armour* (2 vols). Dublin and London.

Hurley, M.F. 1987 Kilferagh, Co. Kilkenny. Corn-drying kiln and settlement site. In R.M. Cleary, M.F. Hurley and E.A. Twohig (eds), *Archaeological excavations on the Cork–Dublin gas pipeline (1981–82)*, 88–100. Cork Archaeological Studies 1.

Ivens, R.J., Simpson, D. and Brown, D. 1986 Excavations at Island MacHugh, 1985—interim report. *Ulster Journal of Archaeology* **49**, 99–103.

Jones-Hughes, T. 1970 Town and baile in Irish place names. In N. Stephens and R.E. Glasscock (eds), *Irish geographical studies*, 244–58. Belfast.

Jope, E.M., Jope, H.M. and Johnson, E.A. 1966 *An Archaeological Survey of County Down*. Belfast.

Jordan, A. 1990 The tower houses of County Wexford. Unpublished PhD thesis, Trinity College Dublin.

Jordan, A.J. 1990–1 Date, chronology and evolution of the County Wexford tower house. *Journal of the Wexford Historical Society* **13**, 30–82.

Kelly, F. 1997 *Early Irish farming*. Dublin.

Kelly, R.J. 1913 Dungory Castle, Kinvara. *Journal of the Royal Society of Antiquaries of Ireland* **33**, 114–31.

Kenyon, J. 1990 *Medieval fortifications*. Leicester and London.

King, D.C. 1988 *The castle in England and Wales*. London and Sydney.

King, H.A. 1984 Late medieval crosses in County Meath, *c.* 1470–1635. *Proceedings of the Royal Irish Academy* **84C**, 79–115.

Langrishe, R. 1906 Notes on Jerpoint Abbey, County Kilkenny. *Journal of the Royal Society of Antiquaries of Ireland* **36**, 179–97.

Lawlor, H.C. 1938 Mote and mote-and-bailey castles in de Courcy's principality of Ulster. *Ulster Journal of Archaeology* **1**, 155–64.

Lawlor, H.C. 1939 Mote and mote-and-bailey castles in de Courcy's principality of Ulster. *Ulster Journal of Archaeology* **2**, 46–54.

Lawlor, H.J. 1917 The monuments of the pre-Reformation archbishops of Dublin. *Journal of the Royal Society of Antiquaries of Ireland* **47**, 109–38.

Lawlor, H.J. 1923 The chapel of Dublin Castle. *Journal of the Royal Society of Antiquaries of Ireland* **53**, 34–73.

Lawlor, H. J. 1928 The chapel of Dublin Castle. *Journal of the Royal Society of Antiquaries of Ireland* **58**, 44–53.

Leask, H.G. 1914 Swords Castle. *Journal of the Royal Society of Antiquaries of Ireland* **64**, 259–63.

Leask, H.G. 1916 Bective Abbey, Co. Meath. *Journal of the Royal Society of Antiquaries of Ireland* **46**, 46–57.

Leask, H.G. 1936 [1937] Irish castles, 1180–1310. *Archaeological Journal* **93**, 143–99.

Leask, H.G. 1937 Clara Castle, Co. Kilkenny. *Journal of the Royal Society of Antiquaries of Ireland* **67**, 284–9.

Leask, H.G. 1941 *Irish castles and castellated houses* (1st edn). Dundalk.

Leask, H.G. 1943 Terryglass Castle, Co. Tipperary. *Journal of the Royal Society of Antiquaries of Ireland* **53**, 141–3.

Leask, H.G. 1944 Ballymoon Castle, Co. Carlow. *Journal of the Royal Society of Antiquaries of Ireland* **74**, 183–90.

Leask, H.G. 1948 Irish Cistercian monasteries: a pedigree and distribution map. *Journal of the Royal Society of Antiquaries of Ireland* **78**, 63–4.

Leask, H.G. 1951 Slade Castle, Co. Wexford. *Journal of the Royal Society of Antiquaries of Ireland* **81**, 198–203.

Leask, H.G. 1953 Rathmacknee Castle, Co. Wexford. *Journal of the Royal Society of Antiquaries of Ireland* **83**, 37–45.

Leask, H.G. 1955–60 *Irish churches and monastic buildings* (3 vols). Dundalk.

Leister, I. 1976 *Peasant openfield farming and its territorial organisation in Co. Tipperary.* Marburg/Lahn.

Long, H. 1994 Three settlements of Gaelic Wicklow: Rathgall, Ballinacor, and Glendalough. In K. Hannigan and W. Nolan (eds), *Wicklow: history and society,* 237–65. Dublin.

Long, H. 1997 Medieval Glendalough: an interdisciplinary study. Unpublished PhD thesis, Trinity College Dublin.

Lucas, A.T. 1973 Irish ploughing practices. Part Two. *Tools and Tillage* **2** (2), 67–83.

Lucas, A.T. 1974 Irish ploughing practices. Part Three. *Tools and Tillage* **2** (3), 149–60.

Lucas, A.T. 1975 Irish ploughing practices. Part Four. *Tools and Tillage* **2** (4), 195–210.

Lucas, A.T. 1989 *Cattle in ancient Ireland*. Kilkenny.

Lydon, J.F.M. 1963 Richard II's expedition to Ireland. *Journal of the Royal Society of Antiquaries of Ireland* **93**, 135–49.

Lydon, J.F.M. 1973 *Ireland in the Later Middle Ages*. Dublin.

Lydon, J.F.M. 1987a The expansion and consolidation of the colony, 1215–54. In A. Cosgrove (ed.), *A New History of Ireland, vol. II. Medieval Ireland, 1169–1534,*

156–78. Oxford.

Lydon, J.F.M. 1987b A land of war. In A. Cosgrove (ed.), *A New History of Ireland, vol. II. Medieval Ireland, 1169–1534*, 240–74. Oxford.

Lydon, J.F.M. 1987c The impact of the Bruce Invasion, 1315–1327. In A. Cosgrove (ed.), *A New History of Ireland, vol. II. Medieval Ireland, 1169–1534*, 275–302. Oxford.

Lynn, C.J. 1975a The dating of raths: an orthodox view. *Ulster Journal of Archaeology* **38**, 45–7.

Lynn, C.J. 1975b The medieval ring-fort—an archaeological chimera. *Irish Archaeological Research Forum* **2**, 29–36.

Lynn, C.J. 1981–2 The excavation of Rathmullan, a raised rath and motte in County Down. *Ulster Journal of Archaeology* **44–5**, 65–171.

Lynn, C.J. 1983 Some early ringforts and crannogs. *Journal of Irish Archaeology* **1**, 47–58.

Lynn, C.J. 1985–6 Some 13th century castle sites in the west of Ireland: notes on a preliminary reconnaissance. *Journal of the Galway Archaeological and Historical Society* **40**, 90–113.

Lyons, P. 1937 Norman antiquities at Lisronagh, Co. Tipperary. *Journal of the Royal Society of Antiquaries of Ireland* **67**, 242–9.

Macalister, R.A.S. 1913 The Dominican church at Athenry. *Journal of the Royal Society of Antiquaries of Ireland* **43**, 197–222.

Macalister, R.A.S. 1928 *The archaeology of Ireland*. London.

McAuliffe, M. 1991a The use of tower houses and fastnesses in the Desmond Rebellions, 1565–1583. *Journal of the Kerry Archaeological and Historical Society* **24**, 105–12.

McAuliffe, M. 1991b The tower houses of County Kerry. Unpublished PhD thesis, Trinity College Dublin.

MacCurtain, M. 1972 *Tudor and Stuart Ireland*. Dublin.

MacCurtain, M. 1988 A lost landscape: the Geraldine castles and tower houses of the Shannon Estuary. In J. Bradley (ed.), *Settlement and society in medieval Ireland*, 429–44. Kilkenny.

MacDermot, D. 1996 *MacDermot of Moylurg*. Manorhamilton.

McDonald, T. 1997 *Achill Island*. Tullamore.

MacNamara, G.V. 1912 The O'Davorens of Cahermacnaughton, Co. Clare. *North Munster Antiquarian Journal* **2** (2), 63–93.

McNeill, T.E. 1975a Medieval raths? An Anglo-Norman comment. *Irish Archaeological Research Forum* **2**, 37–9.

McNeill, T.E. 1975b Ulster mottes; a checklist. *Ulster Journal of Archaeology* **38**, 49–56.

McNeill, T.E. 1977 Excavations at Doonbought Fort, Co. Antrim. *Ulster Journal of Archaeology* **40**, 63–84.

McNeill, T.E. 1980 *Anglo-Norman Ulster*. Edinburgh.

McNeill, T.E. 1981 *Carrickfergus Castle*. Belfast.

McNeill, T.E. 1983 The stone castles of northern Co. Antrim. *Ulster Journal of Archaeology* **46**, 101–28.

McNeill, T.E. 1989–90 Early castles in Leinster. *Journal of Irish Archaeology* **5**, 57–64.

McNeill, T.E. 1990a Trim Castle, Co. Meath; the first three generations. *Archaeological Journal* **147**, 308–36.

McNeill, T.E. 1990b Hibernia pacata et castellata. *Chateau Gaillard* **14**, 261–75.

McNeill, T.E. 1991 Excavations at Dunsilly, Co. Antrim. *Ulster Journal of Archaeology* **54**, 78–112.

McNeill, T.E. 1992a *Castles*. London.

McNeill, T.E. 1992b The origin of tower houses. *Archaeology Ireland* **6** (1), 13–14.

McNeill, T.E. 1993 The outer gate house at Dunamase Castle, Co. Laois. *Medieval Archaeology* **37**, 236–8.

McNeill, T.E. 1997 *Castles in Ireland, feudal power in a Gaelic world*. London and New

York.

Maguire, J.B. 1974 Seventeenth century plans of Dublin Castle. *Journal of the Royal Society of Antiquaries of Ireland* **104**, 5–14.

Mallory, J. and McNeill, T.E. 1991 *The archaeology of Ulster.* Belfast.

Manning, C. 1990 *Clogh Oughter Castle, Cavan.* Cavan.

Meenan, R. 1985 The deserted villages of County Westmeath. Unpublished MLitt thesis, Trinity College Dublin.

Mitchell, F. 1986 *The Shell Guide to reading the Irish landscape.* Dublin.

Mooney, C. 1955 Franciscan architecture in pre-Reformation Ireland. *Journal of the Royal Society of Antiquaries of Ireland* **85**, 133–73.

Mooney, C. 1956 Franciscan architecture in pre-Reformation Ireland. *Journal of the Royal Society of Antiquaries of Ireland* **86**, 125–69.

Mooney, C. 1957 Franciscan architecture in pre-Reformation Ireland. *Journal of the Royal Society of Antiquaries of Ireland* **87**, 1–38, 103–24.

Moore, M. 1987 *Archaeological Inventory of County Meath.* Dublin.

Moore, M. 1996 *Archaeological Inventory of County Wexford.* Dublin.

Murray, H.K. and Murray, J.C. 1993 Excavations at Rattray, Aberdeenshire, a Scottish deserted borough. *Medieval Archaeology* **37**, 109–218.

Murtagh, B. 1993 The Kilkenny Castle archaeological project, 1990–1993: interim report. *Old Kilkenny Review* **45**, 101–17.

Murtagh, B. 1994 Archaeological investigations at Dysart, Co. Kilkenny, 1989–1994: an interim report. *Old Kilkenny Review* **46**, 78–94.

Murtagh, D. 1993 The Anglo-Norman earthworks of Co. Kildare, 1169–1350. Unpublished PhD thesis, Trinity College Dublin.

Mytum, H. 1992 *The origins of Early Christian Ireland.* London.

Newman, C. 1997 *Tara—an archaeological survey.* Discovery Programme Monograph 2. Dublin.

Nicholls, K.W. 1969–72 The Register of Clogher. *Clogher Record* **7**, 361–431.

Nicholls, K.W. 1972 *Gaelic and Gaelicised Ireland in the Middle Ages.* Dublin.

Nicholls, K.W. 1982 Anglo-French Ireland and after. *Peritia* **1**, 370–403.

Nicholls, K.W. 1985 Gaelic landownership in Tipperary from the surviving Irish deeds. In W. Nolan and T.G. McGrath (eds), *Tipperary: history and society*, 92–103. Dublin.

Nicholls, K.W. 1987 Gaelic society and economy in the High Middle Ages. In A. Cosgrove (ed.), *A New History of Ireland, vol. II. Medieval Ireland, 1169–1534,* 397–438. Oxford.

O'Brien, C. and Sweetman, P.D. 1997 *Archaeological Inventory of County Offaly.* Dublin.

Ó Conbhuí, C. 1962 The lands of St Mary's Abbey, Dublin. *Proceedings of the Royal Irish Academy* **62C**, 21–84.

O'Conor, K.D. 1986 The Anglo-Norman period in Co. Laois. Unpublished MA thesis, University College Dublin.

O'Conor, K.D. 1987–91 The later construction and use of motte and bailey castles in Ireland: new evidence from Leinster. *Journal of the Kildare Archaeological Society* **17**, 13–29.

O'Conor, K.D. 1992 Irish earthwork castles. *Fortress* **12**, 1–12.

O'Conor, K.D. 1993 The earthwork castles of medieval Leinster. Unpublished PhD thesis, University College Cardiff.

O'Conor, K.D. 1996 Dunamase Castle. *Journal of Irish Archaeology* **7**, 107–25.

O'Conor, K.D. 1997 The origins of Carlow Castle. *Archaeology Ireland* **11** (3), 13–16.

O'Conor, K.D. 1998 The moated site on Inishatirra Island, Drumharlow Lough, Co. Roscommon. *County Roscommon Historical and Archaeological Society Journal* **7**, 1–3.

O'Conor, K.D. (forthcoming) Anglo-Norman castles in Co. Laois. In P. Lane (ed.), *Laois—history and society.* Dublin.

O'Conor, K.D., Keegan, M. and Tiernan, P. 1996 Tulsk Abbey. *County Roscommon*

Historical and Archaeological Society Journal **6**, 67–9.

Ó Corráin, D. 1972 *Ireland before the Normans*. Dublin.

Ó Corráin, D. 1978 Nationality and kingship in pre-Norman Ireland. *Historical Studies* **11**, 1–35.

Ó Corráin, D. 1989 Prehistoric and Early Christian Ireland. In R. Foster (ed.), *The Oxford illustrated history of Ireland*, 1–52. Oxford.

Ó Cróinín, D. 1995 *Early medieval Ireland, 400–1200*. London.

Ó Danachair, C. 1977–9 Irish tower houses. *Bealoidas* **45–7**, 158–63.

Ó Domhnaill, S. 1946–7 Warfare in sixteenth century Ireland. *Irish Historical Studies* **5** (17), 29–54.

O'Donovan, P.F. 1995 *Archaeological Inventory of County Cavan*. Dublin.

O'Dowd, A. 1989 Folklife and folk traditions. In D. Gillmor (ed.), *The Irish countryside*, 121–60. Dublin.

O'Dowd, M. 1991 *Power, politics and land: Early Modern Sligo 1568–1688*. Belfast.

Ó Floinn, R. (forthcoming) Anglo-Irish material culture—craft and industry in medieval Ireland. In J. Bradley and G. Cooney (eds), *Irish archaeology from the Vikings to AD 1700*, 111–157. Dublin.

Oibre 1965 *Official Journal of the Office of Public Works* **2**, 22. Dublin.

O'Keeffe, T. 1985–6 The castle of Tullow, Co. Carlow. *Journal of the Kildare Archaeological Society* **16**, 528–9.

O'Keeffe, T. 1987 Rathnageeragh and Ballyloo. *Journal of the Royal Society of Antiquaries of Ireland* **117**, 28–49.

O'Keeffe, T. 1990a The archaeology of Norman castles—part I: mottes and ringworks. *Archaeology Ireland* **4** (3), 15–17.

O'Keeffe, T. 1990b The archaeology of Anglo-Norman castles in Ireland. Part 2: stone castles. *Archaeology Ireland* **4** (4), 20–2.

O'Keeffe, T. 1991 The Irish Romanesque style in architecture and architectural sculpture. Unpublished PhD thesis, University College Dublin.

O'Keeffe, T. 1995a The frontier in medieval Ireland: an archaeological perspective. *Group for the Study of Irish Historic Settlement Newsletter* (Spring 1995), 16–18.

O'Keeffe, T. 1995b Tower-houses of the Pale in east County Kildare, Oughterrany. *Journal of the Donadea Local History Group* **1** (2), 4–11.

O'Keeffe, T. 1996 Rural settlement and cultural identity in Gaelic Ireland, 1000–1500. *Ruralia* **1**, 142–53.

O'Kelly, M.J. 1962 Beal Boru. *Journal of the Cork Historical and Archaeological Society* **67**, 1–27.

O'Kelly, M.J. 1989 *Early Ireland*. Cambridge.

O'Loan, J. 1961 The manor of Cloncurry, County Kildare, and the feudal system of land tenure in Ireland. *Department of Agriculture Journal* **58**, 14–36.

Ó Ríordáin, S.P. 1936 Excavations at Lissard, County Limerick, and other sites in the vicinity. *Journal of the Royal Society of Antiquaries of Ireland* **66**, 173–85.

Ó Ríordáin, S.P. 1979 *Antiquities of the Irish countryside* (5th edn). London.

Ó Ríordáin, S.P. and Hunt, J. 1942 Medieval dwellings at Caherguillamore, County Limerick. *Journal of the Royal Society of Antiquaries of Ireland* **72**, 37–63.

Orpen, G.H. 1906a Mote and bretasche building in Ireland. *English Historical Review* **21**, 417–44.

Orpen, G.H. 1906b The castle of Raymond le Gros at Fodredunolan. *Journal of the Royal Society of Antiquaries of Ireland* **36**, 368–82.

Orpen, G.H. 1907a Athlone Castle: its early history with notes on some neighbouring castles. *Journal of the Royal Society of Antiquaries of Ireland* **37**, 257–76.

Orpen, G.H. 1907b Mottes and Norman castles in Ireland. *English Historical Review* **22**, 228–54.

Orpen, G.H. 1907c Motes and Norman castles in Ireland. *Journal of the Royal Society of Antiquaries of Ireland* **37**, 123–52.

Orpen, G.H. 1908a Castrum Keyvini: Castlekevin. *Journal of the Royal Society of*

Antiquaries of Ireland **38**, 17–27.

Orpen, G.H. 1908b Novum Castrum McKynegan, Newcastle, Co. Wicklow. *Journal of the Royal Society of Antiquaries of Ireland* **38**, 126–40.

Orpen, G.H. 1908c Motes and Norman castles in County Louth. *Journal of the Royal Society of Antiquaries of Ireland* **38**, 241–69.

Orpen, G.H. 1909a Dundrum Castle, Co. Down. Identified with 'Castrum de Rath'. *Journal of the Royal Society of Antiquaries of Ireland* **39**, 23–9.

Orpen, G.H. 1909b Notes on some Co. Limerick castles. *Journal of the Royal Society of Antiquaries of Ireland* **39**, 30–41.

Orpen, G.H. 1909c The mote of Knockgraffon. *Journal of the Royal Society of Antiquaries of Ireland* **39**, 275–7.

Orpen, G.H. 1909d Motes and Norman castles in Ossory. *Journal of the Royal Society of Antiquaries of Ireland* **39**, 313–42.

Orpen, G.H. 1910a The mote of Street, County Westmeath. *Journal of the Royal Society of Antiquaries of Ireland* **40**, 214–22.

Orpen, G.H. 1910b The mote of Lissardowlin, County Longford. *Journal of the Royal Society of Antiquaries of Ireland* **40**, 223–5.

Orpen, G.H. 1910c The mote of Castlelost, Co. Westmeath. *Journal of the Royal Society of Antiquaries of Ireland* **40**, 226–8.

Orpen, G.H. 1911–20 *Ireland under the Normans, 1169–1333* (4 vols). Oxford.

O'Sullivan, A. 1994 Harvesting the waters. *Archaeology Ireland* **8** (1), 10–12.

O'Sullivan, A. 1995a Medieval fishweirs on the Deel Estuary, Co. Limerick. *Archaeology Ireland* **9** (2), 15–17.

O'Sullivan, A. 1995b Medieval fishweirs and coastal settlement in north Munster. *Group for the Study of Irish Historic Settlement Newsletter* **4**, 3–5.

O'Sullivan, A. 1997 Medieval fish traps at Bunratty, Co. Clare. *The Other Clare* **21**, 40–2.

Otway-Ruthven, A.J. 1951 The organisation of Anglo-Irish agriculture in the Middle Ages. *Journal of the Royal Society of Antiquaries of Ireland* **81**, 1–13.

Otway-Ruthven, A.J. 1961 Knights' fees in Kildare, Leix, and Offaly. *Journal of the Royal Society of Antiquaries of Ireland* **91**, 163–81.

Otway-Ruthven, A.J. 1965 The character of Norman settlement in Ireland. *Historical Studies* **5**, 75–84.

Otway-Ruthven, A.J. 1968 *A history of medieval Ireland*. London.

Platt, C. 1978 *Medieval England*. London.

Pollock, A.J. and Waterman, D.M. 1963 A medieval pottery kiln at Downpatrick. *Ulster Journal of Archaeology* **26**, 79–104.

Pounds, N.J.G. 1990 *The medieval castle in England and Wales*. Cambridge.

Power, D., Byrne, E., Egan, U., Lane, S. and Sleeman, M. 1992 *Archaeological Inventory of County Cork: Volume 1—West Cork*. Dublin.

Power, D., Byrne, E., Egan, U., Lane, S. and Sleeman, M. 1994 *Archaeological Inventory of County Cork: Volume 2—East and South Cork*. Dublin.

Power, D., Byrne, E., Egan, U., Lane, S. and Sleeman, M. 1997 *Archaeological Inventory of County Cork: Volume 3—Mid-Cork*. Dublin.

Proudfoot, V.B. 1959 Clachans in Ireland. *Gwerin* **2**, 110–22.

Proudfoot, V.B. 1970 Irish raths and cashels: some notes on origin, chronology and survivals. *Ulster Journal of Archaeology* **33**, 37–48.

Proudfoot, V.B. 1977 Economy and settlement in rural Ireland. In L. Laing (ed.), *Studies in Celtic survival*, 83–106. Oxford.

Quiggin, E.C. 1913 O'Conor's house at Cloonfree. In E.C. Quiggin (ed.), *Essays and studies presented to William Ridgeway*, 333–52. Cambridge.

Rae, E.C. 1966 The sculpture of the cloister of Jerpoint Abbey. *Journal of the Royal Society of Antiquaries of Ireland* **96**, 59–91.

Rae, E.C. 1970 Irish sepulchral monuments of the Later Middle Ages. *Journal of the Royal Society of Antiquaries of Ireland* **100**, 1–38.

Rae, E.C. 1971 Irish sepulchral monuments of the Later Middle Ages, part II. The O'Tunney atelier. *Journal of the Royal Society of Antiquaries of Ireland* **101**, 1–40.

Rae, E.C. 1987 Architecture and sculpture, 1169–1603. In A. Cosgrove (ed.), *A New History of Ireland, Vol. II. Medieval Ireland, 1169–1534*, 737–77. Oxford.

Raftery, B. 1970 The Rathgall hillfort, Co. Wicklow. *Antiquity* **44**, 51–4.

Raftery, B. 1994 *Pagan Celtic Ireland*. London.

Rahtz, P.A. and Hirst, S.M. (eds) 1976 *Bordesley Abbey*. Oxford.

Richter, M. 1988 *Medieval Ireland—the enduring tradition*. Dublin.

Roberts, B.K. 1962 Moated sites in midland England. *Transactions of the Birmingham Archaeological Society* **80**, 26–37.

Roberts, B.K. 1968 Study of medieval colonisation in the Forest of Arden, Warwickshire. *Agricultural History Review* **16**, 101–13.

Robinson, P. 1979 Vernacular housing in Ulster in the 17th century. *Ulster Folklife* **25**, 1–28.

Roe, H. 1968 *Medieval fonts of Meath*. Navan.

Rowley, T. and Wood, J. 1982 *Deserted villages*. Princes Risborough.

Rynne, E. 1963 Some destroyed sites at Shannon Airport, Co. Clare. *Proceedings of the Royal Irish Academy* **63C**, 245–77.

Sandes, C. 1993 The redating of Ham Green ware; some reflections on the Irish evidence. *Trowel* **4**, 1–4.

Sandes, C. (forthcoming) Irish medieval pottery—a proposal. *Medieval Ceramics* **22**.

Simms, A. 1979 Settlement patterns of medieval colonisation in Ireland: the example of Duleek in County Meath. In P. Flatres (ed.), *Paysages ruraux europeéns*, 159–77. Rennes.

Simms, A. 1983 Rural settlement in medieval Ireland: the example of the royal manors of Newcastle Lyons and Esker in south County Dublin. In B.K. Roberts and R.E. Glasscock (eds), *Villages, fields and frontiers*, 133–52. British Archaeological Reports. Oxford.

Simms, A. 1988a Core and periphery in medieval Europe: the Irish experience in a wider context. In W.J. Smith and K. Whelan (eds), *Common ground: essays on the historical geography of Ireland*, 22–40. Cork.

Simms, A. 1988b The geography of Irish manors: the example of the Llanthony cells of Duleek and Colp in County Meath. In J. Bradley (ed.), *Settlement and society in medieval Ireland*, 291–326. Kilkenny.

Simms, K. 1975–6 Warfare in medieval Gaelic lordships. *Irish Sword* **12**, 98–108.

Simms, K. 1987 *From kings to warlords*. Woodbridge.

Simms, K. 1989 The Norman Invasion and Gaelic Recovery. In R.F. Foster (ed.), *The Oxford illustrated history of Ireland*, 53–103. Oxford and New York.

Simpson, M.L., Bryan, P.S., Delaney, T.G. and Dickson, A. 1979 An early thirteenth century double-flued pottery kiln at Carrickfergus, County Antrim, 1972–9. *Medieval Ceramics* **3**, 41–51.

Sleeman, M.J. and Hurley, M.F. 1987 Blackcastle, Co. Kildare. In R.M. Cleary, M.F. Hurley and E.A. Twohig (eds), *Archaeological excavations on the Cork–Dublin gas pipeline (1981–1982)*, 101–5. Cork Archaeological Reports 1.

Smyth, A. 1982 *Celtic Leinster*. Dublin.

Smyth, J. 1954 Crannogs in north Monaghan. *Clogher Record* **1** (2), 1–7.

Smyth, W. 1985 Property, patronage and population: reconstructing the human geography of mid 17th century County Tipperary. In W. Nolan (ed.), *Tipperary: history and society*, 104–38. Dublin.

Stalley, R. 1971 *Architecture and sculpture in Ireland, 1150–1350*. Dublin.

Stalley, R. 1973 *Christ Church, Dublin: the late Romanesque building campaign*. Ballycotton.

Stalley, R. 1975 Corcomroe Abbey: some observations on its architectural history. *Journal of the Royal Society of Antiquaries of Ireland* **105**, 21–46.

Stalley, R. 1977 The long Middle Ages: from the twelfth century to the Reformation.

In B. de Breffny (ed.), *The Irish world,* 71–98. London and New York.

Stalley, R. 1984 Irish Gothic and English fashion. In J. Lydon (ed.), *The English in medieval Ireland,* 65–86. Dublin.

Stalley, R. 1987 *The Cistercian monasteries of Ireland.* London and New Haven.

Stalley, R. 1992 The Anglo-Norman keep at Trim: its architectural implications. *Archaeology Ireland* **6** (4), 16–19.

Stout, G. 1984 *Archaeological survey of the Barony of Ikerrin.* Roscrea.

Stout, M. 1997 *The Irish ringfort.* Dublin.

Sweetman, P.D. 1978 Archaeological excavations at Trim Castle, Co. Meath, 1971–4. *Proceedings of the Royal Irish Academy* **78C,** 127–98.

Sweetman, P.D. 1979 Archaeological excavations at Ferns Castle, County Wexford. *Proceedings of the Royal Irish Academy* **79C,** 217–45.

Sweetman, P.D. 1980 Archaeological excavations at Adare Castle, Co. Limerick. *Journal of the Cork Historical and Archaeological Society* **85,** 1–6.

Sweetman, P.D. 1981 Excavations of a medieval moated site at Rigsdale, County Cork, 1977–8. *Proceedings of the Royal Irish Academy* **81C,** 103–205.

Sweetman, P.D. 1992a Dating Irish castles. *Archaeology Ireland* **3** (4), 136–7.

Sweetman, P.D. 1992b Aspects of early 13th century castles in Leinster. *Chateau Gaillard* **15,** 325–33.

Sweetman, P.D. 1995 *Irish castles and fortified houses.* Dublin.

Sweetman, P.D., Alcock, O. and Moran, B. 1995 *Archaeological Inventory of County Laois.* Dublin.

Talbot, E.J. 1972 Lorrha Motte, County Tipperary. *North Munster Antiquarian Journal* **15,** 8–12.

Thompson, M. 1987 *The decline of the castles.* Cambridge.

Twohig, D.C. 1978 Norman ringwork castles. *Bulletin of the Group for the Study of Irish Historic Settlement* **5,** 7–9.

Wallace, P.F. 1984 A reappraisal of the archaeological significance of Wood Quay. In J. Bradley (ed.), *Viking Dublin exposed,* 112–33. Dublin.

Waterman, D.M. 1951 Excavations at Dundrum Castle. *Ulster Journal of Archaeology* **14,** 15–29.

Waterman, D.M. 1954a Excavations at Clough Castle, County Down. *Ulster Journal of Archaeology* **17,** 103–63.

Waterman, D.M. 1954b Excavations at Dromore Motte, County Down. *Ulster Journal of Archaeology* **17,** 164–8.

Waterman, D.M. 1955 Excavations at Seefin Castle and Ballyroney Motte and Bailey. *Ulster Journal of Archaeology* **18,** 83–104.

Waterman, D.M. 1956 Moylough Castle, Co. Galway. *Journal of the Royal Society of Antiquaries of Ireland* **86,** 73–6.

Waterman, D.M. 1958a Excavations at Ballyfounder Rath, County Down. *Ulster Journal of Archaeology* **21,** 39–61.

Waterman, D.M. 1958b Greencastle, Co. Donegal. *Ulster Journal of Archaeology* **21,** 74–88.

Waterman, D.M. 1959a Excavations at Lismahon, Co. Down. *Medieval Archaeology* **3,** 139–76.

Waterman, D.M. 1959b Pipers Fort, Farranfad, County Down. *Ulster Journal of Archaeology* **22,** 83–7.

Waterman, D.M. 1963 Excavations at Duneight, County Down. *Ulster Journal of Archaeology* **26,** 55–78.

Waterman, D.M. 1964 The water supply of Dundrum Castle, Co. Down. *Ulster Journal of Archaeology* **27,** 136–9.

Waterman, D.M. 1968 Rectangular keeps of the thirteenth century, at Grenan (Kilkenny) and Glanworth (Cork). *Journal of the Royal Society of Antiquaries of Ireland* **98,** 67–73.

Waterman, D.M. 1979 St Mary's Priory, Devenish, excavation of the east range. *Ulster*

Journal of Archaeology **42**, 34–50.

Waterman, D.M. and Collins, A.E.P. 1952 Excavations at Greencastle, Co. Down, 1951. *Ulster Journal of Archaeology* **15**, 87–102.

Watt, J.A. 1972 *The church in medieval Ireland*. Dublin.

Watt, J.A. 1987a Approaches to the history of 14th century Ireland. In A. Cosgrove (ed.), *A New History of Ireland, vol. II. Medieval Ireland, 1169–1534*, 303–13. Oxford.

Watt, J.A. 1987b Gaelic polity and cultural identity. In A. Cosgrove (ed.), *A New History of Ireland, vol. II. Medieval Ireland, 1169–1534*, 314–56. Oxford.

Webb, J. 1824 Translation of a French metrical history of the deposition of King Richard the Second. *Archaeologia* **20**, 1–423.

Westropp, T.J. 1897 Prehistoric stone forts of northern Clare. *Journal of the Royal Society of Antiquaries of Ireland* **27**, 116–27.

Westropp, T.J. 1900–2 The churches of County Clare and the origin of the ecclesiastical divisions in that county. *Proceedings of the Royal Irish Academy* **1C**, 100–80.

Westropp, T.J. 1902 The ancient forts of Ireland: being a contribution towards our knowledge of their types, affinities, and structural features. *Transactions of the Royal Irish Academy* **31**, 579–730.

Westropp, T.J. 1903 On the external evidence relating to the historic character of the Wars of Turlough. *Transactions of the Royal Irish Academy* **32**, 134–96.

Westropp, T.J. 1904 Of Irish mottes and early Norman castles. *Journal of the Royal Society of Antiquaries of Ireland* **34**, 313–45.

Westropp, T.J. 1904–5 A survey of ancient churches in the County of Limerick. *Proceedings of the Royal Irish Academy* **25C**, 327–480.

Westropp, T.J. 1905 Irish mottes and alleged Norman castles: notes on some recent contributions to their study. *Journal of the Royal Society of Antiquaries of Ireland* **35**, 402–6.

Westropp, T.J. 1907a The principal ancient castles of Co. Limerick. *Journal of the Royal Society of Antiquaries of Ireland* **37**, 24–40, 153–64.

Westropp, T.J. 1907b The ancient castles of the County of Limerick. *Proceedings of the Royal Irish Academy* **26C**, 55–108, 143–264.

Westropp, T.J. 1908 Carrigunnell Castle and the O'Briens of Pubblebrian, in the County of Limerick. Part II—the ruins and later families. *Journal of the Royal Society of Antiquaries of Ireland* **38**, 141–59.

Westropp, T.J. 1909 The Desmonds' castle at Newcastle Oconyll, Co. Limerick. *Journal of the Royal Society of Antiquaries of Ireland* **39**, 42–58, 350–68.

Westropp, T.J. 1911 Cahermurphy Castle and its earthworks, with certain forts near Miltown Malbay, Co. Clare. *Journal of the Royal Society of Antiquaries of Ireland* **41**, 117–37.

Westropp, T.J. 1915 Paintings at Adare 'Abbey', Co. Limerick. *Journal of the Royal Society of Antiquaries of Ireland* **45**, 151–2.

Westropp, T.J. 1918 'Lady Isabella's Fish Pond', Kilkee, Co. Clare. *Journal of the Royal Society of Antiquaries of Ireland* **48**, 79–80.

Williams, B.B. and Robinson, P.S. 1983 The excavation of Bronze Age cists and a medieval booley house at Glenmakeeran, County Antrim, and a discussion of booleying in north Antrim. *Ulster Journal of Archaeology* **46**, 29–40.

Woodman, P.C. 1995 Who possesses Tara? Politics in archaeology in Ireland. In P.J. Uckro (ed.), *Theory in archaeology—a world perspective*, 278–97. London and New York.

Wood-Martin, W.G. 1886 *The lake dwellings of Ireland*. Dublin.

Wrathmell, S. 1989 *Domestic settlement 2: medieval peasant farmsteads*. York.

Yates, M.J. 1983 Excavations at Carnaghliss. *Moated Site Research Group Report* **10**, 12.

Yeoman, P.A. 1984 Excavations at Castlehill of Strachan 1980–81. *Proceedings of the Society of Antiquaries of Scotland* **114**, 315–64.

Yeoman, P. 1995 *Medieval Scotland*. London.

FURTHER READING

Aalen, F.H.A. 1964 Clochans as transhumance dwellings in the Dingle Peninsula, Co. Kerry. *Journal of the Royal Society of Antiquaries of Ireland* **94**, 39–44.

Aalen, F.H.A. 1966 The evolution of the traditional house in western Ireland. *Journal of the Royal Society of Antiquaries of Ireland* **96**, 47–58.

Aalen, F.H.A. 1978 *Man and the landscape in Ireland.* London.

Ball, F.E. 1900 Monkstown Castle and its history. *Journal of the Royal Society of Antiquaries of Ireland* **30**, 109–17.

Bradley, J. 1984 *Urban Archaeological Survey—County Louth* (limited distribution). Office of Public Works, Dublin.

Bradley, J. 1984 *Urban Archaeological Survey—County Meath* (limited distribution). Office of Public Works, Dublin.

Bradley, J. 1985 *Urban Archaeological Survey—County Westmeath* (limited distribution). Office of Public Works, Dublin.

Bradley, J. 1985 *Urban Archaeological Survey—County Longford* (limited distribution). Office of Public Works, Dublin.

Bradley, J. 1986 *Urban Archaeological Survey—Co. Laois* (limited distribution). Office of Public Works, Dublin.

Bradley, J. 1986 *Urban Archaeological Survey—County Offaly* (limited distribution). Office of Public Works, Dublin.

Bradley, J. and King, H.A. 1991 Archaeological trial excavations at Bunratty, Co. Clare. *North Munster Antiquarian Journal* **33**, 16–21.

Bradley, J., Halpin, A. and King, H.A. 1986 *Urban Archaeological Survey—County Kildare* (limited distribution). Office of Public Works, Dublin.

Bradley, J., Halpin, A. and King, H.A. 1987 *Urban Archaeological Survey—County Kerry* (limited distribution). Office of Public Works, Dublin.

Bradley, J., Halpin, A. and King, H.A. 1987 *Urban Archaeological Survey—County Clare* (limited distribution). Office of Public Works, Dublin.

Brady, N. 1987 A late ploughshare type from Ireland. *Tools and Tillage* **5**, 228–42.

Brady, N. 1988 The plough pebbles of Ireland. *Tools and Tillage* **6**, 47–60.

Brady, N. 1993 Reconstructing a medieval Irish plough. In Dirección Gral de Bellas Artes y Archivos (ed.), *Primeras jornadas sobre technologia agraria tradicional*, 31–44. Madrid.

Buchanan, R.H. 1973 Field systems in Ireland. In A.R.H. Baker and R.A. Butlin (eds), *Studies of field systems in the British Isles*, 580–618. Cambridge.

Butlin, R.A. 1978 Some observations on the field systems of medieval Ireland. *Geographia Polonica* **38**, 31–6.

Claffey, J.A. 1972–3 Ballintubber Castle, Co. Roscommon. *Journal of the Old Athlone Society* **1** (3), 143–6.

Claffey, J.A. 1978 Medieval Rindoon. *Journal of the Old Athlone Society* **2** (1), 11–13.

Colfer, W. 1987 Anglo-Norman settlement in Co. Wexford. In K. Whelan (ed.), *Wexford: history and society*, 65–101. Dublin.

Cosgrove, A. 1981 *Late medieval Ireland, 1370–1541.* Dublin.

Danaher, K. 1938 Old house types in Oighreacht Uí Chonchubhair. *Journal of the Royal Society of Antiquaries of Ireland* **48**, 226–40.

Devitt, M. 1899–1902 The ramparts of the Pale at Clongowes Wood. *Journal of the Kildare Archaeological Society* **3**, 284–8.

Dickinson, C.W. and Waterman, D.M. 1960 Excavations at Castle Screen, Co. Down. *Ulster Journal of Archaeology* **23**, 63–77.

Donnelly, C.J. 1995 John Henry Parrer and his contribution to Irish tower house studies. *Group for the Study of Irish Historic Settlement Newsletter* **5**, 5–7.

Duport, M. 1934 La sculpture irlandaise à la fin du Moyen-Age. *La Revue de L'Art* **30**, 49–62.

Empey, C.A. 1981 The settlement of the kingdom of Limerick. In J.F.M. Lydon (ed.), *England and Ireland in the later Middle Ages,* 1–25. Dublin.

Empey, C.A. 1984 The sacred and the secular: the Augustinian priory of Kells in Ossory, 1193–1541. *Irish Historical Studies* **24**, 131–51.

Empey, C.A. 1986 Conquest and settlement: patterns of Anglo-Norman settlement in north Munster and south Leinster. *Irish Economic and Social History* **13**, 5–32.

Empey, C.A. 1992 Anglo-Norman County Waterford, 1200–1300. In W. Nolan and T.P. Power (eds), *Waterford: history and society,* 131–46. Dublin.

Estyn-Evans, E. 1969 Sod and turf houses in Ireland. In J.G. Jenkins (ed.), *Studies in folk life,* 80–90. London.

Fanning, T. 1970 Excavation of a ringfort at Bowling Green, Thurles, Co. Tipperary. *North Munster Antiquarian Journal* **13**, 6–21.

Fanning, T. and O'Brien, K. 1973–4 Earthworks at Raheen Castle, Co. Limerick. *North Munster Antiquarian Journal* **16**, 29–32.

Foster, R.F. 1988 *Modern Ireland, 1600–1972.* London.

Fowler, P.J. 1966 Some ridge and furrow cultivation at Cush, Co. Limerick. *North Munster Antiquarian Journal* **10** (1), 69–71.

Gailey, A. 1970 Irish corn-drying kilns. In D. McCourt and A. Gailey (eds), *Studies in folklife presented to Emyr Estyn Evans,* 52–71. Ulster Folk Museum.

Gaskell-Brown, C. 1979 Excavations at Greencastle, Co. Down. *Ulster Journal of Archaeology* **42**, 34–50.

Gleeson, D.F. 1937 The silver mines of Ormond. *Journal of the Royal Society of Antiquaries of Ireland* **67**, 101–16.

Gleeson, D.F. 1938 The Priory of St John of Nenagh. *Journal of the Royal Society of Antiquaries of Ireland* **68**, 201–18.

Gleeson, D.F. 1943 The manor of Ballinaclogh in Ormond. *North Munster Antiquarian Journal* **3** (3), 129–43.

Gosling, P. 1991 From Dun Delca to Dundalk: the topography and archaeology of a medieval frontier town. *Journal of the County Louth Archaeological and Historical Society* **22**, 227–353.

Graham, B.J. 1979 Clochan continuity and distribution in medieval Ireland. In P. Flatres (ed.), *Paysages ruraux europeéns,* 147–57. Rennes.

Graham, B.J. 1980 *Medieval Irish settlement; a review.* Norwich.

Guest, E.M. 1936 Irish sheela-na-gigs in 1935. *Journal of the Royal Society of Antiquaries of Ireland* **66**, 107–29.

Guest, E.M. 1937 Some notes on the dating of sheela-na-gigs. *Journal of the Royal Society of Antiquaries of Ireland* **67**, 101–16.

Hall, T. 1907 Crannoge near Belturbet. *Journal of the Royal Society of Antiquaries of Ireland* **37**, 240–1.

Halpin, E. 1994 Excavations at Enniskillen Castle, Co. Fermanagh. *Ulster Journal of Archaeology* **57**, 119–44.

Harbison, P. 1996 Newtown Castle. *Archaeological Journal* **153**, 346–8.

Harbison, S. 1995 Rindown Castle: a royal fortress in Co. Roscommon. *Journal of the Galway Archaeological and Historical Society* **47**, 138–48.

Hodkinson, B. 1992 Serious crime in early 14th century Co. Limerick. *North Munster Antiquarian Journal* **34**, 37–43.

Holland, P. 1987 The Anglo-Normans in Co. Galway: the process of colonization. *Journal of the Galway Archaeological and Historical Society* **41**, 73–89.

Holland, P. 1996 The Anglo-Normans and their castles in County Galway. In G. Moran and R. Gillespie (eds), *Galway: history and society,* 1–26. Dublin.

Hurst, J.G. 1988 Medieval pottery imported into Ireland. In G. Mac Niocaill and P.F. Wallace (eds), *Keimelia—studies in medieval archaeology and history in memory of Tom Delaney,* 220–53. Galway.

Ivens, R.J. 1984 Movilla Abbey, Newtownards, County Down: excavations 1981. *Ulster Journal of Archaeology* **47**, 71–108.

Ivens, R.J. 1991–2 Medieval pottery studies in Ulster: the future. *Ulster Journal of Archaeology* **54–5**, 160–1.

Jager, H. 1983 Land-use in medieval Ireland: a review of the documentary evidence. *Irish Economic and Social History* **10**, 57–65.

Jope, E.M. 1952 Review of 'Excavations at Island MacHugh' by Oliver Davies. *Ulster Journal of Archaeology* **15**, 134–7.

Jope, E.M., Jope, H.M. and Johnson, E.A. 1950 Harry Avery's Castle, Newtownstewart, Co. Tyrone. *Ulster Journal of Archaeology* **13**, 81–92.

Kelly, E.P. 1984 Medieval metal objects from Baunkyle, Co. Clare. *North Munster Antiquarian Journal* **26**, 96–9.

Knox, H.T. 1903 Occupation of Connaught by the Anglo-Normans after AD 1237. *Journal of the Royal Society of Antiquaries of Ireland* **33**, 58–74, 179–89, 284–94.

Knox, H.T. 1911 The Croghans and some Connacht raths and motes. *Journal of the Royal Society of Antiquaries of Ireland* **41**, 93–116.

Leask, H.G. 1928 Taghmon Church, Co. Westmeath. *Journal of the Royal Society of Antiquaries of Ireland* **58**, 102–10.

Lett, H.W. 1905 The island in Lough Briclan (Loughbrickland, County Down). *Journal of the Royal Society of Antiquaries of Ireland* **35**, 249–54.

Loeber, R. 1990 *The geography of the English colonisation of Ireland from 1534 to 1609.* Athlone.

Lucas, A.T. 1953 The horizontal mill in Ireland. *Journal of the Royal Society of Antiquaries of Ireland* **83**, 1–36.

Lucas, A.T. 1970 Turf as a fuel in Ireland. In D. McCourt and A. Gailey (eds), *Studies in folklife presented to Emyr Estyn Evans*, 172–202. Ulster Folk Museum.

Lydon, J.F.M. 1972 *The lordship of Ireland in the Middle Ages.* Dublin.

Lydon, J.F.M. 1984 The middle nation. In J.F.M. Lydon (ed.), *The English in medieval Ireland*, 1–26. Dublin.

Lyons, M.C. 1989 Weather, famine, pestilence and plague in Ireland, 900–1500. In E.M. Crawford (ed.), *Famine: the Irish experience, 900–1900*, 31–74. Edinburgh.

Lyttleton, J.I. 1997 Reassessment of the excavation of Loughpairc crannog near Tuam, County Galway. Unpublished MA thesis, University College Dublin.

Macalister, R.A.S., Armstrong, E.C.R. and Praeger, R.L. 1914 The excavations of Loughpairc crannog near Tuam. *Proceedings of the Royal Irish Academy* **38C**, 69–127.

McCourt, D. 1971 The dynamic quality of Irish rural settlement. In R.H. Buchanan, E. Jones and D. McCourt (eds), *Man and his habitat: essays presented to Emyr Estyn Evans*, 126–64. London.

McCracken, E. 1971 *The Irish woods since Tudor times.* Newtown Abbot.

McEnery, M.J. 1920 The state of agriculture and the standard of living in Ireland in the years 1240–1350. *Journal of the Royal Society of Antiquaries of Ireland* **50**, 1–18.

MacEoin, G. 1978 Craggaunowen crannog: gangway and gate-tower II—some literary evidence on crannog structure. *North Munster Antiquarian Journal* **20**, 52–6.

McErlean, T. 1983 The Irish townland system of landscape organisation. In T. Reeves-Smyth and F. Hamond (eds), *Landscape archaeology in Ireland*, 315–40. British Archaeological Reports, British Series 116. Oxford.

MacLeod, C. 1945 Medieval wooden figure sculpture in Ireland. *Journal of the Royal Society of Antiquaries of Ireland* **75**, 167–95.

MacLeod, C. 1947 Some late medieval wood sculptures in Ireland. *Journal of the Royal Society of Antiquaries of Ireland* **77**, 53–62.

MacNamara, G.V. 1901 Inchiquin, Co. Clare. *Journal of the Royal Society of Antiquaries of Ireland* **31**, 204–27, 341–64.

McNeill, C. 1940 Notes on Dublin Castle. *Journal of the Royal Society of Antiquaries of Ireland* **70**, 194–9.

McNeill, T.E. 1986 Church building in the 14th century and the Gaelic Revival. *Journal of Irish Archaeology* **3**, 61–4.

McNeill, T.E. 1996 Castles of ward and the changing pattern of border conflict in Ireland. *Château Gaillard* **17**, 127–33.

McNeill, T.E. 1997 County Down in the later Middle Ages. In L. Proudfoot (ed.), *Down: history and society*, 103–22. Dublin.

Mac Niocaill, G. 1966 The origins of the betagh. *Irish Jurist* **1**, 292–8.

Meenan, R. 1992 A survey of late medieval and early post-medieval Iberian pottery from Ireland. In D. Gaimster and M. Redknap (eds), *Everyday and exotic pottery from Europe c. 650–1900—studies in honour of John G. Hurst*, 186–93. Oxford.

Mills, J. 1892 Accounts of the earl of Norfolk's estates in Ireland, 1279–94. *Journal of the Royal Society of Antiquaries of Ireland* **22**, 50–62.

Mitchell, G.F. 1965 Littleton Bog, Tipperary: an Irish agricultural record. *Journal of the Royal Society of Antiquaries of Ireland* **95**, 121–32.

Nicholls, K.W. 1971 Rectory, vicarage and parish in the western Irish dioceses. *Journal of the Royal Society of Antiquaries of Ireland* **101**, 53–84.

Nicholls, K.W. 1984 The land of the Leinstermen. *Peritia* **3**, 535–58.

Nicholls, K.W. 1993 The development of lordship in medieval Cork, 1300–1600. In P. O'Flanagan and C.G. Buttimer (eds), *Cork: history and society*, 83–156. Dublin.

Ní Loinsigh, M. 1994 An assessment of castles and landownership in late medieval north Donegal.*Ulster Journal of Archaeology* **57**, 145–58.

O'Brien, A.F. 1993 Politics, economy and society: the development of Cork and the Irish south coast region, *c.* 1170 to *c.* 1583. In P. O'Flanagan and C.G. Buttimer (eds), *Cork: history and society*, 83–156. Dublin.

O'Brien, E. 1989 Excavations at Dundrum Castle, Dundrum, Co. Dublin. *Archaeology Ireland* **3** (4), 136–7.

O'Conor Don 1889 Ballintubber Castle, County Roscommon. *Journal of the Royal Society of Antiquaries of Ireland* **19**, 24–30.

Ó Danachair, C. 1946 The traditional houses of Co. Limerick. *North Munster Antiquarian Journal* **5** (1), 18–32.

Ó Danachair, C. 1957 Materials and methods in Irish traditional building. *Journal of the Royal Society of Antiquaries of Ireland* **87**, 61–74.

Ó Danachair, C. 1964 The combined byre-and-dwelling in Ireland. *Folk Life* **2**, 58–75.

Ó Danachair, C. 1969 Representations of houses on some Irish maps of *c.* 1600. In J.G. Jenkins (ed.), *Studies in folk life: essays in honour of Iorwerth C. Peate*, 91–103. London.

Ó Danachair, C. 1972 Traditional forms of the dwelling house in Ireland. *Journal of the Royal Society of Antiquaries of Ireland* **102**, 77–96.

Ó Floinn, R. 1988 Handmade medieval pottery—Leinster cooking ware. In G. Mac Niocaill and P.F. Wallace (eds), *Keimelia—studies in medieval archaeology and history in memory of Tom Delaney*, 325–48. Galway.

O'Malley, E. 1936 *On another man's wound*. Dublin.

Ó Murchadha, D. 1993 Gaelic land tenure in Co. Cork: Uibh Laoghaire in the seventeenth century. In P. O'Flanagan and C.G. Buttimer (eds), *Cork: history and society*, 83–156. Dublin.

O'Neill, St J.B. 1941 A square fort at Ballyraine, near Arklow. *Journal of the Royal Society of Antiquaries of Ireland* **71**, 26–7.

Orpen, G.H. 1898 Site of Raymond's Fort, Dundonnolf, Baginbun. *Journal of the Royal Society of Antiquaries of Ireland* **28**, 155–60.

Orpen, G.H. 1934 Charters of Earl Richard Marshal of the forests of Ross and Taghmon. *Journal of the Royal Society of Antiquaries of Ireland* **64**, 54–63.

Papazian, C. 1991 Excavations at Athenry Castle, Co. Galway. *Journal of the Galway Archaeological and Historical Society* **42**, 1–45.

Power, P. 1938 The Cistercian abbeys of Munster. *Journal of the Cork Historical and Archaeological Society* **43**, 1–11, 96–100.

Price, L. 1963 A note on the use of the word *baile* in placenames. *Celtica* **6**, 119–26.

Rees-Jones, S. and Waterman, D.M. 1967 Recent work at Harry Avery's Castle, Co.

Tyrone. *Ulster Journal of Archaeology* **30**, 76–82.

Richardson, H.G. 1942 Norman Ireland in 1212. *Irish Historical Studies* **3**, 144–58.

Richter, M. 1985 The interpretation of medieval Irish society. *Irish Historical Studies* **24**, 289–95.

Robinson, D. 1982 Urbanisation in north-west Ulster, 1609–1670. *Irish Geography* **15**, 35–51.

Roe, H. 1966 Some aspects of medieval culture in Ireland—the Presidential Address. *Journal of the Royal Society of Antiquaries of Ireland* **96**, 105–10.

Rynne, E. 1961 Was Desmond Castle, Adare, erected on a ringfort? *North Munster Antiquarian Journal* **8** (4), 193–202.

Rynne, E. 1965 Earthworks around Ballydoyle Castle, Co. Tipperary. *North Munster Antiquarian Journal* **10** (1), 72–4.

Rynne, E. 1978 The Craggaunowen crannog: gangway and gate tower I—the archaeological evidence: crannogs in Cuilmore Lough, near Balla, Co. Mayo. *North Munster Antiquarian Journal* **20**, 47–52.

Seymour, St J.D. 1909 Loughmoe Castle and its legends. *Journal of the Royal Society of Antiquaries of Ireland* **39**, 70–4.

Sheehy, J. and Mott, G. 1980 *The rediscovery of Ireland's past: the Celtic Revival 1830–1930.* London.

Simms, A. 1986 Continuity and change: settlement and society in medieval Ireland, *c.* 500–1500. In W. Nolan (ed.), *The shaping of Ireland,* 44–65. Cork.

Simms, K. 1978 The O'Hanlons, the O'Neills and the Anglo-Normans in 13th century Armagh. *Seanchas Ardmhacha* **9**, 70–94.

Simms, K. 1996 Gaelic warfare in the Middle Ages. In T. Bartlett and K. Jeffrey (eds), *A military history of Ireland,* 99–115. Cambridge.

Simpson, L. 1994 Anglo-Norman settlement in Uí Briúin Cualann. In K. Hannigan and W. Nolan (eds), *Wicklow: history and society,* 191–236. Dublin.

Stalley, R. 1996 Carrigafoyle (Co. Kerry). *Archaeological Journal* **153**, 328–9.

Sweetman, P.D. 1978 Excavation of medieval 'field boundaries' at Clonard, County Meath. *Journal of the Royal Society of Antiquaries of Ireland* **108**, 10–22.

Timoney, M.A. 1972 'Moin na gCaoineach' tower-house, Drimmeen, Co. Clare. *North Munster Antiquarian Journal* **15**, 13–16.

Ua Danachair, C. 1945 Some primitive structures used as dwellings. *Journal of the Royal Society of Antiquaries of Ireland* **75**, 204–12.

Ua Danachair, C. 1945 Traces of the *buaile* in the Galtee Mountains. *Journal of the Royal Society of Antiquaries of Ireland* **75**, 248–52.

Wallace, P.F. 1983 Appendix 2: North European pottery imported into Dublin 1200–1500. In P. Davey and R. Hodges (eds), *Ceramics and trade,* 225–30. Sheffield.

Wallace, P.F. 1985 The archaeology of Anglo-Norman Ireland. In H.B. Clarke and A. Simms (eds), *The comparative history of urban origins in non-Roman Europe,* 379–410. Oxford.

Warner, R.B. 1994 On crannogs and kings (part I). *Ulster Journal of Archaeology* **57**, 61–9.

Westropp, T.J. 1900 Notes on the lesser castles or 'peel towers' of County Clare. *Proceedings of the Royal Irish Academy* **21C**, 348–65.

Westropp, T.J. 1900 The Augustinian houses of Co. Clare: Clare, Killone and Inchicronan. *Journal of the Royal Society of Antiquaries of Ireland* **30**, 118–35.

Westropp, T.J. 1912 The promontory forts and early remains of the coasts of Mayo, part I—the north coast (Tirawley and Erris). *Journal of the Royal Society of Antiquaries of Ireland* **42**, 51–9, 101–39.

Westropp, T.J. 1912 Notes on the promontory forts and similar structures of County Kerry. *Journal of the Royal Society of Antiquaries of Ireland* **41**, 285–324.

Westropp, T.J. 1913 Prehistoric remains (forts and dolmens) in the Corofin district, Co. Clare. *Journal of the Royal Society of Antiquaries of Ireland* **43**, 232–60.

Westropp, T.J. 1915 Prehistoric remains (forts and dolmens) in the Burren and its south-western border, Co. Clare. Part XII: north-western part. *Journal of the Royal Society of Antiquaries of Ireland* **45**, 45–62, 249–74.

Westropp, T.J. 1918 Five large earthworks in the barony of Shelburne, Co. Wexford. *Journal of the Royal Society of Antiquaries of Ireland* **48**, 1–18.

Westropp, T.J. 1919 Notes on several forts in Dunkellin and other parts of southern Co. Galway. *Journal of the Royal Society of Antiquaries of Ireland* **49**, 167–86.

Westropp, T.J. 1921 The promontory forts of Beare and Bantry. *Journal of the Royal Society of Antiquaries of Ireland* **51**, 1–16.

Yates, M.J. 1983 Preliminary excavations at Movilla Abbey, County Down, 1980. *Ulster Journal of Archaeology* **46**, 53–66.

APPENDIX I.

STRATEGIES FOR RESEARCH

I.1—Introduction

A number of priorities for future research on rural settlement in medieval Ireland have been identified in this monograph. These will be summarised briefly here in order to bring together what the present writer perceives as the questions that could be answered by archaeological methods of enquiry in the future.

More than 4000 castles of different types exist throughout the Irish countryside today. There has always been a tendency to see castles as having been purely military in function. However, castles, being private residences, were also the centres of working farms and rural administration, in different ways over time and space (sections 2.1, 2.2, 2.3a). It was argued that one of the main priorities for future research into medieval rural settlement is to comprehensively demonstrate this point and to show, mainly by excavation, that castles had peaceful roles as well (section 2.3b). Arguably, a tower-house could be chosen for this proposed excavation of a castle site, especially as so few of these have been excavated to date in this country (section 1.1c). Yet a lot of information can be gleaned about the way tower-houses were used in the past through architectural analysis, simply because many of these structures are still standing today. In contrast, motte and ringwork castles are usually overgrown earthworks now, as all their original timber buildings have decayed or been burnt over time. Earthwork castles have received far less academic attention than masonry castles. It was suggested, therefore, that the excavation of a motte would not only help to show that castles were the centres of farms and rural administration, thereby substantially adding to the available information on the manorial economy of Anglo-Norman Ireland, but would also help to elucidate the important role played by timber castles across medieval Europe (sections 2.3a–b).

The historical sources suggest that many parts of eastern Ireland, in particular the fertile lowland regions, were colonised by peasants mostly of English origin. This occurred mainly in the first couple of decades of the thirteenth century, at least in Leinster and Meath (section 3.1). Very little archaeological work has been carried out on the nature of this colonisation and the settlement forms actually used by these incoming peasants (sections 3.1, 3.2, 3.3a–b, 3.5a). It was suggested that another important question for future research is how this English settlement developed and declined over time (section 3.5b). It was pointed out that a variety of problems concerning the nature of certain settlement forms and the material culture of rural medieval Ireland could be answered by an archaeological project trying to tackle this broad question (sections 3.5a–b).

Few detailed historical sources relating to the nature of settlement, society and the economy in Gaelic-dominated parts of medieval Ireland survive today. Furthermore, annalistic and literary sources relating to medieval Gaelic society have been under-studied by historians. This suggests that archaeology and archaeologically related methods of enquiry, such as animal bone and pollen analysis, have a large role to play in any future research on this important aspect of medieval rural settlement in Ireland. The discipline of archaeology has the potential to be at the forefront of academic work on Gaelic Ireland in the period from the twelfth century through to the late sixteenth century (section 4.5b). However, very little excavation or even survey work has been carried out to date on Gaelic habitation sites of general medieval date (sections 4.2b–c, 4.5a–b). It was postulated that excavations of specifically targeted medieval native Irish occupation sites, such as certain moated sites, crannogs and natural island fortresses, would yield much-needed information about the material culture and economic basis of Gaelic Ireland (section 4.5b). It was also felt that more information on these matters could be gained by integrating these excavations with a programme of fieldwork and further historical research into the scanty sources that are available for medieval Gaelic Ireland (*ibid.*). It was suggested that any future project on medieval Gaelic Ireland should try to elucidate whether or not some earthen ringforts remained in use in certain parts of the country up until the seventeenth century (sections 4.2c, 4.5b).

The aim of this appendix is to suggest various research strategies that could be used to answer these questions about medieval rural settlement. However, before doing this, it is necessary to discuss two points, which will in turn help to define the most efficient ways in which research by the Discovery Programme on rural settlement should proceed in the future. Firstly, it is important to define the actual strengths of the Discovery Programme, as perceived by the present writer. Secondly, it is important to suggest ways in which the Discovery Programme can look for extra funding for research, in addition to its annual government grant. Both of these topics have implications for future Discovery Programme research on medieval rural settlement in Ireland.

I.2—Discovery Programme strengths

Since the start of its first projects in 1992, the Discovery Programme has clearly built up an expertise in the field of archaeological survey (Eogan 1997, 41–5). Highly detailed plans have been made of important archaeological sites in Ireland, using the most modern survey equipment (e.g. Newman 1997). It is also important to note that the Discovery Programme's survey team, who are primarily qualified surveyors, have become archaeologically competent as well, able to plan and record any given site or site-complex with the minimum of archaeological supervision. This allows the archaeologists working for the Discovery Programme more time for true research work (Eogan 1997, 41). The Discovery Programme uses Geographical Information Systems or GIS in its research and is at the forefront of developing this technology for the benefit of Irish archaeology. The main strength of GIS for any future Discovery Programme project is its ability to compare and manipulate many different sets of data relating to the landscape and to the archaeology within it (*ibid.*, 46–51). The Discovery Programme has also become adept at interpreting information gained from geophysical survey, again using GIS (*ibid.*, 48). Overall, the technical backup for future archaeological projects run by the Discovery Programme will be of the highest quality.

Another strength of the Discovery Programme lies in its administration. For example, outside the Discovery Programme it is common practice for the director of any given archaeological excavation to do his or her own administration and to negotiate for funds. However, in the Discovery Programme, much of the burden of managing projects, such as working out the weekly payment of wages, is dealt with by the administration staff. Again, this leaves

the Discovery Programme archaeologists free to deal with archaeological matters on these excavations. Basically, the Discovery Programme is an institution that gives its archaeologists proper time for comprehensive research.

It seems to the present writer that, in view of the excellent technical and administrative support given to its archaeologists, the Discovery Programme is suited to the running of large archaeological projects, whether short-term or long-term, which individual scholars and other, less well-organised institutions would be wary of starting.

I.3—Extra funding for future Discovery Programme projects

The Discovery Programme's main source of funding at present is an annual government grant, channelled through the Heritage Council, which amounted to £700,000 for 1998. This figure is an indication of the political support the Discovery Programme has gained for itself since 1991 (Eogan 1997, 55–6). Indeed, successive governments have committed themselves to supporting the Discovery Programme. At the same time, meaningful and comprehensive archaeological projects cost a lot of money, especially those using the most modern technology in both the collection of data and at the analytical stage. The Discovery Programme fully realises this and is actively seeking ways of obtaining extra funds for its future research, in addition to its government grant.

Certainly, funding from the European Union should be actively sought by the Discovery Programme. The present writer visited Britain and Northern Ireland on two occasions in 1997 while working for the Discovery Programme. The response amongst academics there to the idea of joint archaeological projects with the Discovery Programme, tapping into EU funds, was very favourable. The general impressions gained by the present writer from these talks and from his own research are that rural settlement has been understudied across Europe in comparison to other aspects of the medieval period, such as urban archaeology, and that there is a strong feeling that this situation should be rectified in the years ahead. For example, very little is known about the nature of rural settlement in medieval Scotland, and its study is clearly a priority for future archaeological research there (Yeoman 1995, 108, 122). Relatively little archaeological work has been carried out in Wales on the nature of Welsh settlement during the medieval period, which was essentially rural in character (N. Edwards, pers. comm.). This suggests that there are numerous potential partners across the European Union for joint projects examining the nature of medieval rural settlement in different countries. One of the first priorities for the director of any future Discovery Programme project dealing with medieval rural settlement in Ireland should be to properly research themes for joint projects with other European institutions. The great strength of the Discovery Programme for future joint projects is that it has its national funds in place because of its annual government grant. Therefore that element of gaining European Union funding would already have been achieved, which should speed the process considerably. It is generally held that the nascent Raphael Programme offers the best opportunity for obtaining EU funds to help future Discovery Programme projects (Eogan 1997, 14). However, other programmes, such as Life, have also reacted favourably to applications for funds to carry out archaeological projects.

Furthermore, in Britain a lot of financial resources are going into the Trusts and to rescue archaeology in general, and consequently far less into research excavations. This in turn means that university departments there cannot find enough suitable excavations for their students, which might offer another opportunity for cooperation. It might be added that such cooperation between the Discovery Programme and various British universities may also qualify for EU funding. The Student Summer Job Scheme in the Republic also offers the Discovery Programme a means of getting excavation staff at little cost to itself.

Another possible additional source of funding for the Discovery Programme may lie in cooperation with institutions in Northern Ireland, such as Queen's University, Belfast, or the Department of the Environment, on archaeological projects straddling the Border counties. In order to gain these funds, it must be shown that the proposed projects have an employment or tourism potential at a local level, even if only temporary.

Lastly, it has been suggested that one indirect way of stretching the financial resources available to the Discovery Programme is to form partnerships with other institutions (such as university departments), who can share the cost of whatever research is being undertaken (Eogan 1997, 20).

Overall, it is abundantly clear that the Discovery Programme is in an ideal position to obtain extra financial resources from both the European Union and other sources, because of its annual funding from the Irish government and its acknowledged

international reputation for research.

I.4—Strategies for research: small-scale projects

I.4a—General
There have been relatively few excavations of medieval rural settlement sites in this country to date, and many of those undertaken were small in scale and often linked to the requirements of development rather than research (sections 1.2a–f, 1.3, 3.5a–b, 4.5a–b). This lack is also partly due to the fact that Irish archaeologists in the past have tended to concentrate their research on the prehistoric and Early Christian periods (section 1.1e). The majority of excavations at medieval sites in Ireland over the last two decades have been urban in character because the archaeological remains at what were our medieval towns are under threat from increased development and urban renewal schemes. These developments have often been funded by the European Union in recent years (section 1.2f). Most of the published work on medieval rural settlement in what were Anglo-Norman-dominated parts of Ireland comes either from an analysis of surviving manorial documents by historians or from fieldwork, which has been carried out as much by historical geographers as by archaeologists (sections 1.1e–f, 1.3; Barry 1996, 136). As noted, there has been very little archaeological work of any sort on medieval Gaelic Ireland (sections 4.5a–b). Therefore, in terms of relatively short-term projects, it is apparent that the main contribution the Discovery Programme can make to the study of the medieval period in both Ireland and Europe is to target and excavate specific rural settlement sites in this country. Indeed, this point has already been partly made in this book (sections 2.3b, 3.5b, 4.5b). However, for the sake of clarity in formulating meaningful future Discovery Programme projects, it is necessary to discuss some of these points again. Therefore, what specific monument types of medieval date could be excavated by the Discovery Programme over a relatively short time-span that would enhance our knowledge of medieval rural settlement?

I.4b—The excavation of a motte castle
One clear priority for future research on medieval rural settlement in Ireland would be to excavate a motte castle in a part of the country where demesne farming took place during the thirteenth century— somewhere in Leinster, Meath, Louth or Tipperary.

The research aims and projected results of such an excavation have already been discussed in detail (sections 2.3a–b), as well as the methods of choosing a suitable site (section 2.3b).

I.4c—The excavation of a moated site
Another target for future research by the Discovery Programme would be to excavate a moated site in a part of eastern Ireland that was relatively well colonised by English peasants in the thirteenth century. Again, the research aims of such a project and the postulated results have been laid out already (sections 3.5a–b).

I.4d—The excavation of a Gaelic habitation site of medieval date
As noted, very little is known about the economy and society of Gaelic Ireland prior to the sixteenth century (sections 4.1, 4.5b). Therefore, it is suggested that one relatively short-term Discovery Programme project would be to excavate a Gaelic occupation site of thirteenth- to fifteenth-century date (section 4.5b). A number of candidates for this excavation have been identified above (sections 4.2a–c, 4.5b).

I.4e—The excavation of a ringfort
There is much debate about whether or not ringforts continued in use in many parts of Ireland beyond the eleventh century and through to the seventeenth century (sections 4.2c, 4.5a). Another possibility for a short-term Discovery Programme project would be to excavate a ringfort, specifically chosen because the available historical sources and its siting suggest that it has the potential to answer questions about the medieval use of this monument type (section 4.5b).

I.4f—Discussion: short-term excavation projects
It is envisaged that these excavations (which would best be spread over two to three seasons) would each take about a year. This would include time for post-excavation research. It is taken for granted that the excavation teams at any given site would be quite large, given the Discovery Programme's ability to provide administrative backup. It is felt that a decision by the Discovery Programme to excavate even one of the above-mentioned sites would be seen as a major contribution to the study of medieval rural settlement in this country, given the lack of archaeological work on the subject as a whole.

Instrument survey, geophysical survey and analysis of the surviving documentary sources would be used in pre-excavation planning, both in choosing specific sites for investigation and in deciding which areas of any given site should actually be excavated. Animal bone analysis and environmental studies would also be part of the overall strategy of any given excavation. The application of these techniques has the potential to yield valuable information about the economic basis of the site under investigation during the medieval period.

I.4g—The field identification of Gaelic habitation sites of twelfth- to fourteenth-century date
It was stated above that there has been little attempt by scholars to locate native Irish occupation sites of thirteenth- and fourteenth-century date in the modern landscape (section 4.1). This proposed short-term project, of about six months' duration, would try to equate Gaelic habitation sites of pre-1400 date mentioned in the surviving sources with actual archaeological monuments in the field today. These sites would then be planned by the Discovery Programme. The project could also include some field-walking in specifically chosen areas for medieval booley houses, although these might be difficult to distinguish on the ground from later houses (section 4.3). The identification and planning of these occupation sites dating from before *c.* 1400 would help to lay the basis for any future archaeological projects on Gaelic settlement and society in medieval Ireland by identifying suitable places for excavation and areas for more intensive fieldwork.

I.5—Strategies for research: medium-term projects

I.5a—The excavation of a deserted village or rural borough site in eastern Ireland
Another major contribution that the Discovery Programme could make to the advancement of the study of medieval rural settlement in Ireland would be to undertake the excavation of a deserted village or rural borough site at an Anglo-Norman manorial centre. It would be hoped that manorial documents relating to the site eventually chosen for excavation would survive. The combined evidence from these documents and a research excavation at such a nucleated rural site would yield much-needed information about the foundation, growth, economic basis and subsequent decline of such colonial settlements (section 3.5b). Additional information about medieval peasant house types and rural industry would also come from such an excavation (*ibid.*). Obviously, the survey and environmental techniques discussed above in the options for short-term

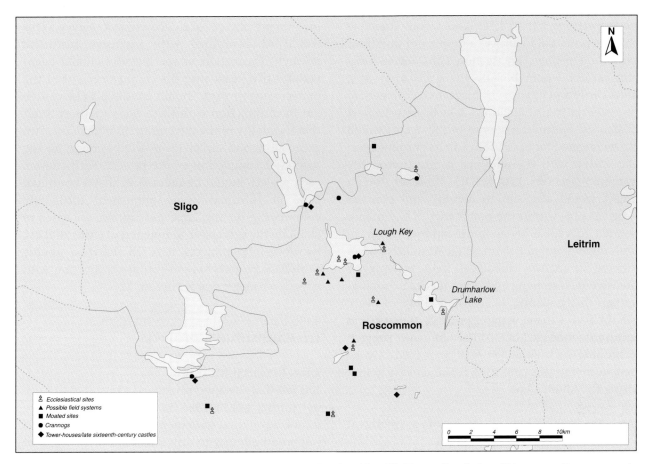

Fig. 22—*Map of the Boyle area in north Roscommon, showing identifiable medieval sites* (Discovery Programme).

projects would also be applied to this proposed excavation. Given the right resources, it is estimated that this project would last about three years, including post-excavation research. The deserted rural borough of Newtown Jerpoint, Co. Kilkenny, would be a good candidate for such an excavation (Barry 1987, 76–81).

I.5b—Archaeological survey of a medieval Gaelic lordship

Another medium-term project for the Discovery Programme might be to carry out an archaeological survey of a medieval native Irish lordship in order to understand more about the economic and social development of Gaelic Ireland throughout the Middle Ages. The first steps in such a project would be to choose a specific area for research and then to plot its geographic extent, using the available historical sources. The next stage would be to identify medieval Gaelic occupation sites within the chosen lordship by carrying out fieldwork, scouring the archives of the Archaeological Survey of Ireland, and examining the available documentary sources. Field-walking and aerial photography would also be used to help identify such things as medieval field systems or booleying areas in order to better under-

stand the economic basis of medieval Gaelic society. Pollen analysis could also be employed to provide additional information about land use. Such a project would comprehensively utilise the survey skills of the Discovery Programme. It is felt that about two years would be needed to bring such a project to publication, using a relatively small team of archaeologists.

I.6—Strategies for research: long-term projects

I.6a—An archaeological study of an Anglo-Norman manor in eastern Ireland

The aim of this project would be to examine the development and decline of settlement, society and the economy within the geographical boundaries of a specifically chosen Anglo-Norman manor in a well-colonised part of eastern Ireland. Again, in order to recreate a better picture of rural medieval life, there should be some surviving documentary evidence for the chosen manor, such as at least one manorial extent. The importance of such a large project would be that it combines a number of the short-term and medium-term projects discussed above (sections I.4b–c, I.5a), and would therefore have the potential to answer a number of questions about rural medieval life (section 3.5b). Such a long-term project would include the excavation of a motte castle and its adjacent nucleated settlement at the manorial centre (sections 2.3a–b, I.4b, I.5a). A moated site within the bounds of the manor would also be targeted for excavation and its chronological relationship with the manorial centre thoroughly examined (sections 3.5a–b, I.4c). However, such a project would also aim to identify and plan all medieval sites within the boundaries of the manor in order to gain a better understanding of life in rural Anglo-Norman Ireland. There would also be an attempt to identify medieval field systems by intensive field-walking and other methods, such as perhaps hedge-dating (e.g. Aston 1985, 136–7). Geophysical survey would be used as much as necessary during the course of the project. Techniques such as pollen analysis would also be used to investigate land use on the chosen manor during the Middle Ages.

I.6b—An archaeological study of a medieval Gaelic lordship in western Ireland

This large project would combine three of the short- and medium-term projects discussed above. It would include the identification and excavation of Gaelic habitation sites of medieval date (section I.4d). Intensive fieldwork and survey would also be carried out to identify other medieval sites and field systems within the lordship (section I.5b). Overall, the aim of such a project would be to employ archaeological survey, excavation, the historical analysis of surviving documentary sources and various environmental techniques to provide a model of how the economy and society of a Gaelic lordship functioned throughout the medieval period. A possible candidate for such a project would be the MacDermot lands of Moylurg in north Roscommon (Fig. 22), a manageable area containing good, well-preserved archaeological remains, including identifiable medieval secular sites, centred on the Rock of Lough Key and the townland of Rockingham Demesne near the modern town of Boyle (e.g. MacDermot 1996).

I.6c—Discussion: long-term projects

It is envisaged that these two long-term projects would each take five years to complete, provided that sufficient funds and manpower are made available. The initial step in both projects would certainly be the gathering of information in the area chosen for research, using non-intrusive archaeological techniques such as fieldwork,

instrument survey and geophysical survey. This would be combined with intensive historical research. Excavation at specific sites should begin perhaps two years after the commencement of the project. Survey work should continue to be carried out in conjunction with these excavations. It is felt that the ability of the director to simultaneously run excavations and survey teams will be crucial for the successful completion of the project. Furthermore, each project should be tailored so that a continual flow of information is published, ultimately culminating in one large publication. In order to facilitate the successful completion of either of these two long-term projects, it is felt that two specific subsidiary projects should run in conjunction with whichever major one is chosen.

I.7—Subsidiary projects

I.7a—Research historian

It is felt that the appointment of a historian to carry out further research on the documentary evidence for medieval rural settlement in Ireland would be an important adjunct to any long-term archaeological project on the subject. A variety of tasks could be undertaken that would be of overall value to the archaeological project. For example, the historian could scour the surviving sources for references to medieval settlements, domestic and farm buildings, and both Gaelic and Anglo-Norman agricultural practices. Such additional information would be integrated into the large archaeological publication on medieval rural settlement that will eventually be published by the Discovery Programme. This historian will be encouraged throughout his or her employment with the Discovery Programme to publish historical material on medieval rural settlement independently of the main project.

It is envisaged that this historian be appointed initially for a two-year period. The post should then be reviewed and its potential to make further contributions to the main archaeological project assessed by the Discovery Programme. Furthermore, it is possible that the Discovery Programme could go into partnership with a university Department of History, north or south of the Border, to meet the cost of this post (section I.3).

I.7b—Medieval pottery research fellow

Pottery is often the only potentially datable artefact that regularly occurs on medieval sites, mainly because it survives well in comparison to other finds. It is therefore important to have a full knowledge of how long individual pottery types lasted over time. Pottery analysis also helps to determine any given site's status and function, as well as establishing its trade connections, at both a local and an international level (Sandes, forthcoming). Obviously, in order to get the fullest possible information from any future Discovery Programme excavations at medieval rural sites, it will be necessary to employ a pottery specialist to help to elucidate the dating, trade connections, function and status of the monuments under investigation. It is possible that quite large pottery assemblages could be uncovered by excavation in both of the proposed long-term projects. Indeed, the possible pottery assemblages from the proposed project dealing with settlement in Gaelic Ireland would be of great interest to medieval scholars since almost nothing is known about Gaelic Irish use of pottery during the medieval period, simply because so few native Irish sites have been excavated to date (*ibid.*). Certain aspects of the medieval pottery that occurs in Ireland are well understood by scholars, but there are still wide gaps in our knowledge (*ibid.*). Therefore it is felt that perhaps the Discovery Programme should employ a pottery specialist as a research fellow for a period of at least three years. The duties of the appointee to this post would be twofold: firstly, to analyse the pottery assemblages from the Discovery Programme's own excavations; secondly, and most importantly, to carry out a research project on Irish medieval pottery in general, specifically targeting areas of the subject that need further elucidation.

It is suggested that the work of this researcher will substantially add to the impact of the project on Irish archaeology in general.

I.8—Other projects on medieval rural settlement in Ireland

It was stated in the Introduction that the main aims of this report were, firstly, to identify gaps in our knowledge of medieval rural settlement in Ireland and, secondly, to isolate ways in which the Discovery Programme could contribute to a greater understanding of the subject. In this regard a series of projects have been proposed that could be carried out in the future by the Discovery Programme to substantially increase knowledge of medieval rural settlement in this country.

However, this does not mean that our understanding of other aspects of medieval rural settlement, not dealt with comprehensively in this report, is complete. For example, it was noted above

that there has been little excavation of tower-houses in Ireland. Certainly, the tower-house is one of the most numerous monument types in the Irish countryside today (section 2.1). Therefore, understandably, the excavation of a tower-house should be a priority for future research into medieval rural settlement. However, it was not recommended to the Discovery Programme in this report as a priority for their future research on the medieval period in Ireland because it is felt that it is important to first understand rural settlement during the twelfth, thirteenth and fourteenth centuries before attempting to study the period from the fifteenth century onwards. Chronologically, in the present writer's opinion, the research excavation of a tower-house should come after the long-term excavation of a late twelfth- to fourteenth-century earthwork or masonry castle.

Furthermore, there is some debate about the actual origins of tower-houses in this country (section 2.1). Most Irish examples belong to the fifteenth century or later. One school of thought, however, believes that tower-houses began to be built in Ireland in the early fourteenth century (e.g. Barry 1987, 186; 1993b; Cairns 1987, 8–9), while another view argues that the tower-house emerged as a monument type during the very late fourteenth and early fifteenth centuries (e.g. Leask 1941, 73–112; McNeill 1997a, 202–3, 225; Sweetman 1995, 36–42; Westropp 1907b, 55–75). A project that attempts to answer the question of exactly when tower-houses began to be built in Ireland is arguably a priority for future research into the medieval period in this country. Possibly the way to proceed with such a project would be to combine comprehensive historical research with intensive fieldwork and survey. This would include tabulating the historical references to castles and fortifications built throughout the whole of the fourteenth century and the very early fifteenth century. The next stage would be to try to identify these sites within the landscape today, and then to try to elucidate what types of castles or fortifications are being referred to in the sources. A good knowledge of more recent work done in Britain and elsewhere on the dating and development of architectural features during the medieval period would be essential, because the present writer feels that much of Leask's dating of specific architectural details seen in Irish castles, and indeed ecclesiastical sites, is too conservative (e.g. Leask 1941, 24). Some of these features, such as plain ogee-headed windows, can be earlier in date than Leask allows for. Overall, in this proposed project, if certain early fourteenth-century historical references to castles correspond to tower-houses on the ground that can be architecturally dated as early, this would be a strong indication that this monument type first appears in Ireland just after *c.* 1300. Alternatively, this project could find out that in fact these early fourteenth-century references to fortifications refer to other forms of castles, such as late hall-houses or even mottes, suggesting that tower-houses are a phenomenon that first appear in Ireland during the very late fourteenth and early fifteenth centuries. As noted, the true *forte* of the Discovery Programme lies in running large projects of different time-scales (section I.2). This was partly the reason why this particular project was not recommended to the Discovery Programme. It is felt that it would be better carried out either by an individual as a PhD thesis or by the Archaeological Survey of Ireland as a thematic survey after fieldwork for the County Inventories has been completed around the year 2000.

Ecclesiastical art and architecture have been continuously studied by scholars in Ireland this century (section 1.3). There are aspects of ecclesiastical rural settlement, however, that have not received much academic attention. Barry (1987, 139–67, 201) has enumerated these and has discussed ways in which the discipline of archaeology can contribute to the study of ecclesiastical settlement throughout the medieval period. It therefore seemed unnecessary to create a specific chapter within the report proper on this particular aspect of medieval rural settlement in Ireland.

However, following on from Barry's recommendations and more recent work such as Aston's (1993) work on monasteries in the English medieval landscape, the present writer sees a number of ways in which archaeology can contribute to a better understanding of medieval ecclesiastical settlement in this country.

The large majority of extant medieval parish churches in this country date from the fifteenth century or later (Barry 1987, 140). What form did the churches at these sites take during the twelfth and thirteenth centuries when parishes were being set up by the lay and ecclesiastical authorities? Careful excavation of well-chosen sites and the architectural survey of standing medieval parish churches could help to answer this question.

In the case of Cistercian abbeys or Augustinian priories, research and excavation have concentrated on the visible architectural remains at these places— usually the church and most of the claustral buildings (Pls 35–6). However, large numbers of other buildings existed at these sites that have left little or no trace in the landscape today. The

discipline of archaeology can help to provide a better picture of how these abbeys looked during the medieval period. For example, the lay-brothers' quarters on the western side of the cloister garths at Cistercian monasteries were poorly built in comparison to the other claustral buildings and therefore little often remains of them today (Barry 1987, 145). Excavation has a part to play in elucidating the layout and nature of the buildings in this part of any given Cistercian abbey (*ibid.*). Furthermore, other buildings existed within the precincts of Cistercian and Augustinian abbeys, beyond the church and the claustral buildings. These include such structures as guest-houses, infirmaries and abbots' lodgings (Aston 1993, 89–110; Barry 1987, 145; Stalley 1987, 172). Many medieval monasteries were not just religious centres but farms too, as the land in their immediate vicinity was cultivated to provide food for the religious communities. Therefore such farm buildings as stables, barns, granaries, pigsties, cattlesheds, dovecotes, buildings for wool and cloth manufacture, watermills, workshops and forges existed beside many monasteries. Fish-ponds, orchards and gardens for herbs and vegetables also occurred beside medieval abbeys (Aston 1993, 89–110; Barry 1987, 145; Stalley 1987, 172). The long-term research excavation of a specifically chosen religious house would uncover evidence for these buildings and provide much-needed information about the economic basis of medieval monasteries. Indeed, Barry (1987, 144) has suggested that the work carried out at the Cistercian house of Bordesley Abbey in Worcestershire should act as a model for any future research excavation of a medieval monastery in Ireland (Rahtz and Hirst 1976). Cistercian and Augustinian granges, defined here as the outfarms of various abbeys on lands away from the monastic centres, have also received little academic attention. One priority for future work on medieval rural settlement in Ireland would be to identify and excavate a grange centre (Graham 1985b, 25–6).

Quite an amount of information exists on the extent of Cistercian and Augustinian estates throughout Ireland during the medieval period (e.g. Ó Conbhuí 1962). Possibly one long-term project for future research would be to archaeologically examine the possessions of one specifically chosen Cistercian or Augustinian house. This would include the excavation of the monastic centre itself and an outlying grange. It would also include fieldwork to examine the settlement forms and field systems visible throughout the whole monastic estate, which would have consisted of parcels of land scattered

Pl. 35—*Cistercian abbey at Corcomroe, Co. Clare.* (Photo: *Dúchas*, The Heritage Service.)

Pl. 36—*Augustinian priory at Kells, Co. Kilkenny.* (Photo: *Dúchas*, The Heritage Service.)

throughout the country. Furthermore, in the case of a Cistercian house, it would be interesting to carry out environmental work to determine how much of its property consisted of land reclaimed by the monks from waste.

These projects were not recommended to the Discovery Programme as a priority for its future research as it is felt that mainstream secular settlement should be studied first. However, given the importance of the Church to medieval society, any long-term study of either a Gaelic lordship or an Anglo-Norman manor would have to address the question of the development of the parish within these areas. Furthermore, given the widespread nature of monastic estates throughout Ireland, it is also clear that these projects would have to elucidate what lands or rights within the study areas belonged to religious houses. Some comment about the nature of the settlement forms, field systems and reclamation works on medieval monastic estates in Ireland would necessarily be included as part of any general work on secular rural settlement. Indeed, it will probably be shown that many of the settlement forms and field systems seen on scattered medieval monastic estates were little different to those on contemporary secular manors and lands.

I.9—Conclusions and recommendations for future research

A variety of short-, medium- and long-term projects have been proposed for future Discovery Programme research on medieval rural settlement (sections I.4a–g, I.5a–b, I.6a–c). It is for the Discovery Programme's Directorate and Council ultimately to choose which of these projects should go ahead. It must be stated that the successful completion of any one of the above-mentioned proposals, even the short-term ones, would be seen as a major contribution to the subject of medieval rural settlement in Ireland. However, in this last section, the present writer will make suggestions as to which of the proposed projects he believes should be chosen by the Discovery Programme.

As noted, few historical documents containing detailed economic or social information relating to medieval Gaelic society survive today (section 4.1), suggesting that this is the sphere in which the discipline of archaeology and the Discovery Programme could make the most impact (section 4.5b). Archaeology and archaeologically related methods of enquiry have the clear potential to provide large amounts of new information about the nature of this society. Since very little archaeological work has been carried out on medieval Gaelic Ireland so far, in terms of both excavation and fieldwork (*ibid.*), it is suggested that the Discovery Programme should opt for any one of the proposed Gaelic projects outlined above. These range from the short-term excavation of a habitation site through to an integrated study of a Gaelic lordship, involving a programme of excavation, environmental sampling and fieldwork (sections I.4d, I.4f, I.5b, I.6b). Much of north Connacht and most of Ulster were Gaelic-dominated parts of medieval Ireland (section 4.1). North Connacht in particular has suffered little from agricultural development in recent years, and whole archaeological landscapes still exist in the region.

Which one of these Gaelic projects should be chosen above the others? It was noted above that archaeological survey using the most modern technology is one of the great strengths of the Discovery Programme, along with a proven ability to administer large projects and excavations (section I.2). In the circumstances it would seem logical for the Discovery Programme to opt for the proposed five-year archaeological study of a Gaelic lordship (section I.6b). This long-term project would be best suited to the skills developed by the Discovery Programme over the years and has the clear potential to provide a huge amount of information on rural settlement in medieval Ireland.